American Indian Law

WILLIAM C. CANBY, JR.

AMERICAN INDIAN LAW

IN A NUTSHELL

Third Edition

By

WILLIAM C. CANBY, JR.
Senior Judge, United States Court of Appeals
For the Ninth Circuit
formerly
Professor of Law,
Arizona State University

WEST
GROUP

ST. PAUL, MINN.
1998

x

Nutshell Series, In a Nutshell, the Nutshell Logo and the West Group symbol are registered trademarks used herein under license.

ISBN 0–314–22637–0

 TEXT IS PRINTED ON 10% POST CONSUMER RECYCLED PAPER

3rd Reprint — 2002

PREFACE

The purpose of this book remains as it was in the first two editions. It is to set forth in succinct form the essentials of the very complex body of federal Indian Law, with attention when necessary to the governmental policies underlying it.

This edition contains two new chapters. One is Chapter X on Indian Gaming, a recent arrival on the scene that simply cannot be ignored. The other is Chapter XIII on Alaska Natives, a subject that has long merited fuller treatment. To keep the work within manageable proportions, I have omitted treatment of some other subjects that fall within the field of Indian Law or are related to it. For example, I have not dealt individually with the special problems peculiar to Oklahoma or New York. Nor have I discussed the serious problems of urban Indians, which are more a function of poverty and dislocation than of Indian status. I have not treated the subject of the Native Hawaiians, who seek to apply some of the principles of Indian Law to their situation.

The original chapters have been revised far more extensively for this edition than they were for the second edition. The necessity for such treatment arises from the significant changes wrought by the Supreme Court in the area of civil jurisdiction over

non-Indians, and by the Court's narrowing approach
to questions of tribal sovereignty generally.

The views expressed in this book are attributable
to me individually as a student and former teacher
of Indian Law. They do not represent the views of
Arizona State University, the United States Court of
Appeals for the Ninth Circuit, or even of myself in
any official capacity.

WILLIAM C. CANBY, JR.

Phoenix, Arizona
April 23, 1998

P022885

OUTLINE

OUTLINE

*

TABLE OF CASES

References are to Pages

A

B

TABLE OF CASES

C

D

G

H

I

J

K

L

M

N

TABLE OF CASES

P

Q

R

S

U

V

W

Y

Z

*

AMERICAN INDIAN LAW

IN A NUTSHELL

Third Edition

*

CHAPTER I

INTRODUCTION

A. THE NATURE AND SCOPE OF INDIAN LAW

The term "Indian Law" is a catchall with various meanings, but it refers primarily to that body of law dealing with the status of the Indian tribes and their special relationship to the federal government, with all the attendant consequences for the tribes and their members, the states and their citizens, and the federal government. In this application, "Indian Law" might better be termed "Federal Law About Indians."

The unique legal posture of the tribes in relation to the federal government is deeply rooted in American history, and a knowledge of historical context is perhaps more important to the understanding of Indian Law than of any other legal subject. Indian Law has always been heavily intertwined with federal Indian policy, and over the years the law has shifted back and forth with the flow of popular and governmental attitudes toward Indians. Yet a few themes have persisted and form the doctrinal bases of present law. At the risk of oversimplification, they may be reduced to four. *First*, the tribes are independent entities with inherent powers of self-

1

government. *Second*, the independence of the tribes is subject to exceptionally great powers of Congress to regulate and modify the status of the tribes. *Third*, the power to deal with and regulate the tribes is wholly federal; the states are excluded unless Congress delegates power to them. *Fourth*, the federal government has a responsibility for the protection of the tribes and their properties, including protection from encroachments by the states and their citizens. These principles, while enduring, are not static. The boundaries of tribal self-government referred to in the first proposition, for example, are constantly being adjusted, particularly with regard to tribal authority over non-Indians. Recent assertions of state power also have subjected the third proposition to great stress.

As all of these themes suggest, Indian Law is greatly concerned with actual or potential conflicts of governmental power. When such conflicts arise in a legal setting, they appear as issues of jurisdiction. It is not surprising, therefore, that controversies in Indian Law usually have at their core a jurisdictional dispute.

Indian Law includes within its scope those situations in which a legal outcome is affected by the Indian status of the participants or the subject matter. Obviously, there are many legal disputes involving Indians that do not turn upon points of Indian Law. If an Indian commits a traffic offense in Chicago, his case will be governed by the same law and decided by the same court that would govern and decide a case against a non-Indian; the defendant's Indian status is irrelevant and Indian Law does not enter at all. But if that same Indian commits a similar offense upon the Navajo Reservation in Arizona, his Indian status and the location will combine to confer jurisdiction upon a different court and will result in the application of different law from that which would decide and govern the case if the defendant were a non-Indian. (See Chapter VII, Section D.) The latter situation is very much controlled by Indian Law—that is, by the federal law which allocates jurisdiction over Indian affairs.

Although the subject of "Indian Law" legitimately might be thought to include the internal law that each tribe applies to its own affairs and members, that is not the common definition nor the one used here. Instead, that body of law is separately referred to as "tribal law," and it may range from oral tradition to entire codes borrowed intact from non-Indian sources. No attempt will be made in this volume to set forth the content of the various bodies of tribal law. Instead, the concern will be to determine *when* tribal law (rather than state or federal law) governs a particular situation.

B. WHAT IS AN INDIAN TRIBE?

The Indian tribe is the fundamental unit of Indian Law; in its absence there is no occasion for the law to operate. Yet there is no all-purpose definition of an Indian tribe. A group of Indians may qualify as a tribe for the purpose of one statute or federal

program, but fail to qualify for others. See Golden
Hill Paugussett Tribe of Indians v. Weicker, 39 F.3d
51, 57–58 (2d Cir.1994). Definitions must accordingly be used with extreme caution.

At the most general level, a tribe is simply a
group of Indians that is recognized as constituting a
distinct and historically continuous political entity
for at least some governmental purposes. See Pau-
gusset Tribe, 39 F.3d at 59. The key problem with
this definition lies in the word "recognized." Recognized by whom? The answer is that recognition may
come from many directions, and the sufficiency of
any given recognition is likely to depend upon the
purpose for which tribal status is asserted. See
Joint Tribal Council of Passamaquoddy Tribe v.
Morton, 528 F.2d 370 (1st Cir.1975).

By far the most important and valuable recognition is that of the federal government. Unequivocal
federal recognition may serve to establish tribal
status for every purpose, and the Department of the
Interior insists upon federal recognition as a prerequisite for entitlement to the many federal Indian
services administered by the Department. Federal
recognition may arise from treaty, statute, executive or administrative order, or from a course of
dealing with the tribe as a political entity. Any of
these events, or a combination of them, then signi-
fies the existence of a special relationship between
the federal government and the concerned tribe
that may confer such important benefits as immunity of the Indians' lands from state taxation. The
Kansas Indians, 72 U.S. (5 Wall.) 737 (1866). In

recognizing a tribe, the federal government has not always been governed by ethnological realities; there are numerous instances where ethnologically distinct tribes or bands were gathered into one common reservation and thereafter treated as a single tribe.

The failure of the federal government to recognize a particular group of Indians as a tribe cannot deprive that group of vested treaty rights. Greene v. Babbitt, 64 F.3d 1266, 1270–71 (9th Cir.1995). The group must have maintained itself as a distinct community, however, with some defining characteristic that permits it to be identified as the group named in the treaty. United States v. Washington, 641 F.2d 1368 (9th Cir.1981), cert. denied, 454 U.S. 1143 (1982).

The action of the federal government in recognizing or failing to recognize a tribe has traditionally been held to be a political one not subject to judicial review. United States v. Holliday, 70 U.S. (3 Wall.) 407, 419 (1866). Although it is still true that Congress or the Executive can establish standards of recognition without court direction, federal courts today will review grants or denials of recognition under the Administrative Procedure Act to determine whether the Department of Interior followed its own regulations and other controlling law, and adhered to the requirements of due process. See Cherokee Nation of Oklahoma v. Babbitt, 117 F.3d 1489, 1499–1500 (D.C.Cir.1997); Greene v. Babbitt, 64 F.3d 1266, 1274–75 (9th Cir.1995). A court may also order the executive branch of the federal government to honor tribal status for a particular purpose when that is deemed to have been the intent of Congress. Joint Tribal Council of Passamaquoddy Tribe v. Morton, 528 F.2d 370 (1st Cir. 1975). There may be other substantive limits to the executive power to recognize in extreme instances; the government would not be permitted to confer tribal status arbitrarily on some group that had never displayed the characteristics of a distinctly Indian community. See United States v. Sandoval, 231 U.S. 28, 46 (1913).

In 1978, the Department of the Interior published criteria for the "acknowledgement" of the status of tribes that were not otherwise federally recognized. The Department revised those criteria in 1994. See 25 C.F.R. Part 83 (1997). The criteria are designed to achieve eligibility for federal services and other benefits of tribal status for Indian groups that have maintained a "substantially continuous tribal existence and which have functioned as autonomous entities throughout history until the present." 25 C.F.R. § 83.3. Acknowledgement thus amounts to recognition. A group seeking acknowledgement may establish the requisite tribal identity by various types of evidence, including dealings as a tribe with federal, state or local governments or other tribes, and recognition by historical records or scholarly opinion. The group must show that it is a distinct community and exercises political influence or authority over its members, and that it has maintained these characteristics from historical times until the present. 25 C.F.R. § 83.7. The Depart-

ment's decision to acknowledge or deny acknowledgement is subject to administrative review before
the Interior Board of Indian Appeals. 25 C.F.R.
§ 83.11.

Even when a tribe clearly has been recognized, as
by a treaty, Congress has the power effectively to
end the recognized status by legislating a "termination" of the tribe's special relationship to the
federal government. (See Chapter III, Section E). In
addition, a tribe may totally lose its tribal status by
voluntarily ceasing to function as a distinct and
identifiable entity. Mashpee Tribe v. New Seabury
Corp., 592 F.2d 575 (1st Cir.), cert. denied, 444 U.S.
866 (1979).

Congress in 1994 required the Secretary of the
Interior to publish annually in the Federal Register
a list of all tribes recognized to be eligible for
federal services because of their Indian status. 25
U.S.C.A. § 479a–1. The 1997 list included more
than 300 recognized tribes in the lower 48 states,
and over 200 recognized Alaska Native entities. 62
Fed. Reg. 55270 (Oct. 23, 1997).

C. WHO IS AN INDIAN?

"Indian" is another term the meaning of which
varies according to the purpose for which the definition is sought. In the most general terms, a person
must meet two requirements to be an Indian: he or
she must (1) have some Indian blood, and (2) be
regarded as an Indian by his or her community. See

F. Cohen, Handbook of Federal Indian Law 2 (1942).

To have Indian blood is to have had ancestors living in America before the Europeans arrived, but this fact is obviously never provable as such. It is enough that a parent, grandparent, or great-grandparent was clearly identified as an Indian. Because the general requirement is only of "some" blood, a person may be classified as an Indian despite a very low quantum of Indian blood, such as one-sixteenth. Particular statutes, however, may set higher blood requirements.

For many federal jurisdictional purposes it is not enough that the individual be regarded as an Indian by his or her community; the person must be considered a member of a *federally recognized* tribe. LaPier v. McCormick, 986 F.2d 303, 305 (9th Cir. 1993); State v. Sebastian, 243 Conn. 115, 701 A.2d 13 (1997), cert. denied, 118 S.Ct. 856 (1998). In that context, individual status follows tribal status, and there can be no Indian without a tribe. See Epps v. Andrus, 611 F.2d 915 (1st Cir.1979). Thus where Congress has terminated a tribe's special relationship with the federal government, the individual members of that tribe are no longer Indians for purposes of federal criminal jurisdiction. United States v. Heath, 509 F.2d 16 (9th Cir.1974). Even in the case of tribes that continue to be federally recognized, individual members have been held in the past to have lost their Indian status by leaving the tribe and adopting non-Indian ways. E.g., Nagle v. United States, 191 Fed. 141 (9th Cir.1911). It is unlikely, however, that such behavior today would be considered an unequivocal abandonment of the tribe by the individual.

It is not always necessary for an individual to be formally enrolled in a recognized tribe to be regarded as a member for jurisdictional purposes. United States v. Broncheau, 597 F.2d 1260 (9th Cir.), cert. denied, 444 U.S. 859 (1979); United States v. Keys, 103 F.3d 758, 761 (9th Cir.1996); but see United States v. Lawrence, 51 F.3d 150 (8th Cir.1995). Nevertheless, enrollment is commonly a prerequisite for acceptance as a member of the tribal community, and it provides by far the best evidence of Indian status. Individual tribes have varying blood requirements for enrollment, with the result that the general definitional requirement of "some" blood may be substantially increased for persons seeking to establish status as members of certain tribes. Many tribes require one-fourth tribal blood, and at least one requires five-eighths.

CHAPTER II

HISTORICAL OVERVIEW OF FEDERAL INDIAN LAW AND POLICY

A. INTRODUCTION

Indian Law is a reflection of national Indian policy, which has undergone numerous shifts in direction in the course of American history. At some times, the prevailing view has regarded the tribes as enduring bodies for which a geographical base would have to be established and more or less protected. At other times, the dominant position has been that the tribes are or should be in the process of decline and disappearance, and that their members should be absorbed into the mass of non-Indian society. Many other views have entered into the debate, but these two polar positions continually reappear and affect legislation, court decisions and the executive administration of Indian affairs. The dominance of one position at any given time does not, of course, mean that the other disappears entirely; its influence is diminished but usually observable. That is as true today as it has been in the past, and the continuing tension between the two views makes it unsafe to assume that national Indian policy has found its final direction.

B. ESTABLISHMENT OF THE FEDERAL ROLE: COLONIAL TIMES TO 1820

During the colonization of America, the British Crown dealt with the Indian tribes formally as foreign sovereign nations. Britain and several of its colonies entered treaties with various tribes. As the colonies grew in strength and population, it became apparent that individual colonists were encroaching upon Indian lands and were otherwise treating the Indians unfairly or worse. In order to avoid prolonged and expensive Indian wars, and perhaps also to enforce a measure of justice, the Crown increasingly assumed the position of protector of the tribes from the excesses of the colonists. It is accordingly not surprising that when the colonies revolted from Britain, nearly all of the tribes allied themselves with the Crown.

Upon independence, the new nation found itself with the same problems of non-Indian aggression and threatened Indian retaliation that had faced the Crown. If Indian affairs were left to the individual states, non-Indian land hunger would almost certainly result in new Indian wars that the exhausted United States was in no position to fight. If stability were to be achieved, it had to be by placing Indian affairs in the hands of the central government. After a period of uncertainty under the Articles of Confederation, the Constitution did just that. Congress was granted the power to "regulate Commerce with the Indian Tribes" while the President was empowered to make treaties, necessarily including Indian treaties, with the consent of the Senate. U.S.Const. Art. I, § 8, cl. 3; Art. II, § 2, cl. 2.

Congress set the basic pattern of federal Indian Law in a series of Trade and Intercourse Acts passed between 1790 and 1834. E.g., 1 Stat. 137 (1790); 2 Stat. 139 (1802); 4 Stat. 729 (1834). The central policy embodied in the Acts was one of separating Indians and non-Indians and subjecting nearly all interaction between the two groups to federal control. The Acts established the boundaries of Indian country and protected against incursion by non-Indians in several ways. Non–Indians were prohibited from acquiring Indian lands by purchase or treaty (other than a treaty entered pursuant to the Constitution), or from settling on those lands or entering them for hunting or grazing. Trading with the Indians was made subject to federal regulation. Depredations by non-Indians against Indians were made a federal crime, with federal compensation to the injured Indians so long as they did not exact private revenge. The federal government likewise guaranteed compensation of non-Indians injured by Indians committing depredations in non-Indian territory, provided again that no private revenge were taken. While regulating relations between Indians and non-Indians comprehensively, the Trade and Intercourse Acts made no attempt to regulate the conduct of Indians among themselves in Indian country; that subject was left entirely to the tribes.

During these years when federal control over Indian affairs was being consolidated, the federal government continued to deal with Indian tribes by treaty. Indian agents were appointed as the federal government's liaison with the tribes. These agents were generally under the jurisdiction of the War Department.

C. THE CHEROKEE CASES AND INDIAN REMOVAL: 1820 TO 1850

Despite the Trade and Intercourse Acts, friction grew between the burgeoning non-Indian population and the tribes, particularly as non-Indian demands for additional land became more acute. As a consequence, the solution of "removal" of the tribes to Indian country beyond the Mississippi gained currency and was espoused by Presidents Monroe, John Quincy Adams and, most vigorously, Jackson. At the same time that this executive policy was hardening, however, the Supreme Court under John Marshall's leadership was independently fashioning legal doctrines that would influence Indian Law for the next century and a half.

The first decision in which the Supreme Court attempted to formulate its views of Indian tribes and their legal and historical relation to the land was Johnson v. McIntosh, 21 U.S. (8 Wheat.) 543 (1823). The case concerned the validity of a grant of land made by tribal chiefs to private individuals in 1773 and 1775 (before passage of the Trade and Intercourse Acts, which would have prohibited such transactions). The Court held the conveyance invalid. Discovery of lands in the new world, said the

Court, gave the discovering European sovereign a title good against all other Europeans, and along with it "the sole right of acquiring the soil from the natives * * *." 21 U.S. at 573. The Indians retained a right of occupancy, which only the discovering sovereign could extinguish, either "by purchase or by conquest." The sovereign (now the United States) was free to grant land occupied by Indians, but the grantee received title subject to that right of occupancy. The result of this decision was to recognize a legal right of Indians in their lands, good against all third parties but existing at the mere sufferance of the federal government. This right of occupancy is frequently referred to as "aboriginal title," or simply "Indian title."

A few years later, the attempts of Georgia to extinguish Indian title within the state gave rise to the Cherokee Cases—perhaps the two most influential decisions in all of Indian Law. The state of Georgia had given up western land claims in return for a federal promise to extinguish Indian title to lands within Georgia, but the state tired of waiting for federal action. Between 1828 and 1830, Georgia enacted a series of laws that divided up the Cherokee territory among several Georgia counties, extended state law to the divided territory, invalidated all Cherokee laws, and made criminal any attempts of the Cherokees to act as a government. To combat these actions of Georgia, the Cherokees brought an original action in the Supreme Court, Cherokee Nation v. Georgia, 30 U.S. (5 Pet.) 1 (1831). The ability of the tribe to bring such a suit depended on its being a "foreign state" within the meaning of Art. III, § 2 of the Constitution, which defines the federal judicial power. Chief Justice Marshall, writing for the Court, first determined that the Cherokee tribe had succeeded in demonstrating that it was a "state," "a distinct political society separated from others, capable of managing its own affairs and governing itself," and that treaties between the tribe and the United States had so recognized it. 30 U.S. (5 Pet.) at 16. But Marshall determined that the tribe could not be considered a "foreign" state:

> Though the Indians are acknowledged to have an unquestionable, and, heretofore unquestioned, right to the lands they occupy, until that right shall be extinguished by a voluntary cession to our government; yet it may well be doubted, whether those tribes which reside within the acknowledged boundaries of the United States can, with strict accuracy, be denominated foreign nations. They may, more correctly, perhaps, be denominated domestic dependent nations. They occupy a territory to which we assert a title independent of their will, which must take effect in point of possession, when their right of possession ceases. Meanwhile, they are in a state of pupilage; their relation to the United States resembles that of a ward to his guardian.

30 U.S. (5 Pet.) at 17. Thus, while the language of the opinion was obviously sympathetic to the Cherokee cause, the tribe was out of court. Marshall's characterization of the tribes as "domestic depen-

dent nations" turns out to have been a mixed blessing for them. Its emphasis on nationhood laid the groundwork for future protection of tribal sovereignty by Marshall and his immediate successors, but the characterization also created an opportunity for much later courts to discover limits to tribal sovereignty inherent in domestic dependent status. Marshall's reference to tribes as "wards" was to have an equally mixed history; it provided a doctrinal basis for protection of the tribes by the federal government, but it also furnished support for those who disagreed with Marshall's view that the tribes were states capable of self-government.

The Cherokee question returned to the Supreme Court the very next term. Several missionaries were arrested by Georgia authorities for violating a state law requiring non-Indians residing in Cherokee territory to obtain a license from the state governor. Two of them appealed their convictions to the Supreme Court in Worcester v. Georgia, 31 U.S. (6 Pet.) 515 (1832). In the course of a lengthy and strongly-worded opinion, Marshall reviewed the history of relations with the Indians, the treaties with the Cherokees, and the Trade and Intercourse Acts which "manifestly consider the several Indian nations as distinct political communities, having territorial boundaries, within which their authority is exclusive * * *." 31 U.S. (6 Pet.) at 557. Marshall then concluded:

The Cherokee nation, then, is a distinct community, occupying its own territory, with boundaries accurately described, in which the laws of Georgia can have no force * * *.

31 U.S. (6 Pet.) at 561. The conviction of the missionaries was thereupon reversed.

Marshall's ruling in *Worcester* was even more pivotal than his language in *Cherokee Nation*. His opinion is the foundation of jurisdictional law excluding the states from power over Indian affairs, and it has much vitality today even though it is not applied to the full extent of its logic. Certainly in its own day, it was an exceptionally forthright declaration against the view that the tribes should be dispossessed at all costs. President Jackson probably did not make the statement about the decision that is popularly attributed to him: "John Marshall has made his decision; now let him enforce it," but there is little question that the decision was not popular with the Jacksonians who were anxious to hasten the exodus of the tribes from lands east of the Mississippi.

In the end, however, those favoring removal had their way. All but a few remnants of tribes east of the Mississippi were moved to the West under a program that was voluntary in name and coerced in fact. The journeys were often attended with extreme hardship and some became virtual symbols of imposed suffering, such as the Trail of Tears traveled by the Five Civilized Tribes (Cherokee, Choctaw, Creek, Chickasaw and Seminole) from the Southeast to what is now Oklahoma. In 1849, with the East nearly free of tribal Indians, the Bureau of

Indian Affairs was moved from the War Department, where it had existed since 1824, to the Department of Interior.

D. MOVEMENT TO THE RESERVATIONS: 1850 TO 1887

As non-Indians continued to move westward, further pressures were exerted upon the Indian land base. The federal government consequently evolved a policy of restricting the tribes to specified reservations. This goal was typically accomplished by treaty, exacted with varying degrees of persuasion and coercion, in which the tribe ceded much of the land it occupied to the United States and reserved a smaller portion to itself. On other occasions, the tribe was moved entirely away from the lands it was occupying to a distant reservation.

In 1871, Congress passed a statute providing that no tribe thereafter was to be recognized as an independent nation with which the United States could make treaties. Existing treaties were not affected. 25 U.S.C.A. § 71. While it is questionable that Congress could limit the constitutional treaty-making power of the President, the statute did effectively end the making of Indian treaties by serving as notice that none would thereafter be ratified. Reservations established after 1871 were accordingly created either by statute or, until Congress ended the practice in 1919, by executive order. 43 U.S.C.A. § 150.

Reservations were originally intended to keep distance and peace between Indians and non-Indians, but they came to be viewed also as instruments for "civilizing" the Indians. Each reservation was placed in charge of an Indian agent whose mission was to supervise the Indian's adaptation to non-Indian ways. The appointment of Indian agents came to be heavily influenced by organized religions, and when reservation schools were first set up in 1865, they too were directed by religious organizations with a goal of "Christianizing" the Indians. In 1878, off-reservation boarding schools were established to permit education of Indian children away from their tribal environments.

In 1883, Courts of Indian Offenses were authorized, with judges to be appointed by the Indian agents. Neither these courts nor the codes they administered were fashioned after indigenous Indian institutions; they were imposed as federal educational and disciplinary instrumentalities in furtherance of the civilizing mission of the reservations. See United States v. Clapox, 35 Fed. 575, 577 (D.Or.1888). Accordingly, certain religious dances and customary practices, as well as plural marriages, were outlawed.

Also in 1883, the Supreme Court decided the case of Ex parte Crow Dog, 109 U.S. 556 (1883), which held that murder of one Indian by another in Indian country was within the sole jurisdiction of the tribe; federal territorial courts had no power over the case. Congress reacted by passing the Major Crimes Act, declaring murder and other serious

crimes committed by an Indian in Indian country to
be federal offenses triable in federal court. The
result was a further erosion of the tribes' traditional role in dispute resolution.

E.   ALLOTMENTS AND ATTEMPTED ASSIMILATION: 1887 TO 1934

In the 1870's and 1880's, there was increasing
dissatisfaction in governmental circles with the reservation policy. Those friendly to the Indians recognized that the tribal economies were frequently a
shambles, that individual Indians were living in
hopeless poverty, and that no progress was being
made toward overcoming either of these conditions.
Others not so friendly resented large tracts of land
being excluded from white settlement. The combination of these two sentiments produced the most
important and, to the tribes, the most disastrous
piece of Indian legislation in United States history:
the General Allotment Act of 1887, also known as
the Dawes Act, 24 Stat. 388.

There is little question that the leadership for
passage of the Dawes Act came from those sympathetic to the Indians. They believed that if individual Indians were given plots of land to cultivate, they
would prosper and become assimilated into the
mainstream of American culture as middle-class
farmers. The tribes, which were viewed as obstacles
to the cultural and economic development of the
Indians, would quickly wither away. Such a prospect was not, of course, offensive in the least to

those non-Indians anxious to break up the tribal land mass.

The Allotment Act authorized the President to allot portions of reservation land to individual Indians. Allotments of 160 acres were to be made to each head of a family and 80 acres to others, with double those amounts to be allotted if the land was suitable only for grazing. (These quantities were subsequently cut in half. 25 U.S.C.A. § 331.) Title to the allotted land was to remain in the United States in trust for 25 years (or longer if extended by the President), after which it was to be conveyed to the Indian allottee in fee free of all encumbrances. The trust period was intended to protect the allottee from immediate state taxation and to permit him to learn the arts of husbandry and to acquire the capacity to manage his land and affairs. The Act provided that upon receiving allotments (or, after amendments in 1906, fee title), the allottees became United States citizens (as did other Indians residing apart from their tribes and adopting "the habits of civilized life"), and were subject to state criminal and civil law. Finally, and perhaps most notably, the Act authorized the Secretary of Interior to negotiate with the tribes for disposition of all "excess" lands remaining after allotments, for the purpose of non-Indian settlement.

The Allotment Act was the first truly wholesale Indian legislation, affecting the internal affairs of nearly all the tribes in the nation. Despite the benevolent posture of its sponsors, the Act was imposed without any requirement of consent (however obtained) of the tribes or Indians affected. Because the goal of the Act was to bring Indians into the non-Indian culture, its administration was attended with ever-increasing efforts to destroy tribal traditions and influence.

The primary effect of the Allotment Act was a precipitous decline in the total amount of Indian-held land, from 138 million acres in 1887 to 48 million in 1934. Of the 48 million acres that remained, some 20 million were desert or semidesert. Much of the land was lost by sale as tribal surplus; the remainder passed out of the hands of allottees. Allottees who received patents after 25 years found themselves subject to state property taxation, and many forced sales resulted from non-payment. In addition, the Indians' new power to sell land provided many opportunities for non-Indians to negotiate purchases of allotted land on terms quite disadvantageous to the Indians. The allottees were frequently left with neither their land nor with any benefits that might have resulted from its disposition.

Other circumstances combined to render the allotment system a failure even where the land remained in trust. Leasing of allotted trust land to non-Indians became common, defeating the intention of the Act to turn the Indians into small farmers. The Allotment Act had subjected allotted land, whether or not in trust, to state intestacy laws that resulted in highly fractionated ownership which effectively rendered the land unusable. Passage of many of the fee allotments out of Indian hands left large "checkerboard" areas of alternate non-Indian and Indian ownership, making sizable farming or grazing projects impractical.

Some reservations, particularly the ones in the West that were established late in the allotment period, largely escaped allotment and its baneful effects. But in much of the country the long-range effect of the Act was to separate Indians from their lands without accomplishing any of the benign purposes intended by the Act's sponsors.

In 1924, as the Allotment period was drawing to a close, Congress passed a statute conferring citizenship upon all Indians born within the United States. 8 U.S.C.A. § 1401(b). This action completed a process by which many Indians had already become citizens under the Allotment Act or other special statutes. By reason of the 14th Amendment, the grant of federal citizenship had the additional effect of making the Indians citizens of the states where they resided.

F. INDIAN REORGANIZATION AND PRESERVATION OF THE TRIBES: 1934 TO 1953

In 1928, the now-famous Meriam Report documented the failure of federal Indian policy during the Allotment period. Institute for Gov't Research, The Problem of Indian Administration (1928). The Report provided part of the impetus for a sweeping change in federal policy marked by passage of the Indian Reorganization Act of 1934, also known as the Wheeler–Howard Act. 25 U.S.C.A. § 461 et seq.

The Indian Reorganization Act was based on the assumption, quite contrary to that of the Allotment Act, that the tribes not only would be in existence for an indefinite period, but that they *should* be. The Act consequently sought to protect the land base of the tribes, and to permit the tribes to set up legal structures designed to aid in self-government.

Perhaps the most important and effective provision of the Indian Reorganization Act was that which ended the practice of allotment, and extended indefinitely the trust period for existing allotments still in trust. The Act also authorized the Secretary of the Interior to restore to tribal ownership any "surplus" lands acquired from the tribes under the Allotment Act, so long as third parties had not acquired rights in that land. The Act authorized the Secretary to acquire lands and water rights for the tribes, and to create new reservations.

To aid in tribal self-government, the Act authorized tribes to organize and adopt constitutions and by-laws subject to ratification by vote of tribal members. This recognition of the tribal right of self-government was not complete, however; the constitutions and by-laws were subject to approval of the Secretary of the Interior. Tribes were authorized to employ their own counsel, but again subject to the approval of the Secretary. The Secretary was also authorized to issue charters of incorporation to petitioning tribes, subject to ratification by a majority of tribal members. Finally, the Act provided that its provisions would not apply to any tribe that voted against its application at a special election to be called by the Secretary within one year of the passage of the Act.

The Act was overwhelmingly successful in preventing further rapid erosion of the tribal land base. Its encouragement of tribal self-government enjoyed a more limited success; the tribal constitutions adopted under the Act were suggested by federal authorities and followed the non-Indian pattern of divided executive, legislative and judicial authority. They were consequently often unsuited to tribal needs and conditions. Some of the tribes rejected coverage of the Act, fearing additional federal direction. But on the whole the Act must be considered a success in providing a framework, however flawed, for growing self-government by the tribes in the twenty years following its passage.

G. TERMINATION AND RELOCATION: 1953 TO 1968

By 1950, fashions in federal Indian policy were beginning once again to change radically. In 1953, Congress formally adopted a policy of "termination," its express aim being "as rapidly as possible, to make the Indians within the territorial limits of the United States subject to the same laws and entitled to the same privileges and responsibilities as are applicable to other citizens of the United States, [and] to end their status as wards of the United States * * *." H.Con.Res. 108, 83rd Cong., 1st Sess., 67 Stat. B132 (1953). Pursuant to this policy, several tribes were "terminated" by statute.

Their special relationship with the federal government was ended, they were subjected to state laws, and their lands were converted into private ownership and in most instances sold. See Chapter III, Section E, infra. While the intentions of many of the congressional supporters of termination had once again been benevolent (one purpose had been to "free" the Indians from domination by the Bureau of Indian Affairs), the results were generally tragic. The two largest terminations, those of the Klamaths of Oregon and the Menominees of Wisconsin, were typical. The Klamath lands were sold and the proceeds quickly dissipated. The Menominees were plunged into even deeper economic troubles than they had previously endured; in 1973 they were successful in securing legislation to restore their special relationship with the federal government and to place their lands back in federal trust. While the number of tribes terminated was a very small percentage of the total, the policy cast a pall over the futures of most of the tribes during the years when it was officially endorsed by Congress.

At the same time that Congress was stressing the goal of termination, the Bureau of Indian Affairs was attempting to encourage Indians to leave the reservation under its "relocation" program. As a response to unquestionably high unemployment rates on the reservations, the B.I.A. offered grants to Indians who would leave the reservation to seek work in various metropolitan centers. Some were successful in securing lasting employment. All too often, however, the effect of the program was to create in the target cities a population of unemployed Indians who suffered all the usual problems of the urban poor along with the added trauma of dislocation.

The final major piece of legislation of the 1950's that further attenuated the relationship between the federal government and the tribes was Public Law 280. 67 Stat. 588 (1953), as amended, 18 U.S.C.A. §§ 1161–62, 25 U.S.C.A. §§ 1321–22, 28 U.S.C.A. § 1360 (1953). That statute extended state civil and criminal jurisdiction to Indian country in five specified states: California, Nebraska, Minnesota (except Red Lake reservation), Oregon (except Warm Springs reservation), and Wisconsin. Alaska was added to the list in 1958. In addition, Public Law 280 provided that any other state could assume such jurisdiction by statute or state constitutional amendment. Several states assumed partial or total jurisdiction pursuant to this authority. See Chapter VIII, infra. Consent of the concerned tribes was not required and in several cases was not sought.

The effect of Public Law 280 was drastically to change the traditional division of jurisdiction among the federal government, the states and the tribes in those states where the law was applied. Assumption of jurisdiction by the state displaced otherwise applicable federal law and left tribal authorities with a greatly diminished role. It ran directly counter to John Marshall's original characterization of Indian country as territory in which the laws of the state "can have no force." Worcester v. Georgia, 31 U.S. (6 Pet.) 515, 561 (1832). Indeed, it went much further, for it not only gave state laws and courts force in Indian country, it gave them power over the Indians themselves. Yet an assumption of Public Law 280 jurisdiction by the state did not amount to a termination of the federal trust relationship. The Act specifically disclaimed any grant to the states of power to encumber or tax Indian properties held in federal trust or to interfere with treaty hunting and fishing rights. The Act was subsequently held not to have conferred upon the states general regulatory power within Indian country. Bryan v. Itasca County, 426 U.S. 373 (1976); see Chapter VIII, infra. In these respects, Public Law 280 represented a compromise between termination and continuation of the relative immunity of the tribes from state jurisdiction. It was a compromise that satisfied almost no one. The tribes, fearing that the extension of state jurisdiction was but a first step toward termination, objected to the lack of any requirement of tribal consent. The states, finding that new enforcement responsibilities involved substantial expense, resented their inability to tax tribal properties to help pay the cost. This latter consideration frequently led to neglect of law enforcement in Indian country by Public Law 280 states, and probably explains the reluctance, despite the assimilationist tenor of the times, of many states to assume general jurisdiction.

H. TRIBAL SELF–DETERMINATION: 1968 TO PRESENT

By the late 1960's, the policy of termination was largely regarded as a failure, and the assimilationist ideal began to fade. Partly as a result of this movement, and partly for independent reasons, Congress passed the Indian Civil Rights Act of 1968. 82 Stat. 77, 25 U.S.C.A. § 1301 et seq.

The primary effect of the Act was to impose upon the tribes most of the requirements of the Bill of Rights. Traditionally, the tribes had not been subject to constitutional restraints in their governmental actions, because those restraints are imposed in terms either upon the federal government or, by the 14th Amendment, upon the states. Since the tribes were neither, the constitutional restrictions did not apply to them. Talton v. Mayes, 163 U.S. 376 (1896). The Civil Rights Act imposed upon the tribes by statute such basic requirements as the protection of free speech, free exercise of religion, due process and equal protection of the laws, among others. See Chapter XI, infra. In so doing, the Act represented a federal incursion upon the independence of the tribes, and some tribal members have opposed it upon that ground. On the other hand, congressional action to require constitutional procedures by tribal governments seemed to contemplate the continued existence of those governments, rather than their withering away. In that sense, the Indian Civil Rights Act had a thrust quite inconsistent with the earlier termination policy.

One provision of the Civil Rights Act of 1968 was unequivocally welcomed by the tribes. The Act amended Public Law 280 so that states could no longer assume civil and criminal jurisdiction over Indian country unless the affected tribes consented at special elections called for the purpose. 25 U.S.C.A. §§ 1321–22, 1326. This amendment brought such extensions of jurisdiction to a virtual halt. In addition, the Act set forth a procedure by which states that had assumed Public Law 280 jurisdiction could retrocede such jurisdiction to the federal government. 25 U.S.C.A. § 1323.

In 1970, President Nixon issued a statement on Indian affairs that clearly set the current direction of federal policy. 116 Cong.Rec. 23258. He declared termination to have been a failure, and called upon Congress to repudiate it as a policy. He stressed the continuing importance of the trust relationship between the federal government and the tribes. Finally, he urged a program of legislation to permit the tribes to manage their affairs with a maximum degree of autonomy.

In the ensuing years, Congress passed several measures along the lines indicated by President Nixon. The Indian Financing Act of 1974, 25 U.S.C.A. § 1451 et seq., established a revolving loan fund to aid in the development of Indian resources. In 1975, Congress passed the Indian Self–Determination and Education Assistance Act, 25 U.S.C.A. § 450 et seq., which authorized the Secretaries of the Interior and of Health, Education and Welfare to enter contracts under which the tribes themselves would assume responsibility for the administration of federal Indian programs.

Congress in 1975 also established the American Indian Policy Review Commission to undertake a comprehensive review of federal Indian policy and to consider, among other things, "alternative methods to strengthen tribal government * * *." 88 Stat. 1910. The Commission, which included Indian representation, issued its report in 1977 and called for a firm rejection of assimilationist policies, reaffirmation of the status of tribes as permanent, self-governing institutions, and increased financial aid to the tribes.

Subsequent congressional and executive policies have continued to favor tribal self-development. The Indian Tribal Government Tax Status Act of 1982, 96 Stat. 2607, accorded the tribes many of the federal tax advantages enjoyed by states, including that of issuing tax-exempt bonds to finance governmental projects. In 1983, President Reagan reaffirmed the policy of strengthening tribal governments, with the additional goal of reducing their dependence upon the federal government. He repeated President Nixon's repudiation of the termination policy. Statement on Indian Policy, 19 Weekly Comp.Pres.Doc. 98 (Jan. 24, 1983). In 1988, Congress declared the nation's commitment to "the development of strong and stable tribal governments," 25 U.S.C.A. § 450a(b), and in 1994, President Clinton instructed each agency of the federal government to operate "within a government-to-government relationship with federally recognized tribal governments." 59 Fed.Reg. 22951 (1994).

At present, then, federal Indian policy seems clearly to be based on a model of continuing pluralism; it recognizes that the tribes are here to stay for the indefinite future, and seeks to strengthen them. The assimilationist viewpoint, which has intermittently predominated in the past, is not now in favor. It is perhaps possible that the contending forces in Indian affairs have reached some sort of final resolution, and that no further major changes of direction will occur. Nothing in the history of federal Indian policy, however, justifies confidence in such a conclusion.

CHAPTER III

THE SPECIAL RELATIONSHIP BETWEEN THE FEDERAL GOVERNMENT AND THE TRIBES

A. INTRODUCTION

Much of American Indian Law revolves around the special relationship between the federal government and the tribes. Yet it is very difficult to mark the boundaries of this relationship, and even more difficult to assess its legal consequences. At its broadest, the relationship includes the mixture of legal duties, moral obligations, understandings and expectancies that have arisen from the entire course of dealing between the federal government and the tribes. In its narrowest and most concrete sense, the relationship approximates that of trustee and beneficiary, with the trustee (the United States) subject in some degree to legally enforceable responsibilities. Unfortunately, the same terms of fiduciary obligation are often used by the courts whether they are referring to the broadest or the narrowest definition. Care must be exercised, therefore, to determine whether the type of fiduciary obligation in question in any given case is merely a moral

33

command or is an enforceable legal duty. The line between the two types of obligation is often not clear, and has increasingly become a subject of dispute as the tribes attempt to hold the federal government legally responsible for failures in its Indian policies or practices.

The degree to which the courts are willing to enforce fiduciary responsibilities of the federal government depends upon both the branch of government involved and the subject matter of the dispute. Although it has been stated on several occasions that Congress owes a fiduciary duty to the tribes, no court has ever enforced such a duty. In the case of Congress, then, the duty is essentially a moral or political obligation. The executive branch, on the other hand, sometimes has been subjected to court enforcement of its trust responsibilities. The duty of the executive branch to the tribes is therefore increasingly a legal one. In general, it has been enforced in regard to the executive's management of Indian lands or other properties, such as water rights. See Section C, infra. It should not be assumed, however, that the broader areas of the special relationship between the federal government and the tribes are unimportant simply because they have not been held to be judicially enforceable on a theory of trust. The entire relationship contributes to the unique legal posture of the tribes, as its historical origins indicate.

B. EVOLUTION OF THE RELATIONSHIP

Some form of special relationship between the federal government and the Indian tribes was probably implicit in the decision, made immediately after the Revolution, to keep Indian affairs in the hands of the federal government as a means of protecting the tribes from the states and their citizens (thereby avoiding Indian wars). See Chapter II, Section B, supra. The evolution of that relationship into fiduciary form took place slowly. The Constitution itself certainly contains no explicit delineation of a relationship, fiduciary or otherwise, but it does grant powers to the federal government that have been held to authorize its role as a trustee. Most crucial are the congressional power to regulate commerce with the Indian tribes, Art. I, § 8, cl. 3, and the presidential power to make treaties, Art. II, § 2, cl. 2. Additional support for the role of trustee sometimes has been found in the congressional power to make regulations governing the territory belonging to the United States, Art. IV, § 3, cl. 2.

Primary support for the trust relationship came, however, from the judiciary, beginning with Chief Justice John Marshall's decision in Cherokee Nation v. Georgia, 30 U.S. (5 Pet.) 1 (1831). There he characterized the tribes as "domestic dependent nations" with a right of occupancy of the land until the federal government chose to extinguish their title. Marshall added:

Meanwhile, they are in a state of pupilage; their relation to the United States resembles that of a ward to his guardian.

30 U.S. (5 Pet.) at 17. While Marshall's reference was perhaps more literary than legal and did not attempt to spell out the incidents of the guardian-ward relationship, his statement served as a conceptual basis for further evolution of the doctrine. Thus, fifty years later the Supreme Court was able to uphold Congress's Major Crimes Act (defining certain offenses committed by Indians as federal crimes), on the following theory:

These Indian tribes *are* the wards of the nation. They are communities *dependent* on the United States,—dependent largely for their daily food; dependent for their political rights. They owe no allegiance to the states, and receive from them no protection. Because of the local ill feeling, the people of the states where they are found are often their deadliest enemies. From their very weakness and helplessness, so largely due to the course of dealing of the federal government with them, and the treaties in which it has been promised, there arises the duty of protection, and with it the power. This has always been recognized by the executive, and by congress, and by this court, whenever the question has arisen.

United States v. Kagama, 118 U.S. 375, 384–85 (1886); see also United States v. Sandoval, 231 U.S. 28 (1913).

This view of the trust relationship as a source of congressional power was buttressed in Lone Wolf v. Hitchcock, 187 U.S. 553 (1903). That case involved a federal statute that distributed certain tribal lands to individual tribal members and provided for sale of other tribal lands, with the proceeds to be held for the benefit of the tribes. Some of the tribal members attacked the statute on the ground that it was inconsistent with a prior treaty which required consent of tribal members for any such distribution of lands. The Court rejected the argument, stating:

> The contention in effect ignores the status of the contracting Indians and the relation of dependency they bore and continue to bear towards the government of the United States. To uphold the claim would be to adjudge that the indirect operation of the treaty was to materially limit and qualify the controlling authority of Congress in respect to the care and protection of the Indians, and to deprive Congress, in a possible emergency, when the necessity might be urgent for a partition and disposal of the tribal lands, of all power to act, if the assent of the Indians could not be obtained.
>
> * * *
>
> Plenary authority over the tribal relations of the Indians has been exercised by Congress from the beginning, and the power has always been deemed a political one, not subject to be controlled by the judicial department of the government.

187 U.S. at 564–565. Thus where Congress was concerned, the trust responsibility had become far more of a sword for the government than a shield for the tribes.

C. ENFORCEMENT OF THE TRUST RESPONSIBILITY

It was with regard to the executive branch that the Supreme Court began to enforce the federal trust responsibility toward the Indians. The guardian-ward relationship was held not to authorize the Secretary of Interior to dispose of lands claimed by an Indian Pueblo in the same manner that he could dispose of other public lands. "That would not be an exercise of guardianship, but an act of confiscation." Lane v. Pueblo of Santa Rosa, 249 U.S. 110, 113 (1919). In Cramer v. United States, 261 U.S. 219, 229 (1923), the Court construed a doubtful statute to protect Indian-occupied lands from being patented to third parties, because to fail to protect the Indians' right of occupancy "would be contrary to the whole spirit of the traditional American policy toward these dependent wards of the nation." It also held that the United States had standing to assert the Indians' interest, by reason of its position as guardian. Some years later, the Court observed that, at least in the case of lands owned by an Indian tribe in fee, the federal powers of management arising from the trust relationship were "subject to limitations inhering in such a guardianship * * * ". United States v. Creek Nation, 295 U.S. 103, 110 (1935). Then, in 1942 the Supreme Court held that where a treaty required the United States to pay funds to tribal members, it was liable when it paid the money instead to the tribal government which was known to be misappropriating it. In regard to the treaty, the Government was more than "a mere contracting party;" it was to "be judged by the most exacting fiduciary standards." Seminole Nation v. United States, 316 U.S. 286, 296–97 (1942); see also Loudner v. United States, 108 F.3d 896, 901–02 (8th Cir.1997); cf. Manchester Band of Pomo Indians, Inc. v. United States, 363 F.Supp. 1238 (N.D.Cal.1973).

The trust responsibility and its consequences were further defined in the 1980's by the Supreme Court in two decisions arising from the same lawsuit. Indian allottees of forested land in the Quinault Reservation sued the United States for damages for mismanagement of the forest resources. In the first decision, United States v. Mitchell, 445 U.S. 535 (1980), the Court held that the General Allotment Act itself "created only a limited trust relationship between the United States and the allottee that does not impose any duty upon the Government to manage timber resources." 445 U.S. at 542. In the second decision, United States v. Mitchell, 463 U.S. 206 (1983), the Court held that a trust duty *did* arise from several statutes and regulations that, unlike the General Allotment Act, expressly authorized or directed the Secretary of Interior to manage forests on Indian lands. E.g., 25 U.S.C.A. §§ 406(a), 466. In addition, the Court stated that a fiduciary relationship necessarily arises when the Government assumes such elaborate control over forests and property belonging to Indians. All of the necessary elements of a common-law trust are present: a trustee (the United States), a beneficiary (the Indian allottees), and a trust corpus (Indian timber, lands, and funds).

463 U.S. at 225. In these circumstances, a trust relationship exists " 'though nothing is said expressly in the authorizing or underlying statute * * * about a trust fund, or a trust or fiduciary connection.' " 463 U.S. at 225 (quoting Navajo Tribe of Indians v. United States, 224 Ct.Cl. 171, 183, 624 F.2d 981, 987 (1980)). The Court went on to hold that "it naturally follows that the Government should be liable in damages for the breach of its fiduciary duties." 463 U.S. at 226. Finally, it held that the Tucker Act, 28 U.S.C.A. § 1491, and the Indian Tucker Act, 28 U.S.C.A. § 1505, waived the sovereign immunity of the United States for such claims.

The Supreme Court has thus demonstrated an increasing willingness to hold the executive accountable for breaches of its fiduciary duties to Indians. It must be kept in mind, however, that in those cases the federal government was acting in its most narrow and specific role as trustee—that of manager of assets held by the United States for the benefit of the Indians. Although the Court relied on the more general, overall trust relationship to buttress its decision in the second *Mitchell* case, 363 U.S. at 225, it has never granted relief for breach of that general duty by itself. Nor is the Court always ready to apply the law of private trusts to the federal trustee, as it appears to have done in *Mitchell*, 363 U.S. at 226. When the United States litigates on behalf of the tribes, the Court has said that the government "cannot follow the fastidious standards of a private fiduciary" with regard to potential conflicts of interest. Nevada v. United States, 463 U.S. 110, 128 (1983).

Several lower courts have invoked the trust responsibility to compel the government to undertake litigation to protect tribal lands or resources. One major example is Joint Tribal Council of Passamaquoddy Tribe v. Morton, 528 F.2d 370 (1st Cir. 1975). In that case the tribe had purported to cede most of its lands to the state by a treaty entered with the state in 1794. The treaty had been entered without the participation of the federal government, despite the provisions of the federal Trade and Intercourse Act of 1790, 1 Stat. 137, which prohibited others than the federal government from acquiring land from "any * * * tribe" of Indians. From 1794 on, all the Tribe's dealings with government had been with the state of Maine (or its predecessor, Massachusetts); it had no dealings with the federal government and Congress passed no legislation specifically in regard to the Passamaquoddy. Then, in 1972, the Tribe sued the federal government to require it to bring an action against Maine for the recovery of the Passamaquoddy lands alleged to have been improperly ceded in 1794. In its decision, the Court of Appeals held: (1) that the

Trade and Intercourse Act of 1790 included the Passamaquoddy within its terms as a "tribe," regardless of the fact that the federal government had not taken any action to "recognize" the tribe; (2) that at least insofar as the preservation of tribal lands was concerned, the Act created a trust relationship between the federal government and the tribe; and (3) that Congress had never acted to terminate this trust relationship. The Government accordingly was ordered to file suit as trustee for the tribe. See also United States v. Oneida Nation of New York, 477 F.2d 939 (Ct.Cl.1973), and United States v. Oneida Nation of New York, 576 F.2d 870 (Ct.Cl.1978); Mashpee Tribe v. New Seabury Corp., 592 F.2d 575 (1st Cir.), cert denied, 444 U.S. 866 (1979); Schaghticoke Tribe v. Kent School Corp., 423 F.Supp. 780 (D.Conn.1976).

The trust responsibility has also figured prominently in litigation concerning water rights of several of the western tribes. One such controversy involved the Pyramid Lake Paiute Tribe, which for years had been aggrieved by the declining water levels in its reservation lake, caused by certain reclamation projects along its feeder streams. After several years of prodding, the tribe succeeded in having the United States bring a water rights suit on its behalf. In the meantime, the tribe successfully attacked a regulation of the Secretary of Interior that allocated water among the various users in the watershed. The Secretary's allocation had been an accommodation to the demands of the competing users (including the tribe) and was defended as a "judgment call." The district court struck down the regulation on the ground that, in making a mere accommodation, the Secretary had failed to fulfill his fiduciary duty to protect the water rights of the tribe. The Secretary not only had to live up to that duty; he had to explain how he had done so in arriving at his particular allocation of water. The court then set forth detailed requirements for a new regulation by the Secretary. Pyramid Lake Paiute Tribe of Indians v. Morton, 354 F.Supp. 252 (D.D.C. 1972)

The courts continue to find new ways to apply trust principles to the management of tribal property. In In re Blue Lake Forest Products, Inc., 30 F.3d 1138 (9th Cir.), cert. denied, 513 U.S. 1059 (1994), the United States and the tribe had sold logs cut on the reservation to a non-Indian buyer off-reservation who received but did not pay for them. In an ensuing bankruptcy, "the heightened protection for property held in trust for Indian tribes" was held to override a state security interest in the logs that a financing bank held under the Uniform Commercial Code.

Courts in recent years have delineated additional characteristics or limitations of the federal trust responsibility. The federal government's responsibility runs to *all* Indian tribes; it therefore cannot be invoked to prevent the Indian Health Service from terminating a program favoring one Indian subgroup in order to use the resources in programs benefitting Indians generally. Lincoln v. Vigil, 508 U.S. 182, 194–95 (1993). Similarly, the United

States cannot adequately represent absent tribes in litigation, when their interests are adverse to other tribes to which the United States owes a trust duty. Shermoen v. United States, 982 F.2d 1312, 1318 (9th Cir.1992), cert. denied, 509 U.S. 903 (1993). A tribe seeking judicial redress for federal mismanagement of its resources ordinarily must first exhaust administrative remedies. White Mountain Apache Tribe v. Hodel, 840 F.2d 675, 677–78 (9th Cir.1988). The trust duty does not extend to the federal government in its disposition of an off-reservation Indian school; the school was not trust property, even though operated for the benefit of Indian tribes. Inter Tribal Council of Arizona, Inc. v. Babbitt, 51 F.3d 199 (9th Cir.1995). Congress may authorize state governments to exercise the trust responsibility in specific instances. See Pelt v. Utah, 104 F.3d 1534 (10th Cir.1996); Peyote Way Church of God, Inc. v. Thornburgh, 922 F.2d 1210, 1219 (5th Cir. 1991).

From time to time Indian litigants have urged the enforcement of a broader trust responsibility, going beyond protection of tribal lands and resources and encompassing a duty to preserve tribal autonomy or to contribute to the welfare of the tribes and their members. As yet these attempts have not met with success in the courts, which tend to insist upon a statute or regulation establishing trust responsibility, or upon the existence of federal supervision over tribal funds or other property. See United States v. Wilson, 881 F.2d 596, 600 (9th Cir.1989). When a generalized trust responsibility has been recognized, as in the case of the Federal Energy Regulatory Commission, it has entitled the tribes to no greater rights than they would otherwise have under the Federal Power Act and agency regulations. Skokomish Indian Tribe v. FERC, 121 F.3d 1303 (9th Cir.1997). The broad view of the trust responsibility is not utterly without effect, however; it can influence the decision of cases brought on other grounds. In McNabb v. Bowen, 829 F.2d 787 (9th Cir.1987), the court required the Indian Health Service to pay for medical care of an Indian child when the state, which arguably had the primary responsibility, refused to do so. The court found the sources of the federal duty in the congressional intent underlying the Indian Health Care Improvement Act, 25 U.S.C.A. § 1601 et seq., "brought into sharper focus by the trust doctrine." 829 F.2d at 793. For the Indian Health Service to refuse payment simply because the state ought to pay, when it would not, was "inconsistent with the trust doctrine." 829 F.2d at 794. The broad trust obligation of the United States thus casts its shadow beyond cases involving Indian lands, resources and proprietary treaty rights. See also Morton v. Ruiz, 415 U.S. 199, 236 (1974). Efforts to expand the enforcement of the doctrine may be expected to continue. See, generally, Chambers, *Judicial Enforcement of the Federal Trust Responsibility to Indians*, 27 Stan. L.Rev. 1213 (1975).

D. ROLE OF THE BUREAU OF INDI-
AN AFFAIRS AND THE DEPART-
MENT OF THE INTERIOR

The primary instrument for carrying out the federal trust responsibility has been the Bureau of Indian Affairs, located for the past one hundred fifty years within the Department of the Interior. From a system of Indian agents under the loose control of a small Washington office, the Bureau has evolved into a complex bureaucracy of many thousands of employees. The Washington office is headed by the Commissioner of Indian Affairs, who reports to the Assistant Secretary of Interior for Indian Affairs (whose position was recently created to reflect an increased executive commitment to tribal development). While the Washington office is at the organizational top of the Bureau, an unusually great degree of decision-making authority has been delegated to the twelve Area Offices, located in various parts of the country and each headed by an Area Director. Below the Area Offices are the eighty-odd agencies, each usually responsible for one or more reservations. The Agencies are located on reservations, and each is directed by a Superintendent who may be viewed as the modern counterpart of the Indian agent.

At one time the Bureau represented virtually the entire governing authority in Indian country, particularly during those times when assimilation was the goal of federal Indian policy and tribal self-government was discouraged. Today the activities of the Bureau are more narrowly directed toward the fulfillment of the federal trust responsibility to the tribes, although its overall influence on tribal affairs remains great. The most substantial activities of the Bureau are probably the provision of education and the management of tribal resources, particularly lands. The Bureau has for years run Indian boarding schools, which were originally designed as instruments of assimilation and which have been the focus of controversy and resentment partly because of that heritage. In recent years, the Bureau has been phasing out its boarding schools in favor of day schools located in reservation communities. The Bureau also has entered contracts permitting local tribal or community control of some of the schools, and this trend is likely to continue. (Much Indian education, of course, is provided by the states, with federal financial assistance. See 20 U.S.C.A. §§ 236–44, 631–47 ("impact aid"); 25 U.S.C.A. §§ 452–54 (Johnson O'Malley Act)).

Management of lands and other resources, including mineral and water rights, held in trust is a very significant portion of Bureau activity. Because the United States is legal titleholder of all trust resources, the federal government is of necessity a participant in all leases or other dispositions of these assets. Even a will by an individual allottee disposing of his or her beneficial interest is invalid without the approval of the Secretary of Interior. 25 U.S.C.A. § 373. Indeed, the Secretary must approve any contract providing for payment or grants of privilege by a tribe in consideration of services for the Indians "relative to their lands." 25 U.S.C.A.

§ 81; see Penobscot Indian Nation v. Key Bank, 112 F.3d 538 (1st Cir.), cert. denied, 118 S.Ct. 297 (1997). The result of trusteeship is therefore a considerable degree of Bureau supervision, whether the assets are held in trust for the tribe or for individual Indians.

There are many other activities of the Bureau too numerous to mention here. Examples are the administration of Bureau housing programs, building and maintenance of roads, licensing of Indian traders, provision of emergency relief, and the administration of various grant programs.

Over the years the Bureau has been subjected to repeated and bitter criticism on a variety of counts. If has been contended that the complex and burdensome administrative structure of the Bureau eats up an undue share of the appropriations that Congress intends for the benefit of the Indians, and that it has "lost" large portions of those appropriations. The Bureau has also been charged with simply not doing its job, and with being more sensitive to non-Indian than to Indian interests. Examples that attracted judicial attention were the Bureau's failure to issue regulations governing Indian traders, see Rockbridge v. Lincoln, 449 F.2d 567 (9th Cir.1971), and its failure in one instance to provide irrigation for Indian farmers while providing it for non-Indians—behavior that the Court of Appeals said "borders on the shocking," Scholder v. United States, 428 F.2d 1123, 1130 (9th Cir.), cert. denied, 400 U.S. 942 (1970).

A far more fundamental complaint against the administration of the trust responsibility goes beyond the Bureau to the Department of the Interior and even to the Department of Justice. The Bureau has the responsibility of defending the tribes' trust assets when they are threatened by other interests. Unfortunately, many of these threats come from other agencies within the Department of the Interior and their constituencies. Indian land and water interests frequently conflict with the activities or designs of the Bureau of Reclamation, the Bureau of Land Management, the National Park Service and, occasionally, the Bureau of Mines and the Office of Surface Mining Reclamation and Enforcement. Indian fishing interests have conflicted with those of the Fish and Wildlife Service. All of these agencies are within the Department of the Interior, and many of them have political support far in excess of that of the Bureau of Indian Affairs. As a result, Indian interests may suffer when compromises are made at the Secretary's level between competing bureaus. Although this type of political compromise goes on within every executive agency, it carries the danger that the tribes will be viewed merely as a weak political interest rather than as a group to whom a fiduciary duty is owed. Thus a federal district court overturned a water allocation that the Secretary of Interior had made as an "accommodation" without adequate attention to the trust responsibility. Pyramid Lake Paiute Tribe v. Morton, 354 F.Supp. 252 (D.D.C.1972).

The trust relationship runs into even more severe problems when the battle for preservation of trust assets becomes a legal one. The Bureau of Indian Affairs is represented initially by the Solicitor of the Department of Interior and, if the matter goes to court, by the Department of Justice. Both of these offices are charged with representing not only Indian interests, but also those of the agencies with which the tribes frequently come into conflict. In addition to the agencies within the Department of Interior listed above, the tribes find themselves competing on occasion with the Forest Service of the Department of Agriculture, which is also represented in court by the Justice Department. A private attorney could not ethically undertake the representation of such clearly competing clients, but the government attorneys regularly do. The Supreme Court has made it clear that, in those circumstances, the government may not disregard its obligations to its other beneficiaries in favor of its responsibility to the tribes. Nevada v. United States, 463 U.S. 110, 127 (1983).

[I]t may well appear that Congress was requiring the Secretary of the Interior to carry water on at least two shoulders when it delegated to him both the responsibility for the supervision of the Indian tribes and the commencement of reclamation projects in areas adjacent to reservation lands. But Congress chose to do this, and it is simply unrealistic to suggest that the Government may not perform its obligation to represent Indian tribes in litigation when Congress has obliged it to represent other interests as well. In this regard, the Government cannot follow the fastidious standards of a private fiduciary * * *.

463 U.S. at 128. Accordingly, the tribes are not relieved of the res judicata effect of a judgment merely because the government represented both the tribes and those who competed with them. 463 U.S. at 134–43; Arizona v. California, 460 U.S. 605, 626–28 (1983).

The tribes believe that the government's representation of conflicting interests results in less-than-satisfactory advocacy of Indian trust interests. One alternative, frequently employed, is for the tribes to use their own attorneys. The tribes generally may intervene in litigation affecting their interests, even if they are already represented by the United States as trustee. E.g., Arizona v. California, 460 U.S. 605, 613–15 (1983). This alternative may be an expensive one, however; the tribe that used its own attorney to sue to enforce the trust responsibility in the *Pyramid Lake* case was unable to recover attorneys' fees from the government after it prevailed on the merits. Pyramid Lake Paiute Tribe v. Morton, 499 F.2d 1095 (D.C.Cir.1974), cert. denied, 420 U.S. 962 (1975).

To avoid these problems of conflict of interest, President Nixon proposed the establishment of an independent Indian Trust Counsel Authority that would undertake legal representation of Indian trust interests. 116 Cong.Rec. 23258, 23261 (1970). The American Indian Policy Review Commission went even further; it recommended a cabinet level Department of Indian Affairs with its own Office of Trust Rights Protection to litigate trust cases. Neither proposal has been enacted by Congress.

The final, recurrent criticism of the federal administration of Indian affairs focuses on the Bureau of Indian Affairs itself. It is the charge of excessive paternalism. There is little question that at one time the Bureau supplied all government to the Indians who had been collected one way or another into reservations. The reservations themselves and the schools established by the Bureau had the very purpose of changing and molding the Indians to the non-Indian way of life—a process that was paternalistic by definition. Today the emphasis of federal policy is upon tribal self-determination, and the Bureau has certainly receded from its monolithic control of tribal affairs. Moreover, the Bureau is no longer the only presence of the federal government within Indian country. The Departments of Health and Human Services, of Education, of Housing and Urban Development, as well as the Legal Services Corporation and other agencies now play a considerable part in tribal development. Nevertheless, the Bureau is still the most important agency for the tribes, and on some occasions may influence tribal affairs to a degree greater than is consistent with present notions of tribal autonomy. There are several reasons for this persistent condition.

The first reason may simply be that old habits die hard; neither a bureaucracy nor those accustomed to relying upon it are likely to change overnight.

Habit in this case is supported by the legal framework. Most tribes have constitutions adopted pursuant to the Indian Reorganization Act of 1934, and those constitutions can only be changed after an election supervised by the Secretary of the Interior, with the Secretary having the power to review determinations of voter eligibility and to disapprove the amendments if they do not comply with federal law. See Shakopee Mdewakanton Sioux (Dakota) Community v. Babbitt, 107 F.3d 667 (8th Cir.1997). Typically, those constitutions provide either that tribal ordinances must be approved by the Secretary of the Interior or that the Secretary has the power to rescind ordinances passed by the tribal council. The Secretary's approval or disapproval is based upon the recommendation of the agency superintendent. While the policy today is that tribal ordinances will be approved almost automatically, there are still exceptions. See Moapa Band of Paiute Indians v. United States Dept. of Interior, 747 F.2d 563 (9th Cir.1984), upholding the Secretary's rescission of a tribal ordinance licensing prostitution. It is consequently quite natural for a tribal council, when considering passage of a controversial measure, to be interested in knowing whether the superintendent approves of it. From this position it is a short step to fairly continual guidance of the council by the superintendent, who is the federal authority consistently on the scene. The degree to which this tendency occurs will depend upon the character of the tribal officials and of the superintendent, the attitudes of both toward tribal independence, and the respect those parties have for each other.

Another reason why the Bureau may continue to guide many tribal affairs is found in the trust responsibility itself. The concept of trusteeship is, unfortunately, opposed in principle and to some degree in practice to that of tribal independence. If the tribal council wants to enter a particular lease upon terms that the bureau deems disadvantageous, the trust responsibility (and the possible trustee liability that follows from it) encourages the Bureau to frustrate the desires of the tribal authorities. A respect for tribal self-government would suggest that the Bureau should accede to the desires of the elected tribal officials even if their decision appeared to be an unwise one. Given this conflict, the Bureau is most likely to insist on following its view of the trust responsibility, because of the threat (hypothetical or not) of trustee liability. While it may be argued that this example arises but rarely (as there are all too many instances of the Bureau's having entered disadvantageous leases), the fact remains that the trust responsibility exerts some pressure toward continued paternalism.

An outsider's reaction to the criticisms of the Bureau might simply be to call for its abolition, but this suggestion inevitably encounters opposition from the tribes. While joining in criticism of the Bureau, tribal leaders recognize that it is much less paternalistic than it once was. It has substantial Indian representation within its ranks, partly as a result of Indian preference. Most important, the

Bureau is seen as the embodiment of the federal trust responsibility. An attempt to end the Bureau is perceived as an attempt to do away with the trust relationship itself—in other words, to "terminate." The experience of the tribes whose relationship with the federal government was terminated in the 1950's was sufficiently dismal that any hint of the policy's revival triggers instant opposition.

E. TERMINATION OF THE FEDERAL– TRIBAL RELATIONSHIP

Termination of the special relationship between the federal government and the tribes became an official goal of Congress in 1953, and was pursued for the following fifteen years. See Chapter II, Section G, supra. During that period, the relationship with over 100 tribes or bands was terminated. Nearly all of these were small, consisting of a few hundred members at most. The two exceptions were the Menominee of Wisconsin, with 3,270 members, and the Klamath of Oregon, with 2,133. All of these terminations were accomplished, as they must be, by acts of Congress. Since the provisions of these acts differ, the particular legal effects of termination upon any given tribe can be determined only by examination of the governing statute. The termination of the Mixed Blood Utes of the Uintah and Ouray Reservation, for example, has spawned endless litigation concerning its effects. See Hackford v. Babbitt, 14 F.3d 1457, 1463–64 (10th Cir.1994). Nevertheless, terminations do have enough common consequences to permit a general description of the effects of the process.

One of the most important features of termination is that the tribal land base passes out of trust into some form of private ownership. This means that the land may be sold or mortgaged. Federal government supervision, for good or ill, is no longer available for land and resource management. The land may be taxed by state and local governments, which was not possible when the land was in federal trust, and non-payment of taxes may result in loss of the land. In the case of many of the terminated tribes, the tribal lands were sold as part of the termination process and the proceeds were distributed to tribal members per capita (often to be consumed by routine living expenses).

Another element of termination is the transfer of jurisdiction over the tribal territory from the federal government to the state. The state and local governments acquire complete legislative power; they can regulate all activity taking place on the former reservation. State laws may be applied to the tribe itself. South Carolina v. Catawba Indian Tribe, Inc., 476 U.S. 498, 506 (1986). The state also acquires judicial jurisdiction; civil and criminal matters that were formerly tried in federal or tribal court go to state court instead. Individual members of the tribe, should they be found in Indian country, will not even be considered "Indians" for purposes of jurisdictional questions arising there. United States v. Heath, 509 F.2d 16 (9th Cir.1974).

Termination also brings to an end a number of federal services arising from the trust responsibility. Virtually all services administered by the Bureau of Indian Affairs including education, housing and emergency welfare are discontinued. Tribal members are no longer eligible for health care provided by the Indian Health Service. The tribe itself loses the ability to participate in a number of federal grant programs available to federally recognized tribes. A few federal programs serving "Indians" remain available to individual members, however, because the governing statute or regulation does not make eligibility depend upon federal recognition of the tribe.

A common practical result of termination is the disappearance of the entire tribal governmental structure. While termination statutes do not decree such a result, it is hardly surprising that the structure of self-government collapses when there is no tribal land base and no area of legislation or adjudication reserved for the exercise of tribal authority. Without territory and without government, tribal identity itself is severely threatened. While it is technically inaccurate to refer to "terminated tribes" because it is the federal-tribal relationship and not the tribe that is terminated by statute, that common shorthand term sometimes reflects the true state of affairs.

If the tribe is able to maintain its existence, termination will not put an end to its treaty rights in the absence of a clear expression of legislative intent to accomplish that purpose. Thus the Menominee and Klamath tribes were held to have hunting and fishing rights that survived each tribe's "termination." Menominee Tribe v. United States, 391 U.S. 404 (1968); Kimball v. Callahan, 493 F.2d 564 (9th Cir.), cert. denied, 419 U.S. 1019 (1974), and Kimball v. Callahan, 590 F.2d 768 (9th Cir.1979), cert. denied, 444 U.S. 826 (1979).

The social and economic effects of termination were almost uniformly disastrous. See Chapter II, Section G, supra. After several years of political effort, the Menominees in 1973 convinced Congress to restore the federal-tribal relationship and place their remaining lands back in federal trust. 25 U.S.C.A. §§ 903–903f (Supp.1980). Since that time, Congress has taken the same action in regard to a few other tribes or bands. The American Indian Policy Review Commission has recommended general legislation permitting restoration of any "terminated" tribe whose members vote for it. In the meantime, however, many tribes or bands continue a precarious existence without the benefits, flawed as they may be, of a special relationship with the federal government.

CHAPTER IV

INDIAN TRIBAL GOVERNMENTS

A. ORGANIZATION OF THE TRIBES; TRIBAL CONSTITUTIONS

At the time of their first contact with the Europeans, Indian tribes were characterized by a variety of traditional forms of government. As the tribes were pushed westward and ultimately confined to reservations, these ancient systems were totally disrupted. The social fabric of most of the tribes was severely damaged, and federal administration replaced traditional forms of communal decision-making and internal control. Only a few tribes, most notably the Pueblos, escaped this fate and retained most of their customary ways.

Tribal organization was further distorted by the tendency of the federal government to create a tribe where none existed. In cases where independent bands shared a common language, federal authorities sometimes found it convenient to lump them all together into a "tribe" that could enter a single treaty opening up Indian lands for settlement. On some occasions the federal government selected "chiefs" to sign these treaties even though the concept of a chief (or the choice of those particular chiefs) was wholly foreign to the existing traditional system. The federal government in several instances also gathered disparate or even hostile groups together on one reservation and dealt with them administratively as a single unit.

Federally induced erosion of tribal organization reached its peak during the period of allotment of Indian lands, when the professed goal of national policy was to break up the Indian tribes. See Chapter II, Section E. By the 1920's, when that policy came to be acknowledged as a failure, very little was left of the once-healthy tribal structures. The Indian Reorganization Act of 1934, which marked the shift in federal policy toward preservation of the tribes, did little to revive them in their familiar form. Instead, the Act built upon the tribal situation as it found it, and created an entirely new framework for tribal self-government.

The Indian Reorganization (Wheeler–Howard) Act provided that any tribe or tribes "residing on the same reservation" had the right to organize and adopt a constitution and by-laws which became effective upon a majority vote of the adult members of the tribe and upon approval by the Secretary of the Interior. 25 U.S.C.A. § 476. The Act also permitted the tribe to incorporate under a charter issued by the Secretary and approved by a majority vote of the members. 25 U.S.C.A. § 477. Under these provisions, a large number of the tribes adopted constitutions within a few years of passage of the Act, and many also became incorporated as an aid to the transaction of tribal business. Because these measures were adopted for entire reservations, the new constitutional "tribes" often included more than one ethnic tribe.

In light of the degree of tribal disorganization prevailing at the time of passage of the Reorganization Act and the novelty of the governmental structures proposed by the Act, it is not surprising that the newly constituted tribes were in a poor position to take immediate charge of their destinies. Nor was the Act designed to confer complete autonomy; the Secretary's approval was required for all new constitutions. The conditions for continued federal guidance were abundantly present. As a consequence, virtually all of the new constitutions were reproductions, with insignificant variations, of a model produced in Washington with little attention to the needs of individual tribes.

The standard constitution contained provisions describing the tribal territories, specifying eligibility for membership, and establishing the governing bodies and their powers. It also contained provisions for amendment (subject, of course, to the approval of the Secretary of the Interior), and many of the tribes have since revised their constitutions to reflect individual tribal concerns and a desire to exercise more complete tribal autonomy. Nevertheless, the original structure persists in most cases, so that it is still possible to generalize about the components of tribal government with the caveat that individual tribal constitutions should be consulted to resolve specific problems.

B. THE TRIBAL COUNCIL

Most of the tribes vest the legislative authority in a tribal council, although it is not always called by that name. The council members are normally elected for a specified number of years. In some tribes they are elected by district, in others at large. The council is given general governmental powers over internal affairs of the tribe, with one important qualification. Virtually all ordinances or resolutions of the tribal council that have an operative effect are subject to review by the Secretary of the Interior. Some constitutions provide that the ordinances and resolutions are not effective until the Secretary approves; others provide that the Secretary may rescind ordinances of which he disapproves. Either way, the requirement represents a very substantial limitation upon the self-government of the tribes.

It is true that the present policy of the Secretary (through the Bureau of Indian Affairs) is to approve nearly all ordinances, but the existence of the veto power has its effect nonetheless. Particularly where the council is unsure of itself, or where the agency superintendent or area director is particularly assertive, the council may seek guidance from those federal officials before taking important action.

C. THE TRIBAL CHAIRMAN

Most of the tribal constitutions provide for a tribal chairman, sometimes called president or governor. In some of the tribes, the chairman is elected by a vote of the council; in others, he or she is directly elected by the voting tribal members. The chairman is commonly perceived as the leader and spokesperson for the tribe, but the duties and powers of the position are often not set forth in the constitution. Tribal by-laws typically recite that it is the chairman's duty to preside over the tribal council, and then confer varying degrees of executive authority. The role of the chairman consequently differs substantially from tribe to tribe, depending upon both the governmental structure of the tribe and the individual characteristics of the particular chairman.

D. TRIBAL COURTS

The tribal courts have a history long antedating the Indian Reorganization Act. Their forerunners were Courts of Indian Offenses, first established in the eighteen-eighties by the Secretary of the Interior to help "civilize" the Indians. Those courts administered a code promulgated by the Secretary and incorporated in volume 25 of the Code of Federal Regulations (C.F.R.). Courts of Indian Offenses continued in existence even after the passage of the Indian Reorganization Act, because the tribes lacked the resources to establish new courts on their own authority. Some still function today. During the past thirty years, however, most tribes have organized their own tribal courts that administer tribal codes passed by the council and approved by the Secretary of the Interior. The jurisdiction of these courts is discussed in Chapter VII, Section

D(2) and F(2) infra. Tribal court systems vary from the highly structured, multiple court system of the Navajo Nation, served by tribal prosecutors and defense advocates, to very informal single-judge courts operated on a part-time basis without supplementary services. Some of the Pueblos utilize their traditional governing councils to adjudicate cases under the guidance of customary law. In recent years there has been an emphasis on re-establishing traditional methods of dispute-resolution, either by creating alternative courts such as the Navajo Peacemaker Court, or by providing alternative litigation tracks in existing tribal courts.

In many tribes, the tribal judges are popularly elected; in some others, they are appointed by the tribal council. They are usually, but not always, tribal members. Until the last decade, tribal judges rarely were lawyers, but recently the numbers of law-trained tribal judges has been increasing. Even if not lawyers, nearly all tribal judges undergo some form of training while in office. They commonly serve for a fixed term, although in at least one case (the Navajo) they enjoy indefinite appointments. The degree to which the judges are independent of the tribal council and its political forces varies widely, depending upon the method of judicial selection, the traditions of the council, and the character of the individual judge. In the strongest systems there is a high degree of independence, and the trend is unquestionably in that direction.

Appellate court structures have only recently been developed by most of the tribes. In many tribes, panels of tribal judges are assembled *ad hoc* for each appeal. In others, judges from other tribes are used. Some tribal appellate courts employ outside lawyers or law professors as judges. In the Navajo system, there is a regularly sitting supreme court that issues written opinions.

E. THE TRIBAL ATTORNEY

While not a part of the formal tribal government, the tribal attorney is often a major influence on tribal affairs, particularly the tribe's dealings with third parties. The hiring of attorneys by the tribal council is generally authorized by tribal constitutions, but is made subject to approval of the Secretary of the Interior, as required by statute. 25 U.S.C.A. §§ 81–82a. This requirement became an obvious source of conflict of interest on the part of the federal government when tribes began to engage in litigation against federal authorities for breach of their trust responsibilities. The Department of Interior could, by design or inadvertence, forestall hostile litigation simply by failing to approve the tribal attorney's contract. Inaction by the Department became such a severe problem for the tribes that Congress included in the Indian Civil Rights Act of 1968 a provision that failure of the Secretary to approve or disapprove an attorney's contract within ninety days resulted in automatic approval. 25 U.S.C.A. § 1331.

The client of the tribal attorney is the entire tribe, not its individual members. Of necessity the attorney's relationship is with the tribal council or the tribal chairman, and that fact creates a potential for the tribe's interest to be confused with its leaders' individual interests (much as representation of a corporation sometimes results in confusion of the interests of the corporation with those of its officers). The problem is diminished somewhat by the fact that most tribal attorneys concentrate their efforts on the tribe's external affairs—particularly its dealings with the federal government and with third parties involved in the development of tribal resources or in conflict over them. The more complicated these matters are, the more the tribal council and its chairman find it necessary to rely on the guidance of the attorney. Because the tribal attorneys are often not tribal members or even Indians, they must to some degree be considered an outside influence affecting tribal self-government.

F. TRIBAL CORPORATIONS

Those tribes that incorporated under the provisions of the Indian Reorganization Act did so under charters that were also formulated in Washington and standardized to a greater degree even than the tribal constitutions. These charters, designed to permit the tribes to engage in economic activity in corporate form, created perpetual membership corporations encompassing all tribal members. Usual corporate powers were conferred, but many actions such as the pledging of tribal income or the entering of leases were made subject to approval of the

Secretary of the Interior. The charters also provided for termination of the Secretary's supervisory powers upon a vote of the tribe, but again with the requirement that the Secretary approve such termination. The corporate power to "sue and be sued" has caused conflict in the courts over whether the tribes by those terms have waived their sovereign immunity. See Chapter V, Section C, infra.

G. TRIBES NOT ORGANIZED UNDER THE INDIAN REORGANIZATION ACT

The Indian Reorganization Act (I.R.A.) provided that tribes could vote not to be governed by its organizational provisions, and several tribes rejected application of the Act. The Navajos and many of the Pueblos are examples. As a consequence, these tribes do not necessarily follow the constitutional pattern described above, and it is unsafe to generalize about their characteristics. For example, the Navajo Nation has no written constitution although provisions are made for one in the Navajo–Hopi Rehabilitation Act of 1950, 25 U.S.C.A. § 631 et seq. Yet the Navajos operate under a detailed tribal code, and have an elected tribal council and chairman in much the same manner as the I.R.A. tribes. On the other hand, many of the Pueblos operate entirely under unwritten customary law, with traditional leaders and a governmental structure wholly different from the I.R.A. constitutional model.

CHAPTER V

INDIAN TRIBAL SOVEREIGNTY

A. ORIGINS AND DEVELOPMENT
OF TRIBAL SOVEREIGNTY

Sovereignty is a word of many meanings, and it is used frequently and loosely in Indian affairs. At its most basic, the term refers to the inherent right or power to govern. At the time of the European discovery of America, the tribes were sovereign by nature and necessity; they conducted their own affairs and depended upon no outside source of power to legitimize their acts of government. By treating with the tribes as foreign nations and by leaving them to regulate their own internal affairs, the colonial powers and later the federal government recognized the sovereign status of the tribes. On the other hand, the Europeans clearly claimed dominion over all the territories of the new world, and those claims seemed to limit in some degree the sovereignty of the tribes living there. The legal status of the tribes as nations was therefore clouded by uncertainties, and it was left to the Supreme Court to attempt to resolve them.

In Johnson v. McIntosh, 21 U.S. (8 Wheat.) 543 (1823), Chief Justice Marshall held that Indian tribes had no power to grant lands to anyone other than the federal government. In describing the effects of European discovery on the tribes, Marshall said:

> [T]he rights of the original inhabitants were, in no instance, entirely disregarded; but were, necessarily, to a considerable extent, impaired. They were admitted to be the rightful occupants of the soil * * * but their rights to complete sovereignty, as independent nations, were necessarily diminished, and their power to dispose of the soil, at their own will, to whomsoever they pleased, was denied by the original fundamental principle, that discovery gave exclusive title to those who made it.

21 U.S. (8 Wheat.) at 574. The principles of discovery were, of course, European (and, by adoption, federal) law which the Indian tribes might have thought quite irrelevant, but in Marshall's view that was the only kind of law that the Supreme Court could apply.

Having thus established a serious limitation on tribal sovereignty, Marshall ten years later emphasized the affirmative governmental power of the tribes. In Cherokee Nation v. Georgia, 30 U.S. (5 Pet.) 1 (1831), the Court held that the Cherokees could not be regarded as a "foreign state" within the meaning of Article III of the Constitution, so as to bring them within the federal judicial power and permit them to maintain their action in the Supreme Court. But in ruling the tribe not "foreign,"

Marshall was careful to acknowledge that it qualified as a "state":

> So much of the argument as was intended to prove the character of the Cherokees as a state, as a distinct political society separated from others, capable of managing its own affairs and governing itself, has, in the opinion of a majority of the judges, been completely successful.

30 U.S. (5 Pet.) at 16. He then went on to characterize the tribes, in a famous phrase, as "domestic dependent nations."

In Worcester v. Georgia, 31 U.S. (6 Pet.) 515, 559 (1832), Marshall had a further opportunity to discuss the status of the tribes.

> The Indian nations had always been considered as distinct, independent, political communities, retaining their original natural rights, as the undisputed possessors of the soil, from time immemorial, with the single exception of that imposed by irresistible power, which excluded them from intercourse with any other European potentate than the first discoverer of the coast of the particular region claimed * * *.

The opinion then went on to hold that the laws of Georgia could have no force in Cherokee territory.

Marshall, then, left a view of the tribes as nations whose independence had been limited in only two essentials—the conveyance of land and the ability to deal with foreign powers. For all internal purposes, the tribes were sovereign and free from state intrusion on that sovereignty. Although Marshall's position has been subject to some modification, it still provides the foundation for determining the governmental role of the tribes.

One consequence of the view of tribes as sovereign is that, when a dispute arises over the exercise of tribal powers of self-government, the decisionmaker must begin with the assumption that the power exists. In other words, a tribe is quite unlike a city or other subdivision of a state. When a question arises as to the power of a city to enact a particular regulation, there must be some showing that the state has conferred such power on the city; the state, not the city, is the sovereign body from which power must flow. A tribe, on the other hand, is its own source of power. Thus a tribe's right to establish a court or levy a tax is not subject to attack on the ground that Congress has not authorized the tribe to take these actions; the tribe is sovereign and needs no authority from the federal government. Iron Crow v. Oglala Sioux Tribe, 231 F.2d 89 (8th Cir.1956); Merrion v. Jicarilla Apache Tribe, 455 U.S. 130, 149 (1982). The relevant inquiry is whether any limitation exists to *prevent* the tribe from acting, not whether any authority exists to *permit* the tribe to act. See National Farmers Union Ins. Cos. v. Crow Tribe, 471 U.S. 845, 852–53 (1985). As a sovereign, it is free to act unless some federal intrusion has affirmatively modified that sovereignty. To determine whether sovereignty has been modified, it may be necessary to examine relevant statutes, treaties, executive policies, and administrative or judicial decisions. Id. at 855–56.

Two additional consequences have followed from the fact that tribal powers are inherent and not derived from the federal government. The provisions of the Bill of Rights that restrict the federal government have been held not to apply to the tribes. Talton v. Mayes, 163 U.S. 376 (1896); see Chapter XI, infra. Nor does it violate the Fifth Amendment provision against double jeopardy for the tribe and the federal government to prosecute a defendant for the same offense; both independent sovereigns are entitled to vindicate their identical public policies. United States v. Wheeler, 435 U.S. 313 (1978).

The self-governing character of the tribes also has enabled Congress to delegate power to them that could not properly be delegated to a non-governmental private association. In United States v. Mazurie, 419 U.S. 544 (1975), the Supreme Court upheld a federal statute prohibiting the introduction of liquor into Indian country unless the tribe involved permitted it. The delegation was valid because the tribes already possessed some independent regulatory authority over the subject matter.

B. TRIBAL SOVEREIGNTY TODAY; ITS MEANING AND LIMITS

1. DOMESTIC DEPENDENT STATUS

John Marshall described only two disabilities arising from the domestic dependent status of the tribal sovereigns-tribes could not freely alienate their land and they could not treat with foreign powers. For nearly 150 years following the Cherokee cases, no additional limitations on tribal sovereignty were found to inhere in domestic dependent status. Then, in Oliphant v. Suquamish Indian Tribe, 435 U.S. 191 (1978), the Supreme Court announced another. That case raised the issue of the tribe's power to exercise criminal jurisdiction over non-Indians on the reservation. The tribe relied upon its inherent sovereignty, and argued that no treaty or act of Congress took away its criminal authority over non-Indians. The Supreme Court held that the exercise of criminal jurisdiction over non-Indians was inconsistent with the domestic dependent status of the tribes. The Court also referred to 200 years of federal legislation that seemed to assume an absence of tribal criminal jurisdiction over non-Indians, but those statutes were not held to have removed such jurisdiction by their own operative effect. The Court based its decision squarely on the status of the tribes. While the two limitations originally delineated by Chief Justice Marshall were almost inevitable concomitants of dependent status, that of *Oliphant* was considerably less so.

By opening the door to discovery of new inherent limitations on tribal sovereignty, *Oliphant* represented a significant potential threat to tribal governmental power. The threat was not long in being realized. Tribes were held, rather surprisingly, to have lost any preemptive power to regulate liquor

sales on their reservations, as a consequence of
domestic dependent status. Rice v. Rehner, 463 U.S.
713, 726 (1983). Two years earlier, in Montana v.
United States, 450 U.S. 544 (1981), the Court held
that, at least where there was no showing that
tribal interests were affected, a tribe lacked inherent power to regulate hunting and fishing by non-
Indians on non-Indian-owned land within its reservation. Ownership of land within a reservation had
not previously been held relevant to determinations
of jurisdiction. The Court recited that tribes retained inherent power to protect self-government
and to control "internal relations," which the Court
described quite narrowly as including "the power to
punish tribal offenders, . . . to determine tribal
membership, to regulate domestic relations among
members, and to prescribe rules of inheritance for
members." 450 U.S. at 564. The Court then stated:

> But exercise of tribal power beyond what is neces-
> sary to protect tribal self-government or to con-
> trol internal relations is inconsistent with the
> dependent status of the tribes, and so cannot
> survive without express congressional delegation.

450 U.S. at 564. Non–Indian hunting and fishing on
non-Indian fee lands, according to the Court, bore
no clear relation to tribal self government or internal relations. The Court then added two qualifications to its ruling. Tribes retained inherent sovereign power, even on fee lands: (1) to regulate by
taxation, licensing or other means, activities of nonmembers who enter consensual relationships with
the tribe or its members, as by commercial dealings;

and (2) to regulate conduct of non-Indians that threatens or directly affects "the political integrity, the economic security, or the health or welfare of the tribe." 450 U.S. at 565–66.

Although *Montana* announced an exception to the general rule that a tribe has governmental power over its territory unless some statute or treaty takes it away, subsequent Supreme Court opinions have tended to refer to the *"Montana* rule," not the *"Montana* exception." Thus the plurality opinion in Brendale v. Confederated Tribes and Bands of the Yakima Indian Nation, 492 U.S. 408 (1989), applied the "general principle" of *Montana* to preclude a tribe from zoning fee lands within the reservation that were owned by nonmembers. Because of split votes of other Justices, the judgment in *Brendale* permitted the tribe to zone non-member fee lands in the "closed" portion of the reservation but not in the "open" portion—a territorial distinction that had never before been made. Justice Blackmun in dissent argued that *Montana* should be recognized as a relatively narrow exception to the presumption of tribal governmental power. 492 U.S. at 450–51.

In Duro v. Reina, 495 U.S. 676 (1990), the Supreme Court held that the retained sovereignty of an Indian tribe did not include criminal jurisdiction over nonmember Indians on its reservation, despite a pattern of federal criminal legislation classifying Indians, rather than members, for jurisdictional purposes. See, e.g., 18 U.S.C.A. §§ 1152, 1153. Congress promptly overruled the Court, recognizing and affirming "the inherent power of Indian tribes

* * * to exercise criminal jurisdiction over all Indians." 25 U.S.C.A. § 1301(2).

Finally, in Strate v. A–1 Contractors, 117 S.Ct. 1404 (1997), the Supreme Court held that a tribal court lacked jurisdiction over a civil case between nonmembers arising out of a vehicle accident on a state highway traversing the reservation. The Court held that the grant of right-of-way to the state, which precluded the tribe from exercising proprietary rights of exclusion, rendered the highway the equivalent of non-Indian fee land. 117 S.Ct. at 1413. The Court stated that *"Montana* thus described a general rule that, absent a different congressional direction, Indian tribes lack civil authority over the conduct of nonmembers on non-Indian land within a reservation." The only exceptions were for nonmembers with consensual relationships and activities affecting "the tribe's political integrity, economic security, health, or welfare." 117 S.Ct. at 1409. The tribe's interest in safe driving within the reservation was not sufficient to qualify for the second *Montana* exception, because such a construction "would severely shrink the [*Montana*] rule." 117 S.Ct. at 1415.

Strate is thus the culmination of a series of cases that has reversed the usual presumption regarding sovereignty when the tribe's power over nonmembers on non-Indian fee lands (or the equivalent) is concerned. Instead of presuming that tribal power exists, and searching for statutes or treaties that negate the presumption, the Court presumes that power is absent unless Congress has said otherwise.

117 S.Ct. at 1409; see also South Dakota v. Bourland, 508 U.S. 679, 695 n. 15 (1993). *Strate* also
limits tribal court power over nonmembers to the
Montana formula, which is a departure from the
normal approach to civil judicial jurisdiction. Most
courts can entertain transitory causes of action,
with no requirement that the parties be subject to
regulatory or legislative power within the jurisdiction. The Supreme Court, therefore, appears to
have firmly cemented its view that tribes, as domestic dependent nations, have no authority over nonmembers on non-Indian fee lands, and no criminal
authority over non-Indians anywhere. Whether
Strate presages further limitations on tribal jurisdiction over nonmembers is not clear; its holding
was limited to a state right-of-way, but the Court
stated that it "express[ed] no view on the governing
law or proper forum when an accident occurs on a
tribal road within a reservation." 117 S.Ct. at 1407.
The Ninth Circuit has interpreted *Strate* to preclude tribal court jurisdiction over a civil suit by a
tribal member against a nonmember arising from a
vehicle accident on a state highway within a reservation. Wilson v. Marchington, 127 F.3d 805 (9th
Cir.1997), cert. denied, 118 S.Ct. 1516 (1998). Even
more broadly, it has held that *Strate* precludes
tribal court jurisdiction over a suit by tribal members against non-Indian officers for false arrest on
reservation fee lands that may have been Indian-
owned; the ownership was held to be irrelevant so
long as the defendant officers, who exercised Public
Law 280 jurisdiction, had a right to be there. Coun-

ty of Lweis v. Allen, 1998 WL 191233 (9th Cir. 1998).

A larger question is presented by the Supreme Court's line of cases from United States v. Wheeler, 435 U.S. 313 (1978), through *Montana* to *Strate*. Sovereign power, even when exercised by democratically elected officials, is typically both coercive and territorial. These Supreme Court decisions, however, emphasize two factors not previously considered to be of jurisdictional importance: tribal membership (as opposed to Indian status), and land ownership (as opposed to reservation status as Indian country). Each factor inclines toward a view of tribal power that is not necessarily sovereign and governmental. Private clubs may regulate the conduct of members, but that membership-based power is not governmental; the members may resign and the club has no ability to regulate nonmembers. Private landowners can establish rules of behavior for those who wish to remain on their lands, but that power, too, is not governmental. The question raised by the line of cases from *Wheeler* to *Montana* to *Strate*, which stress membership and rights of land ownership as sources of tribal power, is whether the Supreme Court is evolving, purposefully or not, toward a nongovernmental view of tribal power and, if so, how far and fast that evolution will proceed.

On the other hand, a governmental view of tribal power (including the power over its members) is still dominant in several areas. *Wheeler*'s actual holding was that an exercise by a tribe of criminal

jurisdiction over one of its members was the act of
an independent sovereign. 435 U.S. at 327. The
Court also has never called into question its decisions that tribes as domestic dependent sovereigns
have the power to tax non-Indians for their activities on the reservation. Washington v. Confederated
Tribes of the Colville Indian Reservation, 447 U.S.
134, 152–54 (1980); Merrion v. Jicarilla Apache
Tribe, 455 U.S. 130, 149 (1982); see also Mustang
Production Co. v. Harrison, 94 F.3d 1382, 1385
(10th Cir.1996), cert. denied, 117 S.Ct. 1288 (1997).
The tradition of tribal sovereignty running from
Cherokee Nation v. Georgia embraces a governmental theory of tribal power, and it is unlikely that it
will lose all of its vitality.

2. PREEMPTION OF STATE LAW

Tribal sovereignty has operated to a considerable
degree as a shield against intrusions of state law
into Indian country. Chief Justice Marshall's view,
as described above, was that state laws could simply
"have no force" in Indian territory. Worcester v.
Georgia, 31 U.S. (6 Pet.) 515, 561 (1832). That rule
was modified some fifty years later, however, to
permit state law to apply to a crime by a non-Indian
against a non-Indian on an Indian reservation.
United States v. McBratney, 104 U.S. 621 (1882);
Draper v. United States, 164 U.S. 240 (1896). But
the Supreme Court has almost always held the line
against permitting state law to apply to Indians in
Indian country. In Williams v. Lee, 358 U.S. 217

(1959), a unanimous Court ruled that state courts had no jurisdiction over a civil claim by a non-Indian against an Indian for a transaction arising on the Navajo reservation. The Court stated that state law had been permitted to intrude only where "essential tribal relations" were not involved, and that "absent governing Acts of Congress, the question has always been whether the state action infringed on the right of reservation Indians to make their own laws and be governed by them." To permit state court jurisdiction in this instance, said the Court, "would undermine the authority of the tribal courts over Reservation affairs and hence would infringe on the right of the Indians to govern themselves." 358 U.S. at 220, 223.

In McClanahan v. Arizona State Tax Comm'n, 411 U.S. 164 (1973), the Supreme Court made it clear that state law would be permitted to intrude into Indian country only if both of two conditions were met: (1) there was no interference with tribal self-government; and (2) non-Indians were involved. Thus the Court held that Arizona could not tax the income of an Indian earned on the reservation. In so holding, however, the Court articulated a new approach to the doctrine of tribal sovereignty.

[T]he trend has been away from the idea of inherent Indian sovereignty as a bar to state jurisdiction and toward reliance on federal preemption. * * * The modern cases thus tend to avoid reliance on platonic notions of Indian sovereignty and to look instead to the applicable treaties and statutes which define the limits of state power. * * *

The Indian sovereignty doctrine is relevant, then, not because it provides a definitive resolution of the issues in this suit, but because it provides a backdrop against which the applicable treaties and federal statutes must be read. It must always be remembered that the various Indian tribes were once independent and sovereign nations, and that their claim to sovereignty long predates that of our own Government.

411 U.S. at 172 (footnote omitted). Reading the inexplicit treaty and statutes with "this tradition of sovereignty in mind," the Court found that they precluded state taxation.

Even though *McClanahan* reached a result highly protective of tribal sovereignty, it launched a methodology that may often have the opposite effect. By reducing sovereignty to a backdrop and relying on the preemptive effect of federal law to exclude state power, *McClanahan*'s analysis appears to alter the presumption that the tribe has governmental power over all matters affecting the tribe on the reservation, and that the state does not. It seems instead to assume that the state has power unless federal law (including federal Indian policy) has preempted it.

Because Congress is rarely explicit in preempting state law, the preemption analysis following *McClanahan* often involves a weighing and balancing of the competing state and federal interests.

State jurisdiction is preempted by the operation of federal law if it interferes with or is incompatible with federal and tribal interests reflected in federal law, unless the state interests at stake are sufficient to justify the assertion of state authority.

New Mexico v. Mescalero Apache Tribe, 462 U.S. 324, 334 (1983). Under the previous, more formalistic approach of Williams v. Lee, 358 U.S. 217, 220 (1959), state law simply could not be applied if it interfered with the right of Indians to make their own laws and be governed by them. True, the standard could be weakened by taking a very narrow view of the area of tribal self-government. See *McClanahan*, 411 U.S. at 179–80. But a narrow view usually was not adopted, and if Indian interests were affected, the state law could not apply no matter how important the state interest was. Under the preemption analysis, considered by itself, an extremely important state interest may interfere with and override tribal interests in self-government.

The rule of *Williams v. Lee* that state law may not interfere with tribal self-government remains in effect as an independent test to be applied along with preemption analysis, New Mexico v. Mescalero Apache Tribe, 462 U.S. 324, 334 n. 16 (1983), but tribal self-government no longer seems to be generously defined to include everything that affects Indian interests. See Strate v. A–1 Contractors, 117 S.Ct. 1404, 1416 (1997). As a consequence, most cases involving the application of state law in Indian country are decided on preemption grounds.

In general, the Supreme Court in applying its preemption analysis has considered tribal self-determination to be a weighty federal interest. It has declined, however, to entertain a presumption that all on-reservation activities affecting the tribes are beyond the reach of state power as a necessary implication of the dormant Indian commerce clause, U.S. Const., Art. I, § 8, cl. 3. Ramah Navajo School Bd., Inc. v. Bureau of Revenue, 458 U.S. 832, 845–46 (1982).

Because preemption analysis is highly fact-specific and depends upon the interplay of the particular statutes, treaties, regulations and interests involved, it is less predictable than a more formalistic prescription for protecting Indian sovereignty. When preemption is employed, generalizations become more than usually suspect, and cases must be analyzed in light of their own facts. Yet, a few patterns have emerged. The states have been categorically precluded from directly taxing reservation lands or reservation Indians. See County of Yakima v. Confederated Tribes and Bands of the Yakima Indian Nation, 502 U.S. 251, 257 (1992); Oklahoma Tax Comm'n v. Chickasaw Nation, 515 U.S. 450, 458 (1995). States also have been largely unsuccessful in taxing non-Indian contractors doing business with tribes on reservations. White Mountain Apache Tribe v. Bracker, 448 U.S. 136 (1980); Ramah Navajo School Bd., Inc. v. Bureau of Revenue, 458 U.S. 832 (1982); Central Machinery Co. v. Ari-

zona State Tax Com'n, 448 U.S. 160 (1980). They
have, however, succeeded in taxing cigarette sales to
non-members of the tribes on reservations, and
even in requiring the tribal seller to collect and
remit the tax. Moe v. Confederated Salish and Kootenai Tribes of Flathead Reservation, 425 U.S. 463
(1976); Washington v. Confederated Tribes of the
Colville Indian Reservation, 447 U.S. 134 (1980);
Oklahoma Tax Comm'n v. Citizen Band of Potawatomi Indian Tribe, 498 U.S. 505 (1991). The state is
not preempted even when the tribe imposes its own
cigarette tax. Colville, supra. States have also succeeded in imposing severance taxes on non-Indian
oil and gas producers in Indian country, despite a
similar tribal tax. Cotton Petroleum Corp. v. New
Mexico, 490 U.S. 163 (1989).

A state has been held not preempted from regulating liquor sales by a tribal member on reservation; indeed, in reasoning not since repeated, the
tribe itself was held to be preempted by the exercise
of federal regulation. Rice v. Rehner, 463 U.S. 713
(1983). States have been preempted, however, from
regulating hunting and fishing by non-Indians on
the reservation when the tribe regulated extensively, New Mexico v. Mescalero Apache Tribe, 462 U.S.
324 (1983), and from regulating high stakes bingo
and poker games operated by tribes on reservations,
California v. Cabazon Band of Mission Indians, 480
U.S. 202 (1987).

Protection of tribal sovereignty under the preemption analysis of *McClanahan* has therefore been
substantial but not unwavering. There is one area

in which the Supreme Court appears willing to protect tribal sovereignty from state intrusion without weighing the importance of the state interest. The state courts will not be allowed to exercise civil jurisdiction that interferes with tribal court jurisdiction involving tribal members on the reservation. *Williams v. Lee* governs. See Iowa Mut. Ins. Co. v. LaPlante, 480 U.S. 9, 15 (1987). Although Strate v. A–1 Contractors, 117 S.Ct. 1404, 1412–13 (1997) refused to apply a presumption of tribal jurisdiction to nonmember activities on fee land, it did not limit the applicability of *Williams v. Lee* in cases involving members and reservation activity.

3. PLENARY POWER OF CONGRESS

Although there may be argument over the extent to which the courts may properly limit tribal sovereignty, there has never been any doubt that Congress is legally free to do so. Talton v. Mayes, 163 U.S. 376, 384 (1896); Santa Clara Pueblo v. Martinez, 436 U.S. 49, 56 (1978). Congress' power over Indian affairs is plenary. Plenary power, of course, is subject to constitutional restraint when, for example, Congress deals with recognized Indian property interests, see Babbitt v. Youpee, 117 S.Ct. 727 (1997). As yet, however, no court has found a constitutionally protectible interest in tribal sovereignty itself, and numerous examples exist of federal statutes limiting it. The Major Crimes Act, 18 U.S.C.A § 1153, is an example of federal intrusion on the tribe's traditional power to punish its own members for crime. See United States v. Kagama, 118 U.S. 375 (1886); Ex parte Crow Dog, 109 U.S. 556 (1883). Public Law 280, 67 Stat. 588, which extended state civil and criminal jurisdiction over certain tribes, and the Civil Rights Act of 1968, 25 U.S.C.A. § 1301 et seq., which imposed most of the restraints of the Bill of Rights on the tribes, were both examples of federal legislation interfering substantially with tribal self-government. Finally, federal statutes terminating the special relationship between the federal government and the tribes have the effect of subjecting virtually all tribal affairs to state jurisdiction and causing the ultimate erosion of tribal government. See Chapter III, Section E, supra. Although the doctrine of plenary power of Congress over tribal sovereignty has its critics, see Red Lake Band of Chippewa Indians v. Swimmer, 740 F.Supp. 9, 11–12 (D.D.C.1990), it remains in full strength in the courts, so long as Congress makes its intent to limit sovereignty clear. See, e.g., Fletcher v. United States, 116 F.3d 1315, 1327 (10th Cir.1997). One court has found the Fair Labor Standards Act sufficiently unclear that it would not be applied to tribal off-reservation fish and wildlife police, thus "making federal law bear as lightly on Indian tribal prerogatives as the leeways of statutory interpretation allow." Reich v. Great Lakes Indian Fish & Wildlife Comm'n, 4 F.3d 490, 496 (7th Cir.1993). Such an approach to statutory interpretation does not, however, negate congressional power. Thus it may be said with accuracy that, however useful tribal sovereignty is as a source of inherent tribal power and as a shield against state intrusion, such sovereignty exists entirely at the sufferance of Congress. Political restraints may, of course, keep Congress from eliminating or greatly diminishing tribal sovereignty, but legal restraints do not.

C. SOVEREIGN IMMUNITY OF THE TRIBES

The principle that tribes enjoy the sovereign's common law immunity from suit is well established. Santa Clara Pueblo v. Martinez, 436 U.S. 49, 58 (1978). The immunity extends to agencies of the tribes. Weeks Construction, Inc. v. Oglala Sioux Housing Authority, 797 F.2d 668 (8th Cir.1986). It applies in both state and federal court. See Pan American Co. v. Sycuan Band of Mission Indians, 884 F.2d 416 (9th Cir.1989). Tribal immunity extends to claims for declaratory and injunctive relief, not merely damages, and it is not defeated by a claim that the tribe acted beyond its power. Imperial Granite Co. v. Pala Band of Mission Indians, 940 F.2d 1269 (9th Cir.1991). Sovereign immunity also protects the tribes against enforcement of subpoenas. United States v. James, 980 F.2d 1314, 1319–20 (9th Cir.1992), cert. denied, 510 U.S. 838 (1993).

Inclusion of a group of Indians on the Federal Register list of recognized tribes (see Chapter I, Section B) is ordinarily sufficient to establish entitlement to immunity, unless the suit in issue concerns the validity of that listing. Cherokee Nation of

Oklahoma v. Babbitt, 117 F.3d 1489, 1499 (D.C.Cir. 1997).

Tribal sovereign immunity is a controversial subject, partly because tribal immunity retains its full vitality in an era when other governments are limiting their general immunity. States that have abandoned their own immunity from tort liability must nevertheless honor the immunity of the tribes. See Morgan v. Colorado River Indian Tribe, 103 Ariz. 425, 443 P.2d 421 (1968). The tribes, however, must honor the immunity of states from suit in tribal court; the inherent sovereignty of the tribes has been held not to abrogate the states' immunity, even when the state has waived immunity in its own courts. Montana v. Gilham, 127 F.3d 897 (9th Cir.1997). The tribes are also prevented by the Eleventh Amendment from suing states in federal court without their consent. Seminole Tribe of Florida v. Florida, 517 U.S. 44 (1996); Idaho v. Coeur d'Alene Tribe, 117 S.Ct. 2028 (1997).

Tribes are not immune from suits by the United States. United States v. Yakima Tribal Court, 806 F.2d 853, 861 (9th Cir. 1986), cert. denied, 481 U.S. 1069 (1987); United States v. Red Lake Band of Chippewa Indians, 827 F.2d 380 (8th Cir.1987), cert. denied, 485 U.S. 935 (1988). Here, however, the situation is not reciprocal. The United States remains immune from suit in tribal court. United States v. Yakima Tribal Court, 806 F.2d 853 (9th Cir.1986), cert. denied, 481 U.S. 1069 (1987).

At least two state courts have held that a tribe loses its immunity from suit when it conducts commercial enterprises off the reservation. Aircraft Equip. Co. v. Kiowa Tribe of Okla., 939 P.2d 1143 (Okla. 1997), pet. for cert. filed, 66 U.S.L.W. 3130 (1997); Padilla v. Pueblo of Acoma, 107 N.M. 174, 754 P.2d 845 (1988), cert. denied, 490 U.S. 1029 (1989). The Supreme Court has agreed to review another such decision in Kiowa Tribe of Okla. v. Manufacturing Technologies, Inc., 117 S.Ct. 2506 (1997). Despite these state-court rulings, the prevailing view has been to the contrary: the tribes retain their immunity when conducting commercial enterprises, on the reservation or off it. See In re Greene, 980 F.2d 590 (9th Cir.1992), cert. denied, 510 U.S. 1039 (1994); Sac and Fox Nation v. Hanson, 47 F.3d 1061 (10th Cir.1995), cert. denied, 516 U.S. 810 (1995); Morgan v. Colorado River Indian Tribe, 103 Ariz. 425, 443 P.2d 421 (1968). The prevailing view also gained some support from Oklahoma Tax Comm'n v. Citizen Band Potawatomi Indian Tribe, 498 U.S. 505 (1991), which rejected a state argument that a tribal cigarette sales operation on allotted land should not be immune. The discussion in *Potawatomi* causes some confusion, however, because it does not always differentiate between sovereign immunity of tribes from suit and immunity of tribes and Indians from state taxation in Indian country, which is a matter of preemption.

Sovereign immunity prevents a court from entering orders against the tribe itself in the absence of an effective waiver, but it does not prevent a court from adjudicating the rights of individual tribal members. Puyallup Tribe, Inc. v. Washington Game Dept., 433 U.S. 165 (1977).

The fact that a tribe cannot be sued does not defeat all challenges to the exercise of its power. The Supreme Court has held that a tribal officer is not protected by the tribe's immunity from suit. Santa Clara Pueblo v. Martinez, 436 U.S. at 59. If the official acts beyond his or her authority, or beyond the authority that the tribe had the power legally to confer, the official may be sued. See Baker Elec. Co-op., Inc. v. Chaske, 28 F.3d 1466, 1471–72 (8th Cir.1994); Tenneco Oil Co. v. Sac and Fox Tribe, 725 F.2d 572, 574–75 (10th Cir.1984). Thus a party claiming that a tribe had no power under federal law to impose a tax can sue tribal officials to enjoin enforcement, just as state taxpayers can sue state officials under Ex Parte Young, 209 U.S. 123 (1908). Burlington Northern R. Co. v. Blackfeet Tribe, 924 F.2d 899 (9th Cir.1991), cert. denied, 505 U.S. 1212 (1992); see also Arizona Public Service Co. v. Aspaas, 77 F.3d 1128, 1133–34 (9th Cir.1995).

On the other hand, if tribal officials act within the scope of their lawful authority, they share the tribe's immunity from suit. E.g., Fletcher v. United States, 116 F.3d 1315, 1324 (10th Cir.1997); Hardin v. White Mountain Apache Tribe, 779 F.2d 476, 479 (9th Cir.1985). Wholly apart from questions of sovereign immunity, tribal officers may also be immune from liability for damages by reason of their status as judges or officers acting in good faith. Cf.

United States v. Yakima Tribal Court, 806 F.2d 853, 861 (9th Cir.1986), cert. denied, 481 U.S. 1069 (1987); Kennerly v. United States, 721 F.2d 1252, 1259–60 (9th Cir.1983).

It is clear that Congress can waive a tribe's immunity from suit, but that waiver must be clearly expressed. The Supreme Court refused to find a congressional waiver in the passage of the Civil Rights Act of 1968, which imposed some of the restrictions of the Bill of Rights upon the tribes. Santa Clara Pueblo v. Martinez, 436 U.S. at 58–59. But when a federal statute, such as the Hazardous Materials Transportation Act, clearly indicates that it applies to Indian tribes, tribal sovereign immunity cannot bar enforcement of the statute. Northern States Power Co. v. Prairie Island Mdewakanton Sioux Indian Community, 991 F.2d 458 (8th Cir. 1993). Thus tribes may be sued in federal court under the "citizen suit" provisions of the Resource Conservation and Recovery Act (RCRA). Blue Legs v. U.S. Bureau of Indian Affairs, 867 F.2d 1094, 867 F.2d 1094 (8th Cir.1989). Federal officials acting without congressional authorization are not capable of waiving tribal immunity. United States v. United States Fidelity & Guar. Co., 309 U.S. 506, 513 (1940).

While the earlier cases dealing with waiver of tribal immunity concern themselves only with congressional waiver, later decisions allow waiver by the tribe alone. Recent Supreme Court discussions of waiver assume that the tribe alone could waive its immunity. See Three Affiliated Tribes of Fort

Berthold Reservation v. Wold Engineering, 476 U.S. 877 (1986); Puyallup Tribe, Inc. v. Department of Game of Washington, 433 U.S. 165 (1977); Oklahoma Tax Comm'n v. Citizen Band Potawatomi Indian Tribe, 498 U.S. 505 (1991). Lower courts have now accepted the view that a tribe can waive its immunity if it does so unequivocally. E.g., Weeks Construction, Inc. v. Oglala Sioux Housing Authority, 797 F.2d 668 (8th Cir.1986); Atkinson v. Haldane, 569 P.2d 151 (Alaska 1977). A waiver will not be implied. Maynard v. Narragansett Indian Tribe, 984 F.2d 14 (1st Cir.1993); but cf. Sokaogon Gaming Enterprise Corp. v. Tushie–Montgomery Assoc., 86 F.3d 656, 659–60 (7th Cir.1996).

A tribe does not waive its immunity from counterclaims, even "compulsory" ones, by bringing an action. Oklahoma Tax Comm'n v. Citizen Band Potawatomi Indian Tribe, 498 U.S. 505, 509 (1991). It also does not waive immunity for other related but collateral claims. Pit River Home and Agr. Co-op. Ass'n v. United States, 30 F.3d 1088, 1100–01 (9th Cir.1994). McClendon v. United States, 885 F.2d 627 (9th Cir.1989). The tribe does consent to a full adjudication of the claim it sues upon, however, United States v. Oregon, 657 F.2d 1009 (9th Cir. 1981), and to claims of recoupment or set-off that arise from the transaction sued upon and do not exceed the tribe's claim. Rosebud Sioux Tribe v. A & P. Steel, Inc., 874 F.2d 550 (8th Cir.1989); Jicarilla Apache Tribe v. Andrus, 687 F.2d 1324 (10th Cir.1982). A tribe that brings a quiet title action and invites adverse claims waives its immunity to those claims. Rupp v. Omaha Indian Tribe, 45 F.3d 1241 (8th Cir.1995). A tribe that participates as a creditor in a bankruptcy proceeding waives immunity for adjudication of its claim. In re White, ___ F.3d ___, 1998 WL 125092 (9th Cir.1998). A tribe that becomes a party to federal administrative proceedings does not thereby waive its immunity from suit brought by another party seeking review of the agency decision. Quileute Indian Tribe v. Babbitt, 18 F.3d 1456 (9th Cir.1994); Kescoli v. Babbitt, 101 F.3d 1304 (9th Cir.1996).

Most of the lower courts to consider the question have held that a tribe, by conducting gaming under the Indian Gaming Regulatory Act, waives sovereign immunity for the limited purpose of enforcing compliance with the Act. See, e.g., Montgomery v. Flandreau Santee Sioux Tribe, 905 F.Supp. 740 (D.S.D.1995); Maxam v. Lower Sioux Indian Community of Minnesota, 829 F.Supp. 277 (D.Minn. 1993); but see Davids v. Coyhis, 869 F.Supp. 1401 (E.D.Wis.1994).

A tribe may waive its sovereign immunity by contract. Nenana Fuel Co. v. Native Village of Venetie, 834 P.2d 1229 (Alaska 1992). A mere agreement to arbitrate disputes under a contract has been held not to waive sovereign immunity. Pan American Co. v. Sycuan Band of Mission Indians, 884 F.2d 416 (9th Cir.1989). When such an agreement contemplates possible judicial enforcement of the award, however, immunity has been held to be waived. Sokaogon Gaming Enterprise Corp. v. Tushie–Montgomery Assoc., 86 F.3d 656 (7th Cir.

1996); Rosebud Sioux Tribe v. Val–U Construction Co., 50 F.3d 560 (8th Cir.1995), cert. denied, 516 U.S. 819 (1995). The waiver is only for arbitration and its enforcement, however; it does not extend to all kinds of litigation that might arise from the subject matter of the contract. See Tamiami Partners, Ltd. v. Miccosukee Tribe of Indians, 63 F.3d 1030, 1048–49 (11th Cir.1995).

Many of the tribes have formed tribal corporations under a provision of the Indian Reorganization Act of 1934, 25 U.S.C.A. § 477, which authorized the Secretary of Interior to issue to the tribes corporate charters conferring certain stated powers and "such further powers as may be incidental to the conduct of corporate business." Many of the charters issued pursuant to the Act conferred the power to "sue and be sued." Some courts have construed the term to constitute a waiver of tribal immunity. See, e.g., Rosebud Sioux Tribe v. A & P. Steel, Inc., 874 F.2d 550 (8th Cir.1989); Fontenelle v. Omaha Tribe, 430 F.2d 143 (8th Cir.1970); Martinez v. Southern Ute Tribe, 150 Colo. 504, 374 P.2d 691 (1962); see also Weeks Construction, Inc. v. Oglala Sioux Housing Authority, 797 F.2d 668 (8th Cir.1986). Other courts have held, however, that a "sue and be sued" clause in the tribal corporate charter was insufficient to waive the tribe's general immunity; it applied at most to the tribe's economic dealings for which the corporation was formed. Atkinson v. Haldane, 569 P.2d 151 (Alaska 1977); Boe v. Fort Belknap Indian Community, 455 F.Supp. 462 (D.Mont.1978). Similarly, incorporation of a tribal subentity under state laws enabling corporations to sue and be sued does not waive immunity. Ransom v. St. Regis Mohawk Educ. & Community Fund, Inc., 86 N.Y.2d 553, 562–64, 635 N.Y.S.2d 116, 121–22, 658 N.E.2d 989, 994–95 (1995). If a tribally-chartered corporation operates independently of the tribal government and does not engage in governmental functions, however, it may not qualify for immunity in the first place because it is not an arm of the tribe. See Dixon v. Picopa Constr. Co., 160 Ariz. 251, 772 P.2d 1104 (1989).

CHAPTER VI

INDIAN TREATIES

A. TREATY RIGHTS, PAST AND PRESENT

When Europeans first established colonies in America, they had little choice but to deal with the Indian tribes as the independent nations that they were. Terms of peace and exchanges of land were accordingly accomplished by treaty between the colonial governments and the tribes. After the Revolution, the federal government continued to deal with the tribes by treaty, although it also regulated various aspects of Indian affairs by statute.

From the first treaty with the Delawares in 1787 until the end of treaty-making in 1871, hundreds of agreements were entered between the federal government and various bands and tribes of Indians. Provisions of the treaties differed widely, but it was common to include a guarantee of peace, a delineation of boundaries (often with a cession of specific lands from the tribe to the federal government), a guarantee of Indian hunting and fishing rights (often applying to the ceded land), a statement that the tribe recognized the authority or placed itself under the protection of the United States, and an agreement regarding the regulation of trade and travel of persons in the Indian territory. Treaties also commonly included agreements by each side to punish and compensate for acts of depredation by "bad men" among their own number, a clause that still can support a claim against the United States. See Tsosie v. United States, 825 F.2d 393 (Fed.Cir. 1987).

In the early years of the Republic, the tribes negotiated from positions of some strength, because they retained much of their original integrity and power and because the federal government was exhausted by the Revolutionary War and was anxious to avoid others. As time went on, of course, the bargaining positions changed drastically and by the end of the treaty period the federal government was in a position to dictate terms. After 1850, those terms sometimes included an extension of federal authority over the internal affairs of the tribe—a type of provision that would have been unthinkable forty years earlier.

Even when the tribes possessed some bargaining power, the treaty-making process put them at a disadvantage. Treaties were written in English, and their terms were often explained inexactly to the Indian signatories. The very concepts of land ownership and governmental relations embodied in the treaties were often wholly foreign to the tribal cultures. Moreover, the federal government frequently negotiated with individuals whom it had selected and who were not the traditional leaders of the concerned tribes. All of these factors contributed to overreaching on the part of the federal government.

Nevertheless, important rights were guaranteed to the tribes by treaty, and many of these rights continue to be enforceable. Rights secured to the tribes by treaty today include beneficial ownership of Indian lands, hunting and fishing rights, and entitlement to certain federal services such as education or health care. This is not to say that all such present rights are secured by treaty; many of them are the product of statute or executive agreement. A substantial number, however, still arise from treaties.

A tribe need not be federally recognized to establish that it is the beneficiary of a treaty. United States v. Suquamish Indian Tribe, 901 F.2d 772 (9th Cir.1990); Greene v. Babbitt, 64 F.3d 1266, 1270 (9th Cir.1995). It is enough that a group establish that it has preserved an organized tribal structure that it can trace back to the treaty. United States v. Oregon, 29 F.3d 481, amended 43 F.3d 1284 (9th Cir.1994), cert. denied, 515 U.S. 1102 (1995).

Indian treaties stand on essentially the same footing as treaties with foreign nations. Because they are made pursuant to the Constitution, they take precedence over any conflicting state laws by reason of the Supremacy Clause. U.S.Const., Art. VI, § 2; Worcester v. Georgia, 31 U.S. (6 Pet.) 515 (1832). They are also the exclusive prerogative of the federal government. The First Trade and Intercourse

Act, 1 Stat. 137 (1790), forbade the transfer of Indian lands to individuals or states except by treaty "under the authority of the United States." This provision, repeated in later Trade and Intercourse Acts, has become of tremendous importance in recent years, for several eastern states negotiated large land cessions from Indian tribes near the end of the eighteenth century. In County of Oneida v. Oneida Indian Nation, 470 U.S. 226 (1985), the Court held invalid a treaty entered in 1795 between the Oneidas and the State of New York. The treaty, which had been concluded without the participation of the federal government, transferred 100,000 acres of Indian lands to the state. The Court held that the tribe still had a viable claim for damages. Similar claims exist in other eastern states; in Maine, the likely invalidity of a 1795 state-tribal treaty clouded land titles covering about sixty percent of the state until legislation settled the issue. See Joint Tribal Council of Passamaquoddy Tribe v. Morton, 528 F.2d 370 (1st Cir.1975); Maine Indian Claims Settlement Act, P.L. 96–420, 94 Stat. 1785 (1980).

Not only is the treaty-making power exclusively federal, it is almost entirely presidential. While it is true that two-thirds of the Senate must concur in any treaty, the initiation of the process and the terms of negotiation are inevitably controlled by the executive branch. (Indeed, there were many instances, especially in California, where executive officials negotiated treaties and acted upon them despite the failure of the Senate to ratify them.) In the middle of the eighteenth century, Congress and particularly the House of Representatives grew increasingly resentful of being excluded from the direction of Indian affairs. The ultimate result was the passage in 1871 of a rider to an Indian appropriations act providing that "No Indian nation or tribe * * * shall be acknowledged or recognized as an independent nation, tribe, or power with whom the United States may contract by treaty * * *." 25 U.S.C.A. § 71. The rider also specified that existing treaty obligations were not impaired. As an attempt to limit by statute the President's constitutional treaty-making power, the rider may well be invalid, but it accomplished its purpose nonetheless by making it clear that no further treaties would be ratified. Indian treaty-making consequently ended in 1871, and formal agreements made with the tribes thereafter were either approved by both houses of Congress or were simply embodied in statutes.

B. CONSTRUCTION OF TREATIES

To compensate for the disadvantage at which the treaty-making process placed the tribes, and to help carry out the federal trust responsibility, the Supreme Court has fashioned rules of construction sympathetic to Indian interests. Treaties are to be construed as they were understood by the tribal representatives who participated in their negotiation. Tulee v. Washington, 315 U.S. 681, 684–85 (1942). They are to be liberally interpreted to accomplish their protective purposes, with ambiguities to be resolved in favor of the Indians. Carpenter v. Shaw, 280 U.S. 363 (1930).

One of the most important applications of these rules of construction is found in Winters v. United States, 207 U.S. 564 (1908), which dealt not with a treaty but with an Indian agreement made in 1888 and ratified by an act of Congress. The tribes involved in that agreement had ceded to the United States a large tract of land to be opened up for settlement, while reserving to themselves other lands, bordered by a flowing stream, which became the Fort Belknap Reservation in Montana. Non–Indian settlers diverted the stream, and the United States brought suit on behalf of the Indians. The settlers argued that lands would not have been ceded for settlement without also ceding the water that would permit them to become fruitful. The United States argued that lands would not have been reserved for the tribes unless water also had been reserved to make the reservation productive. Faced with these plausible contradictory interpretations, the Court chose to construe the agreement from the standpoint of the Indians and to resolve the conflict in their favor. The resulting decision has become the foundation of all Indian water law. See Chapter XIV, Section B, infra.

Interpretation of treaties as the Indians understood them has also preserved extremely important fishing rights. Treaties in the Pacific Northwest that guaranteed Indians the right of "taking fish" at customary stations off-reservation "in common with all citizens of the Territory" were held to guarantee up to half of the harvestable fish; they did not merely guarantee the same rights as those enjoyed by non-Indians. See, e.g., Washington v. Washington State Commercial Passenger Fishing Vessel Ass'n, 443 U.S. 658 (1979). A similar result has been reached regarding rights to shellfish in natural beds off-reservation. See United States v. Washington, 135 F.3d 618 (9th Cir.1998). A parallel treaty provision guaranteeing "the right, in common with the citizens of the United States, to travel upon all public highways" has been held to confer immunity from state truck license and permit fees. Yakama Indian Nation v. Flores, 955 F.Supp. 1229 (E.D.Wash.1997).

If the language of a treaty is clear, it will be applied whether or not the outcome is favorable to the Indians. Oregon Dept. of Fish and Wildlife v. Klamath Indian Tribe, 473 U.S. 753, 774 (1985). Thus an income tax exemption will not result from a treaty when there is no language that could reasonably be construed to confer it. Lazore v. C.I.R., 11 F.3d 1180, 1185 (3d Cir.1993). Even where the treaty provisions are unclear, the tribes do not inevitably win every dispute over their interpretation. See Puyallup Tribe v. Department of Game, 391 U.S. 392 (1968). Thus a treaty right to hunt on ceded lands "so long as game may be found thereon" was held to be a transitory right that did not survive the later incorporation of the lands into the State of Wyoming. Crow Tribe of Indians v. Repsis, 73 F.3d 982 (10th Cir.1995), cert. denied, 116 S.Ct. 1851 (1996). Similarly, in Montana v.

United States, 450 U.S. 544 (1981), the Supreme Court held that a treaty setting aside lands for the Crow Tribe did not convey title to the bed of a river within those lands. The Court relied on the presumption that the United States holds title to navigable waterways in trust for the states, which receive the title upon their admission to the Union on an "equal footing" with other states. Subsequent lower court decisions, however, have applied sympathetic construction and held that the bed of navigable waters is conveyed to a grantee tribe if the tribe was known to be dependent upon fishing at the time of the treaty. E.g., Puyallup Indian Tribe v. Port of Tacoma, 717 F.2d 1251, 1258 (9th Cir.1983), cert. denied, 465 U.S. 1049 (1984); Confederated Salish & Kootenai Tribes v. Namen, 665 F.2d 951 (9th Cir.), cert. denied, 459 U.S. 977 (1982). On balance, then, the rules of construction continue to have a very substantial effect favorable to Indian interests, not only in water and property rights but in other important areas such as immunity from state taxation. See McClanahan v. Arizona State Tax Com'n, 411 U.S. 164 (1973).

The rule of sympathetic construction has been carried over from treaties to statutes dealing with Indian matters, as well as to executive orders establishing reservations. See Confederated Tribes of the Chehalis Indian Reservation v. Washington, 96 F.3d 334, 342 (9th Cir.1996), cert. denied, 117 S.Ct. 1432 (1997). The Supreme Court on numerous occasions has adhered to "the general rule that statutes passed for the benefit of the dependent Indian tribes or communities are to be liberally construed, doubtful expressions being resolved in favor of the Indians." Alaska Pacific Fisheries Co. v. United States, 248 U.S. 78, 89 (1918). This rule of sympathetic construction has been held to overcome the rule of deference to the interpretation of an administrative agency. Ramah Navajo Chapter v. Lujan, 112 F.3d 1455 (10th Cir.1997). The Supreme Court resolved ambiguity in favor of the tribes in construing Public Law 280, a statute that deals with Indians but was not necessarily passed for their benefit. Bryan v. Itasca County, 426 U.S. 373, 392–93 (1976). On the other hand, the Supreme Court rejected a "sympathetic" construction of a statute giving Kansas jurisdiction over major crimes by Indians, partly because it doubted that the statute was passed for the benefit of the Indians. Negonsott v. Samuels, 507 U.S. 99, 110 (1993). The rule of sympathetic construction also simply has been ignored on occasion. Mountain States Tel. & Tel. Co. v. Pueblo of Santa Ana, 472 U.S. 237 (1985).

C. ABROGATION OF TREATIES

One of the least understood facts about Indian treaties is that they may be abrogated unilaterally by Congress. Because treaties often contain recitals that they will remain in effect "as long as the grass shall grow" or for some other equally eternal length of time, many people assume that any alterations in terms would have to be mutually negotiated by the federal government and the tribes. The law, however, is to the contrary.

Indian treaties as well as international treaties stand on the same footing as federal statutes. Like federal statutes, they can be repealed or modified by later federal statutes. Thus if the United States enters a treaty with a foreign nation and Congress subsequently passes a statute inconsistent with the provisions of the treaty, the statute will control and the treaty is abrogated, at least to the extent of the inconsistency. Whatever may be the implications of the abrogation for purposes of international law, there is no question that the abrogating statute becomes the governing internal law of the United States. Chae Chan Ping v. United States (The Chinese Exclusion Case), 130 U.S. 581 (1889).

The Supreme Court's first application of the same principle to Indian treaties came in The Cherokee Tobacco, 78 U.S. (11 Wall.) 616 (1871), which upheld a federal tax on tobacco sold within Cherokee territory despite a prior treaty that guaranteed an exemption. The decision most often cited for the proposition that Congress may abrogate an Indian treaty, however, is Lone Wolf v. Hitchcock, 187 U.S. 553 (1903). That case involved a treaty with the Kiowas and Comanches which set aside lands to be held communally by the tribes and provided that no further cessions of those lands could be made without the consent of three-fourths of the adult male Indians of the tribes. Many years later, a further cession was arranged by the federal government but the number of adult males who consented fell short of three-fourths. Congress nevertheless passed a statute putting the cession into effect. The Court

upheld the statute, stating that a treaty could not
be given a legal effect that would restrict the future
exercise of Congress' plenary power over Indian
affairs. The Court also elaborated:

> The power exists to abrogate the provisions of an
> Indian treaty, though presumably such power will
> be exercised only when circumstances arise which
> will not only justify the government in disregard-
> ing the stipulations of the treaty, but may de-
> mand, in the interest of the country and the
> Indians themselves, that it should do so. When,
> therefore, treaties were entered into between the
> United States and a tribe of Indians it was never
> doubted that the *power* to abrogate existed in
> Congress, and that in a contingency such power
> might be availed of from considerations of govern-
> mental policy, particularly if consistent with per-
> fect good faith towards the Indians.

187 U.S. at 566. While it well might be questioned
whether the land cession in *Lone Wolf* properly
could be characterized as consistent with perfect
good faith towards the Indians, the outcome left no
doubt about Congress's ability to abrogate.

The mere fact that Congress has the *power* to
abrogate does not mean, however, that every statute that is potentially inconsistent with a treaty
effects an abrogation. If Congress expressly states
that it is modifying a particular treaty, then the
deed is done and the courts have no room to maneu-
ver. It is far more common for Congress to pass
legislation seemingly inconsistent with a treaty

without mentioning (or perhaps even considering) the effect that the statute is to have on treaty rights. In such cases, the courts have an opportunity to consider whether the unexpressed intent of Congress was indeed to abrogate, or whether congressional purposes would be better served by implying exceptions to the statute that will prevent impairment of the treaty. The nature of the judicial function in this type of case is similar to that in cases involving a question of implied repeal of a statute or of preemption of state law by a federal statute. The outcome depends in part on the nature and scope of the particular statute involved, and may also depend upon a weighing and balancing of policy issues that exist quite independently of the intent or purposes of Congress. These characteristics make it difficult to reduce decisions of this type to a pattern.

It seems clear enough that the trust relationship between the federal government and the Indian tribes ought to weigh heavily against implied abrogation of treaties. It has been urged that abrogation ought never to be found in the absence of Congress' direct statement that it intends to do just that. See Wilkinson and Volkman, *Judicial Review of Indian Treaty Abrogation: "As Long as Water Flows, or Grass Grows Upon the Earth"—How Long a Time is That?*, 63 Cal.L.Rev. 601 (1975). While some lower court and earlier Supreme Court decisions seem to support that position, e.g., Frost v. Wenie, 157 U.S. 46 (1895), the courts in recent years have not gone that far. In holding that the Eagle Protection Act abrogated a treaty right of hunting, the Supreme Court rejected a *per se* rule requiring an explicit statement from Congress:

What is essential is clear evidence that Congress actually considered the conflict between its intended action on the one hand and Indian treaty rights on the other, and chose to resolve that conflict by abrogating the treaty.

United States v. Dion, 476 U.S. 734, 738–740 (1986). See also Seneca Nation v. Brucker, 262 F.2d 27 (D.C.Cir.1958), cert. denied, 360 U.S. 909 (1959).

A tribe's treaty right to the "exclusive use and benefit" of all of the land within a reservation, and a right to regulate conduct that may go with it, has been held to be lost with regard to land that passed into non-Indian hands under subsequently enacted Allotment Acts. Brendale v. Confederated Tribes and Bands of the Yakima Indian Nation, 492 U.S. 408, 422–23 (1989) (plurality opinion); Montana v. United States, 450 U.S. 544, 559 & n. 9 (1981). Similarly, the taking by the United States of a portion of a reservation for a dam and reservoir was held to abrogate the tribe's treaty right to regulate non-Indian hunting and fishing in the taken area. South Dakota v. Bourland, 508 U.S. 679 (1993).

Where there is room for doubt as to congressional intent, the Supreme Court has sometimes gone to considerable lengths to avoid the destruction of treaty rights. Menominee Tribe v. United States, 391 U.S. 404 (1968), provides the cardinal example. An 1854 treaty set aside lands for the Menominee "to be held as Indian lands are held." The Court, appropriately enough, interpreted this phrase sympathetically to guarantee hunting and fishing rights on the reservation lands. In 1954, Congress passed a Termination Act which provided that in 1962 the special relationship between the Menominee Tribe and the federal government would end and that

"all statutes of the United States which affect Indians because of their status as Indians shall no longer be applicable to members of the tribe, and the laws of the several States shall apply to the tribe and its members in the same manner as they apply to other citizens or persons within their jurisdiction."

25 U.S.C.A. § 899 (1954), repealed 25 U.S.C.A. § 903a(b) (1973). No mention was made in the Termination Act of the Menominee's treaty hunting and fishing rights. Wisconsin argued that the statute necessarily extinguished those treaty rights and subjected the Menominee who hunted and fished on the former reservation to state licensing and regulatory laws. A majority of the Court held, however, that the Termination Act did not abrogate the treaty hunting and fishing rights. It pointed out that Congress in other statutes had carefully preserved Indian treaty rights, and that the Termination Act referred to federal *statutes* becoming inapplicable but said nothing of treaties. In concluding, the majority stated, "[w]e decline to construe the Termination Act as a backhanded way of abrogating the hunting and fishing rights of these Indians" and "[w]e find it difficult to believe that Congress

without explicit statement would subject the United States to a claim for compensation by destroying property rights conferred by treaty * * *." 391 U.S. at 412–413. While these remarks cannot now be read as requiring an explicit congressional statement for every abrogation, the *Menominee* case is unquestionably strong authority for the proposition that congressional intent to abrogate a treaty is not easily to be implied.

As the concluding language of the *Menominee* case indicates, abrogation of a treaty may give rise to a claim of compensation. Where a treaty creates property rights, Congress' power to abrogate the treaty does not free it from the duty to compensate for the destruction of the property rights involved. The abrogation itself is effective, but the tribe is entitled to a claim for a "taking" under the Fifth Amendment. See United States v. Creek Nation, 295 U.S. 103 (1935).

CHAPTER VII

CRIMINAL AND CIVIL JURISDICTION IN INDIAN COUNTRY

A. INTRODUCTION

The most complex problems in the field of Indian Law arise in jurisdictional disputes among the federal government, the tribes and the states. To resolve those problems it is essential to know the basic limits of jurisdiction of each of the three contending powers. Although ambiguities still remain in abundance, those limits have been most thoroughly defined in regard to criminal and civil *adjudicatory* jurisdiction, which is discussed in this chapter. The more uncertain area of regulatory jurisdiction is dealt with in Chapter IX, infra. The division of jurisdiction set forth in this chapter is that which prevails in the absence of any federal statute such as Public Law 280, which grants criminal and civil jurisdiction to the states. The effects of Public Law 280 are discussed in Chapter VIII, infra. Other specialized statutes, such as Indian claims settlement acts, may allocate jurisdiction in atypical ways. See, e.g., Rhode Island v. Narragansett Indian Tribe, 19 F.3d 685 (1st Cir.1994); Charles v.

Charles, 243 Conn. 255, 701 A.2d 650 (1997), pet. for cert. filed, 66 U.S.L.W. 3598 (1998).

Subject matter jurisdiction of federal, tribal or state courts usually depends heavily upon two issues: (1) whether the parties involved are Indians, and (2) whether the events in issue took place in Indian country. The question of who is an Indian is discussed in Chapter I, Section C; for jurisdictional purposes it generally may be said that an Indian is one who has Indian blood and is recognized as a member of a tribe having a special relationship with the federal government. An Indian who is a member of a "terminated" tribe is not an Indian for purposes of adjudicatory jurisdiction. United States v. Heath, 509 F.2d 16 (9th Cir.1974).

Traditionally, membership did not need to be in the particular recognized tribe in whose territory the jurisdictional issue arose; a Navajo on an Apache reservation was treated jurisdictionally as an Indian. Recent opinions of the Supreme Court have cast doubt on this practice, at least in some areas. In United States v. Wheeler, 435 U.S. 313 (1978), the Court continually referred to a tribe's inherent criminal jurisdiction over its *members*, although nothing turned on the distinction between tribal members and other Indians in that case. In Washington v. Confederated Tribes of the Colville Indian Reservation, 447 U.S. 134 (1980), the Court permitted a state to impose a sales tax on Indians making purchases on a reservation other than their own. The Court stated that "[f]or most practical purposes those Indians stand on the same footing as non-Indians resident on the reservation." 447 U.S. at 161. Then, in Duro v. Reina, 495 U.S. 676 (1990), the Court held that tribes were precluded by their domestic dependent status from exercising criminal jurisdiction over nonmember Indians. Congress quickly overruled *Duro*, recognizing and affirming "the inherent power of Indian tribes * * * to exercise criminal jurisdiction over all Indians." 25 U.S.C.A. § 1301(2). Thus an Indian of any recognized tribe remains an Indian for criminal jurisdictional purposes. For purposes of civil adjudication, however, the Supreme Court has made clear its preference for drawing jurisdictional lines between members and nonmembers, rather than between Indians and non-Indians. See Strate v. A–1 Contractors, 117 S.Ct. 1404 (1997).

B. INDIAN COUNTRY

The question of what is "Indian country" has been even more troublesome than the question of who is an "Indian." After many years of change and development, the concept of Indian country was given its present definition by Congress in 1948. 18 U.S.C.A. § 1151 provides:

[T]he term "Indian country", as used in this chapter, means (a) all land within the limits of any Indian reservation under the jurisdiction of the United States government, notwithstanding the issuance of any patent, and, including rights-of-way running through the reservation, (b) all dependent Indian communities within the bor-

ders of the United States whether within the
original or subsequently acquired territory thereof, and whether within or without the limits of a
state, and (c) all Indian allotments, the Indian
titles to which have not been extinguished, including rights-of-way running through the same.

Although this definition is for purposes of the criminal code, it is also used for civil jurisdiction. DeCoteau v. District County Court, 420 U.S. 425, 427 n.
2 (1975); see Oklahoma Tax Comm'n v. Chickasaw
Nation, 515 U.S. 450, 453 & n. 2 (1995).

Subsection (a) includes all of the territory within
an Indian reservation. It is most important to note
that even land owned by non-Indians in fee simple
(i. e., where there has been "issuance of any patent") is still "Indian country" if it is within the
exterior boundaries of an Indian reservation. There
exist within many reservations large tracts of land
long since settled by non-Indians, and even entire
towns incorporated by non-Indians under state law,
but all of those tracts and towns are Indian country
for purposes of jurisdiction. Seymour v. Superintendent, 368 U.S. 351 (1962).

The fact that fee land within a reservation is
Indian country retains its full significance for purposes of criminal jurisdiction, and presumably for
civil jurisdiction involving tribal members, but the
Supreme Court in recent years has introduced a
qualification with regard to civil jurisdiction over
nonmembers. In Montana v. United States, 450
U.S. 544 (1981), the Court held that a tribe had no

power to regulate hunting and fishing by non-Indians on non-Indian-owned fee land within the reservation. The Court stated that the tribe's domestic dependent status disabled it from exercising power over non-Indians on non-Indian fee land unless the non-Indians were in a consensual relationship with the tribe or its members, or their conduct threatened or directly affected "the political integrity, the economic security, or the health or welfare of the tribe." 450 U.S. at 564; see also South Dakota v. Bourland, 508 U.S. 679 (1993). This ruling most recently has been extended to preclude tribal court jurisdiction over a dispute between nonmembers arising from a traffic accident on a state highway within the reservation; the state highway right-of-way was regarded as the equivalent of non-Indian fee land. Strate v. A–1 Contractors, 117 S.Ct. 1404 (1997). Thus, while non-Indian fee lands within the reservation remain Indian country, that fact seems to have lost much of its significance for purposes of civil jurisdiction over nonmembers. One court of appeals has even held that a tribal court has no jurisdiction over a claim by a *tribal member* against a nonmember arising out of a vehicle accident on a state right-of-way within a reservation. Wilson v. Marchington, 127 F.3d 805 (9th Cir.1997) cert. denied, 118 S.Ct. 1516 (1998); see also County of Lewis v. Allen, 1998 WL 191233 (9th Cir.1998).

Although the mere opening up of a reservation for non-Indian settlement does not remove the newly settled lands from Indian country, a congressional decision to abandon the reservation status of those lands does. In cases where Congress has opened reservations to heavy settlement, there is often a difficult question of fact whether the intent was to permit non-Indians to live and own land on a reservation or whether it was to extinguish a portion of the reservation and open it for settlement as public, non-Indian land. The answers to this fact-bound inquiry have not been very predictable in the past. Thus in Seymour v. Superintendent, 368 U.S. 351 (1962), and Mattz v. Arnett, 412 U.S. 481 (1973), the Supreme Court held that extensive allotment and settlement of the Colville and Klamath River Reservations, respectively, did not end the reservation status of those lands. But in DeCoteau v. District County Court, 420 U.S. 425 (1975), and Rosebud Sioux Tribe v. Kneip, 430 U.S. 584 (1977), the Court found that Congress had terminated the entire Lake Traverse Reservation and large tracts of land in the Rosebud Reservation, respectively.

In Solem v. Bartlett, 465 U.S. 463 (1984), the Court reviewed these cases and stated that they "have established a fairly clean analytical structure" for determining whether a reservation had been diminished. Most important was the language of the statute: "[e]xplicit reference to cession or other language evidencing the present and total surrender of all tribal interests" was strongly indicative of intent to diminish, and created an almost insurmountable presumption when combined with a commitment to compensate the tribe for the opened land. 465 U.S. at 470–71. Even without language of cession, a diminishment could be found from other factors, although it would not lightly be implied. The other factors were the manner in which the transaction was arranged or considered at the time; subsequent treatment of the area by the concerned governments; and later demographic consequences of the opening. Considering all of these factors in order, the Court in Solem v. Bartlett found that operative statutory language merely providing for sale of the land did not indicate an intent to diminish, even though stray language elsewhere in the statute referred to the opened lands as being in "the public domain" and to the unopened areas as "the reservation thus diminished." 465 U.S. at 475. Contemporaneous circumstances did not show an intent to diminish, and subsequent treatment of the area by the concerned governments was too contradictory to be useful. Finally, relatively few non-Indians had settled on the opened lands, while a majority of present tribal members resided there. Accordingly, the Court held that there had been no diminishment.

With regard to the final factor, demographic results, the the Court in Solem v. Bartlett stated:

[W]e have recognized that who actually moved onto opened reservation lands is also relevant to deciding whether a surplus land Act diminished a reservation. Where non-Indian settlers flooded into the opened portion of a reservation and the area has long since lost its Indian character, we have acknowledged that *de facto*, if not *de jure*, diminishment may have occurred.

465 U.S. at 471. Despite the strength of this wording, demographic results should probably not be viewed as sufficient by themselves to establish that a surplus land act was intended to diminish a reservation; the demographic results are best seen as one post-event clue to Congress' intent regarding the future of the reservation. See South Dakota v. Yankton Sioux Tribe, 118 S.Ct. 789 (1998). There are numerous instances of existing reservations containing substantial tracts of fee land heavily populated by non-Indians. See, e.g., Duncan Energy Co. v. Three Affiliated Tribes of the Fort Berthold Reservation, 27 F.3d 1294, 1297–98 & n. 4 (8th Cir.1994), cert. denied, 513 U.S. 1103 (1995); Oliphant v. Suquamish Indian Tribe, 435 U.S. 191, 193 n. 1 (1978).

In two recent diminishment cases, the Supreme Court applied the factors set forth in Solem v. Bartlett and found that Congress had intended in surplus land acts to diminish, respectively, the Uintah Reservation in Utah and the Yankton Sioux Reservation in South Dakota. Hagen v. Utah, 510 U.S. 399, 413 (1994); South Dakota v. Yankton Sioux Tribe, 118 S.Ct. 789 (1998). In *Hagen*, the Court rejected a contention that Congress was required clearly to state its intention of modifying the reservation boundaries. Applying the factors of Solem v. Bartlett, the Court found that contemporary understanding and later demographics supported diminishment, and that subsequent treatment of the area by government was not illuminating. Most significant, however, was the operative language of the act directing that surplus lands "be restored to the public domain." That language, said the Court, denoted a congressional intent to end the reservation status of those lands. The Court did not state that this language was conclusive of the issue, but it emphasized the wording so heavily that it seems doubtful that the Court would fail to find diminishment when those words appear in the operative portion of the statute. One court of appeals, however, has subsequently held that a provision in executive orders that lands be restored to the public domain was overridden by strong evidence of executive intent not to diminish the reservation. Confederated Tribes of the Chehalis Indian Reservation v. Washington, 96 F.3d 334 (9th Cir.1996), cert. denied, 117 S.Ct. 1432 (1997). In addition, the Tenth Circuit, in subsequently dealing with the same reservation involved in *Hagen*, adhered in the interest of finality to its earlier decision that lands of Reservation not directly covered by *Hagen* remained part of the reservation although in part they may have been ordered restored to the public domain. Ute Indian Tribe of the Uintah and Ouray Reservation v. Utah, 114 F.3d 1513 (10th Cir.1997), cert. denied, 118 S.Ct. 1034 (1998). Any inconsistency with the rationale of *Hagen* was outweighed by the need for finality. Id.

In *Yankton Sioux Tribe*, the Supreme Court applied the "almost insurmountable" presumption of diminishment that *Solem* derived from clear statutory language of cession combined with a commitment by the United States to pay for the ceded lands. The Court also found support for the presumed diminishment in the manner of negotiation and the assumption of jurisdiction by South Dakota immediately after cession. The Court rejected the tribe's claim that the surplus land act, by disclaiming any abrogation of the treaty establishing the reservation, compelled a finding of no diminishment. Because the act clearly modified some portions of the treaty, the Court concluded that the disclaimer applied primarily to payments promised in the treaty. Finally, the Court stated that it was sufficient to find diminishment to resolve the question before it, so it would not rule on whether the entire reservation had been disestablished.

When a reservation is diminished or disestablished, the area excluded from the reservation is no longer Indian country under subsection (a) of 18 U.S.C.A. § 1151, which refers to "all land within the limits of any Indian reservation." Particular sub-portions of the excluded area, however, may still qualify as Indian country under subsections (b) and (c) of § 1151–as dependent Indian communities or allotments in trust. See Mustang Production Co. v. Harrison, 94 F.3d 1382, 1385 (10th Cir.1996), cert. denied, 117 S.Ct. 1288 (1997); United States v. Stands, 105 F.3d 1565, 1572 (8th Cir.), cert. denied, 118 S.Ct. 120 (1997).

Subsection (b) of 18 U.S.C.A. § 1151, which incorporates "dependent Indian communities" into the definition of Indian country, is a codification of the Supreme Court's holding in United States v. Sandoval, 231 U.S. 28 (1913). That case involved the New Mexico Pueblos, which held their land in fee simple under Spanish grants and which were not formally designated as reservations. The Court held that the Pueblo lands were Indian country nevertheless, since the Pueblos were wards dependent upon the federal government's guardianship. Id.; see also Indian Country, U.S.A. v. Oklahoma Tax Comm'n, 829 F.2d 967 (10th Cir.1987), cert. denied, 487 U.S. 1218 (1988). The Court later held that the Pueblo lands could not be alienated without the consent of the United States. United States v. Candelaria, 271 U.S. 432 (1926). Dependent Indian communities, then, are Indian country whether or not they are located within a recognized reservation.

The Supreme Court has recently delineated the elements of a dependent Indian community. The case arose in Alaska, where the issue was of extreme importance because of the unique corporate system under which nearly all Native groups held their land. See Chapter XIII, Section C(2). The Court held that the two essential characteristics of a dependent Indian community were that the land be set aside for the use of Indians, and that the land (not merely the tribe) must be under the superintendence of the federal government. Alaska v. Native Village of Venetie Tribal Government, 118 S.Ct. 948 (1998). Federal superintendence means that the community must be "sufficiently 'dependent' upon the Federal Government that the Federal Government and the Indians involved, rather than the States, are to exercise primary jurisdiction over the land in question." Id. at ___. Although the Court did not forbid consideration of other factors, those factors must not be balanced against or used to dilute the two requirements of federal set-aside and federal superintendence. Id. at ___ n.7.

Earlier cases had established that, when the United States retains or acquires title to the land and sets it aside for use by Indians, a dependent Indian community results. See United States v. McGowan, 302 U.S. 535 (1938). Other factors considered by courts in the past were the nature of the area, the relationship of the inhabitants to tribes and to the federal government, the practice of federal agencies toward the area, and the degree of cohesiveness of the community. Pittsburg & Midway Coal Mining Co. v. Watchman, 52 F.3d 1531 (10th Cir.1995); United States v. South Dakota, 665 F.2d 837 (8th Cir.1981), cert. denied, 459 U.S. 823 (1982). Thus a housing project for Indians of a particular tribe, on land deeded by a church to the United States for that purpose, was held to be a dependent Indian community. *South Dakota*, supra. A region in Maine was held to be a dependent Indian community because it lay within a township 94% populated by Passamaquoddy Indians and largely owned by the Passamaquoddy Tribe, which recently had been recognized and furnished with certain services by the federal government. United States v. Levesque, 681 F.2d 75 (1st Cir.), cert. denied, 459 U.S. 1089 (1982). These cases may be relied upon today, of course, only to the degree that the two mandatory requirements of *Venetie* were met in them. Although land may be set aside for Indian use without the establishment of trust status, such cases have been the exception, and the absence of trust status weighs against a finding of Indian country. Narragansett Indian Tribe v. Narragansett Elec. Co., 89 F.3d 908, 920–21 (1st Cir.1996). Mere concentrated occupancy of land by Indians is not enough to create a dependent Indian community, however; the absence of a defined community and of a setting aside of the land for use of Indians will defeat a claim of Indian country status. See United States v. Adair, 111 F.3d 770 (10th Cir.1997); Blatchford v. Sullivan, 904 F.2d 542 (10th Cir.1990), cert. denied, 498 U.S. 1035 (1991).

Subsection (c) of § 1151 is self-explanatory; it includes within Indian country any allotment still in trust (which necessarily means that it is beneficially owned by an Indian), whether it is located within a reservation or not. United States v. Sands, 968 F.2d 1058, 1062 (10th Cir.1992), cert. denied, 506 U.S. 1056 (1993).

C. HISTORICAL BACKGROUND OF JURISDICTION IN INDIAN COUNTRY

1. INITIAL JURISDICTION OF THE TRIBES AND THE GROWTH OF FEDERAL AUTHORITY

In colonial days, the Indian territory was entirely the province of the tribes, and they had jurisdiction in fact and theory over all persons and subjects present there. Shortly after the Revolution, federal jurisdiction was extended to non-Indians commit- ting crimes against Indians in Indian territory, as part of the overall federal policy of providing a buffer between the non-Indian and Indian popula- tions. 1 Stat. 138 (1790); 1 Stat. 743 (1799); 2 Stat. 139 (1802). Federal jurisdiction was further extend- ed in 1817 to cover crimes by both Indians and non- Indians in Indian country with the notable excep- tion of crimes by Indians against Indians; the latter were left entirely to be dealt with by tribal law or custom. 3 Stat. 383. That 1817 statute extending federal criminal law into Indian country has under- gone several revisions and is now codified as 18 U.S.C.A. § 1152; it is commonly known as the Gen- eral Crimes Act or sometimes the Federal Enclaves Act or the Indian Country Crimes Act. The federal jurisdiction over non-Indians conferred by the 1817 Act and its predecessors was not necessarily exclu- sive; several treaties provided that signatory tribes could exercise jurisdiction over non-Indians commit- ting crimes within their domain. See, generally, Clinton, *Development of Criminal Jurisdiction Over Indian Lands: The Historical Perspective*, 17 Ariz. L.Rev. 951 (1975).

This pattern, emphasizing federal jurisdiction over crimes between non-Indians and Indians while maintaining exclusive tribal jurisdiction over all- Indian crimes, continued until Congress modified it in reaction to the Supreme Court's decision in Ex parte Crow Dog, 109 U.S. 556 (1883). *Crow Dog* involved the conviction of an Indian in territorial court for the murder of another Indian in Indian country. The murder was alleged to have violated the general federal statute against murder, extended to Indian country by the General Crimes Act. The Supreme Court held that there was no jurisdiction, because the General Crimes Act excluded from coverage crimes by an Indian against an Indian. The Court left no doubt of its conviction that in justice the matter should be handled by the tribe:

> It is a case where, against an express exception in the law itself, that law * * * is sought to be extended over aliens and strangers; * * * and to subject them to the responsibilities of civil conduct, according to rules and penalties of which they could have no previous warning; which judges them by a standard made for others, and not for them, which takes no account of the conditions which should except them from its exactions, and makes no allowance for their inability to understand it.

109 U.S. at 571. The Court's heartfelt defense of tribal jurisdiction did not seem to impress Congress; it reacted to *Crow Dog* by promptly passing the Major Crimes Act, which created federal jurisdiction over seven crimes (including murder) committed by Indians in Indian country, whether the victim were Indian or non-Indian. 23 Stat. 362, 385 (1885). Subsequent amendments have expanded the number of major crimes to fourteen. 18 U.S.C.A. § 1153. To the considerable extent that it covered crimes by Indians against Indians, the Major Crimes Act was the first systematic intrusion by the federal govern-

ment into the internal affairs of the tribes. The Supreme Court held that this exercise of congressional power was justified by the dependent status of the tribes as wards of the federal government. United States v. Kagama, 118 U.S. 375 (1886).

Despite the Major Crimes Act, the tribes continued to exercise very substantial jurisdiction over Indians in Indian country. Non-major crimes by Indians were within the exclusive jurisdiction of the tribes, and remain so today (assuming, as we do throughout this chapter, that the crime is committed in a state where Public Law 280 does not apply; see Chapter VIII, infra.) The tribes also retained jurisdiction to punish minor crimes by Indians against non-Indians, a jurisdiction shared with the federal government under 18 U.S.C.A. § 1152. Many tribes even continued to punish Indians for conduct that constituted a major crime, effectively exercising jurisdiction concurrent with that conferred upon the federal courts by Congress. See Wetsit v. Stafne, 44 F.3d 823 (9th Cir.1995). Federal enforcement was often lax (and virtually non-existent in the case of larceny, which Congress had included among the major crimes), and the tribes tended to fill the vacuum when federal authorities refused or failed to prosecute. Recently, the Supreme Court decided that tribes as domestic dependent sovereigns had no power to exercise criminal jurisdiction over Indians who were not members of the tribe. Duro v. Reina, 495 U.S. 676 (1990). Congress promptly overturned that ruling, however, recognizing and affirming "the inherent power of

Indian tribes * * * to exercise criminal jurisdiction over all Indians * * * * '' 25 U.S.C.A. § 1301(2). Thus tribal exercise of power over Indians has been and still is extensive.

On the other hand, tribal jurisdiction over non-Indians, embodied in several early treaties, ceased to be exercised as the federal government assumed primary responsibility under the General Crimes Act, 18 U.S.C.A. § 1152. During the periods of removal to reservations and the Allotment Act, the declining power of the tribes left them in no position to enforce their laws against non-Indians. The Law and Order Codes written by the Department of Interior for use in Courts of Indian Offenses covered only crimes by Indians, and tribal codes adopted after passage of the Indian Reorganization Act of 1934 followed the same pattern. In the 1970's, however, several tribes that had become dissatisfied with the state of law enforcement against non-Indians responded by asserting tribal jurisdiction over crimes committed by them. The tribes contended that such jurisdiction was inherent in tribal self-government. The Supreme Court rejected the tribal position in Oliphant v. Suquamish Indian Tribe, 435 U.S. 191 (1978), and held that the tribes lacked criminal jurisdiction over non-Indians. The Court said that to exercise such jurisdiction in the absence of an authorizing statute of Congress would be inconsistent with the status of the tribes as dependent nations. Unless Congress alters the pattern, then, the inherent tribal jurisdiction over crimes is restricted to those committed by Indians.

One additional federal limitation on tribal jurisdiction over internal affairs is found in the Indian Civil Rights Act of 1968, 25 U.S.C.A. § 1301 et seq., more fully described in Chapter XI, infra. The act imposed most of the requirements of the Bill of Rights upon the tribes in the exercise of their jurisdiction. Tribal courts are consequently required to observe due process and enforce other rights analogous to those arising under the First, Fourth, Fifth, Sixth, Eighth and Fourteenth Amendments. Persons held in tribal custody in violation of the provisions of the Act are afforded a right of review in federal court by habeas corpus. The Act also limits the sentences that may be imposed by tribal courts to a maximum of a $5,000 fine and one year in jail for any one crime. For all practical purposes, therefore, tribal courts are limited to misdemeanor jurisdiction in criminal cases. There are no comparable maximum limits placed upon their civil jurisdiction.

2.   THE SELECTIVE EXTENSION OF STATE LAW INTO INDIAN COUNTRY

One of the basic premises underlying the constitutional allocation of Indian affairs to the federal government was that the states could not be relied upon to deal fairly with the Indians. Severe limitations upon the exercise of state power in Indian territory therefore seemed implicit in the nation's early Indian policy, but the extent of these limitations was not dealt with authoritatively until John Marshall's decision in the second of the famous Cherokee cases, Worcester v. Georgia, 31 U.S. (6 Pet.) 515 (1832). At the heart of the case lay Georgia's attempt to exercise total jurisdiction within Cherokee territory—to divide that territory among several Georgia counties, to apply Georgia law to all persons within the area, and to prohibit the Cherokees from exercising any governmental powers of their own. It was made a crime under state law for any person to hold court under color of Cherokee law for the purpose of hearing either criminal or civil cases. Chief Justice Marshall's opinion for the Court totally rejected Georgia's attempt, and characterized the Cherokee territory as one "in which the laws of Georgia can have no force * * *." 31 U.S. (6 Pet.) at 561. Marshall reviewed the history of governmental relations with the Indian tribes, the treaties entered with the Cherokees, and the constitutional provision for congressional regulation of commerce with the Indian tribes. All of these, said Marshall, reinforced the tribal right of self-government and the exclusively federal right to govern relations between the tribe and outsiders. The Georgia laws interfered with these rights and were a nullity.

For fifty years, Marshall's view that state law and power could not intrude into Indian country held sway. Then a major change occurred in United States v. McBratney, 104 U.S. 621 (1881). In that case a non-Indian had been convicted in federal circuit court of murdering another non-Indian on the Ute reservation in Colorado. The Supreme Court, in a highly doubtful construction of the applicable federal statutes, first held that the federal court could only exercise criminal jurisdiction over places within the *exclusive* jurisdiction of the federal government. If the state had any jurisdiction over this crime, then the federal court necessarily had none. The state of Colorado must have jurisdiction, the Court then ruled, because Congress had admitted it to the union "upon an equal footing with the original States" and no exception was made for jurisdiction over the Ute reservation. The laws of Colorado therefore extend throughout the state, including the Ute reservation, insofar as they relate to crimes by non-Indians against non-Indians. The federal conviction was accordingly reversed, and the lower court was directed to deliver the defendant to state authorities.

The *McBratney* decision is subject to severe criticism on a number of grounds, not the least of which is that it seems utterly inconsistent in principle with Worcester v. Georgia, supra. Its outcome was nevertheless repeated in even more unlikely circumstances some fifteen years later. In Draper v. United States, 164 U.S. 240 (1896), the Supreme Court was presented with virtually the same facts as in *McBratney*, with one exception that ought to have been crucial. The murder of a non-Indian in *Draper* had occurred on the Crow reservation in Montana, and the congressional act enabling Montana's admission to the union provided that the people of Montana forever disclaimed all title to Indian lands and that "said Indian lands shall remain under the absolute jurisdiction and control of the Congress of the United States * * *." 25 Stat. 676, 677 (1889). Despite this language, the Supreme Court ruled that the state and not the federal courts had jurisdiction over the crime involved. While agreeing that the enabling act might have foreclosed state jurisdiction over crimes by or against Indians, the Court stated that Congress could not have intended any result so drastic as the exclusion of state power to punish wholly non-Indian crimes in Indian country.

Despite the dubious statutory and judicial underpinnings for the *McBratney* and *Draper* decisions, they have become firmly entrenched in existing law. New York ex rel. Ray v. Martin, 326 U.S. 496 (1946). Even *Draper's* disregard of the jurisdictional provision in the state's enabling act remains authoritative for purposes of state power over non-Indians in Indian country. The Supreme Court has subsequently explained that the state's disclaimer is of title, not jurisdiction, and the provision for "absolute" federal jurisdiction does not necessarily mean "exclusive" federal jurisdiction! Organized Village of Kake v. Egan, 369 U.S. 60, 68 (1962).

At first glance, *McBratney* and *Draper* might seem to have had a very limited effect on Indian affairs, since they dealt only with crimes where no Indians were involved as either victims or perpetrators. In both theoretical and practical terms, however, the decisions had an enormous and complicating impact on the law of jurisdiction in Indian country, for they made it impossible ever after to deal with questions of state jurisdiction on a purely geographical basis. Marshall's rule in *Worcester* that state law can have no force in Indian country had several virtues, but perhaps the greatest was simplicity. When tribal and state powers were viewed in purely territorial terms, it was only necessary to discover the location of a transaction or occurrence in order to determine which of two competing systems of law and courts had control over it. *McBratney* and *Draper*, on the other hand, require not only a determination of location, but also an inquiry into the nature of the subject matter and the identity of the parties involved in the case. They open the door to judicial balancing of state and tribal interests whenever arguable questions of jurisdiction arise. Cases since *McBratney* and *Draper* have often involved such a weighing of competing interests in their attempts to determine how far state law reaches into Indian country.

The Supreme Court's clearest subsequent articulation of the test of state jurisdiction in Indian country came many years later in a civil case. Williams v. Lee, 358 U.S. 217 (1959), was a suit brought in state court by a non-Indian against an Indian couple for the purchase price of goods sold to the Indians on the Navajo reservation in Arizona. The Supreme Court held that the state courts had no jurisdiction over the action. Justice Black's opinion for the majority laid heavy emphasis upon Worcester v. Georgia and Marshall's proposition that state laws can "have no force" in Indian country, and then added:

Over the years this Court has modified these principles in cases where essential tribal relations were not involved and where the rights of Indians would not be jeopardized, but the basic policy of *Worcester* has remained. * * * Essentially, absent governing Acts of Congress, the question has always been whether the state action infringed on the right of reservation Indians to make their own laws and be governed by them.

358 U.S. at 219–220. The Court also pointed out that Congress in Public Law 280 had provided the sole means for a state to acquire civil and criminal jurisdiction in Indian country and Arizona had not availed itself of that procedure. The Court concluded:

There can be no doubt that to allow the exercise of state jurisdiction here would undermine the authority of the tribal courts over Reservation affairs and hence would infringe on the right of the Indians to govern themselves.

358 U.S. at 223. It is noteworthy that the Court easily assumed that even *concurrent* state jurisdiction would unduly interfere with the powers of the tribal courts.

While the result in Williams v. Lee was highly protective of tribal jurisdiction, the test it announced was capable of being interpreted to permit increased exercise of state power within Indian country. In the subsequent case of Organized Village of Kake v. Egan, 369 U.S. 60 (1962), for example, the Court clearly suggested that state law and state court jurisdiction could be extended to Indians as well as non-Indians in Indian country, so long as there did not seem to be a direct interference with the tribal government itself. This rather expansive view of state power co-existed for several years with the more restrictive approach previously taken in Williams v. Lee, resulting in considerable uncertainty. This particular dispute regarding the proper application of Williams v. Lee was put to rest a decade later in McClanahan v. Arizona Tax Com'n, 411 U.S. 164 (1973), but *McClanahan* also introduced new subtleties to the subject of state jurisdiction in Indian country.

McClanahan involved an attempt by the state of Arizona to collect state income tax on the earnings of an Indian who resided on the Navajo Reservation and whose income was derived entirely from personal services performed on that reservation. One of the arguments raised by the state was that a tax on the income of an individual Indian did not interfere with tribal government and therefore was permissible under the test of Williams v. Lee, supra. In rejecting that contention, the Court first noted that it was not convinced that an individual income tax avoided infringing upon tribal self-government. But the primary defect in the state's argument, according to the Court, was that the test of Williams v. Lee was never intended to apply to attempted exercises of state jurisdiction over Indians. It was only when the state asserted power over *non-Indians* in Indian country that it was appropriate to balance the state and tribal interests by determining whether or not state jurisdiction would infringe upon tribal self-government. When the state attempted to reach Indians in Indian country, the legality of the state's action had to be determined by reference to applicable federal statutes and treaties, interpreted in light of a history of Indian tribal sovereignty and independence from state law. In the case of the Navajo reservation, those sources made it clear that the state had no power to impose its tax.

The subtlety that *McClanahan* introduced into jurisdictional analysis was its preemption approach. Notions of Indian sovereignty, which had loomed large in Williams v. Lee, were reduced to a "backdrop against which the applicable treaties and federal statutes must be read" to determine whether state law was preempted. 411 U.S. at 172. *McClanahan*'s analysis assumes that state law applies if not preempted, which is a reversal of previous presumptions that state law did not apply to matters affecting Indians in Indian country.

Although *McClanahan* applied its preemption analysis only to the question whether state law could reach Indians on the reservation, it soon was employed to determine whether state law could apply to non-Indians there as well. E.g., Washington v. Confederated Tribes of the Colville Indian Reservation, 447 U.S. 134 (1980); New Mexico v. Mescalero Apache Tribe, 462 U.S. 324 (1983). Because federal treaties and statutes rarely preempt state law expressly, preemption analysis often becomes a matter of weighing and balancing the competing interests.

State jurisdiction is preempted by the operation of federal law if it interferes with or is incompatible with federal and tribal interests reflected in federal law, unless the state interests at stake are sufficient to justify the assertion of state authority.

New Mexico v. Mescalero Apache Tribe, 462 U.S. at 334. In theory at least, this formula permits a state law that serves an extremely important state interest to interfere even with tribal self-government. The previous standard of Williams v. Lee, on the other hand, precluded application of *any* state law that "infringed on the right of reservation Indians to make their own laws and be governed by them." 358 U.S. at 220. The *Williams* rule is still employed as a test for the application of state law in Indian country, 462 U.S. at 334 n.16, but the area of tribal self-government that it absolutely protects is no longer construed to include everything affecting tribal interests. In most current clashes between state law and tribal authority, preemption analysis seems to predominate over the approach of Williams v. Lee. An example is Cotton Petroleum Corp. v. New Mexico, 490 U.S. 163 (1989), upholding the state's right to impose a severance tax on non-Indian oil and gas lessees operating on the reservation, even though the tribe also imposed a severance tax.

The Court now recognizes that in "exceptional circumstances" state law may be applied even to tribes and tribal members in Indian country. California v. Cabazon Band of Mission Indians, 480 U.S.

202, 215 (1987); New Mexico v. Mescalero Apache Tribe, 462 U.S. 324, 331–32 (1983). Such applications have occurred, but they have indeed been exceptional. States have been permitted to tax sales of cigarettes to nonmembers by a tribal shop, and to require the tribal seller to collect and remit the tax (although the state must depend on methods of enforcement other than suing the tribe). Washington v. Confederated Tribes of Colville Reservation, 447 U.S. 134 (1980); Oklahoma Tax Comm'n v. Citizen Band Potawatomi Indian Tribe, 498 U.S. 505 (1991). They have been permitted to regulate liquor sales by a licensed tribal member on-reservation, when federal legislation and the tribe's dependent status had traditionally precluded the tribe from doing so. Rice v. Rehner, 463 U.S. 713 (1983); see Fort Belknap Indian Community v. Mazurek, 43 F.3d 428 (9th Cir.1994),, cert. denied, 516 U.S. 806 (1995). Finally, in a most unusual case (see Chapter XV, Section C), a state has been permitted to regulate Indian fishing for conservation purposes, in places that unexpectedly turned out to be within a reservation. Puyallup Tribe, Inc. v. Department of Game, 433 U.S. 165 (1977).

On the other hand, the Supreme Court still presumes that states are preempted from taxing Indian activities, income, or property in Indian country. See Oklahoma Tax Comm'n v. Sac and Fox Nation, 508 U.S. 114, 126 (1993); Oklahoma Tax Comm'n v. Chickasaw Nation, 515 U.S. 450 (1995). States have been preempted from regulating hunting and fishing by *non-Indians* on trust lands within a reservation, where the tribe and the federal government had extensively regulated. New Mexico v. Mescalero Apache Tribe, 462 U.S. 324 (1983). They have also been preempted from regulating gambling operations conducted by tribes on their reservations. California v. Cabazon Band of Mission Indians, 480 U.S. 202 (1987). Finally, states regularly have been preempted from taxing non-Indian contractors who do business with tribes on the reservations. E.g., White Mountain Apache Tribe v. Bracker, 448 U.S. 136 (1980); Ramah Navajo School Bd., Inc. v. Bureau of Revenue, 458 U.S. 832 (1982).

The preemption doctrine, which is somewhat more fully discussed in Chapter V, Section B, has therefore made it quite difficult to draw bright jurisdictional lines for the application of state law in Indian country. Its primary impact, however, has been in the areas of taxation and regulation, rather than adjudicatory jurisdiction. The Supreme Court, at least until very recently, has been extraordinarily protective of the civil jurisdiction of tribal courts. Thus, in a case brought in federal court, the Supreme Court held that the federal question of a tribal court's jurisdiction over a reservation-based suit against a non-Indian must be determined in the first instance by the tribal court itself. National Farmers Union Ins. Cos. v. Crow Tribe, 471 U.S. 845 (1985). Later, the Court imposed the same requirement in a federal diversity case when the matter in litigation was also the subject of a tribal court action brought by an Indian against non-Indians. The Court stated:

If state-court jurisdiction over Indians or activities on Indian lands would interfere with tribal sovereignty and self-government, the state courts are generally divested of jurisdiction as a matter of federal law.

Iowa Mut. Ins. Co. v. LaPlante, 480 U.S. 9, 15 (1987). This statement is notable for its absence of weighing and balancing. It applies the more protective test of Williams v. Lee, which it cites. The Court also stated that civil jurisdiction over the activities of non-Indians on reservation lands "presumptively lies in the tribal courts unless affirmatively limited by a specific treaty provision or federal statute." 480 U.S. at 18.

The Supreme Court has recently reinterpreted this language, however, in a case involving tribal court jurisdiction over a tort suit between nonmembers arising from an accident on a state highway within a reservation. In Strate v. A–1 Contractors, 117 S.Ct. 1404 (1997), the Court held that a tribe, by reason of its domestic dependent status, lacked civil jurisdiction over such a case. It held that a state highway right-of-way was the equivalent of non-Indian fee land, and that tribes had no jurisdiction over nonmember activities on such land under Montana v. United States, 450 U.S. 544 (1981). The language quoted above from *LaPlante* was said to stand for "nothing more than the unremarkable proposition" that "where tribes possess authority to regulate activities of nonmembers," jurisdiction presumptively lies in the tribal court. *Strate*, 117 S.Ct. at 1413. The Supreme Court also reemphasized *Montana*'s narrow description of inherent tribal power: the power to punish members, determine membership, regulate domestic relations among members, and prescribe rules of inheritance for members. 117 S.Ct. at 1416. (If this list is to be deemed exhaustive of tribal powers, there would seem to be no occasion for the *LaPlante* presumption of tribal court jurisdiction over nonmembers to operate.) The consequence of the ruling in *Strate* is that state courts have exclusive jurisdiction over suits between nonmembers arising on non-Indian fee lands within a reservation. That result is not a new intrusion of state power into Indian country, because state courts previously had civil jurisdiction over such a suit. What is new is that the state jurisdiction is now exclusive of the tribe, and neither state nor federal courts are required to abstain in favor of tribal courts in such an action. 117 S.Ct. at 1416 n.14.

Although *Strate*, like *Montana*, involved activities only of nonmembers (indeed, non-Indians), it phrased the question for decision as whether a tribal court could "entertain a civil action against" nonmembers. 117 S.Ct. at 1407. One court of appeals, relying on *Strate*'s narrow view of tribal interests, has subsequently held that a tribal court could not exercise jurisdiction of an action by a *tribal member* against a non-Indian arising out of a vehicle accident on a state right-of-way. Wilson v. Marchington, 127 F.3d 805 (9th Cir.1997), cert. denied, 118 S.Ct. 1516 (1998). It has further held that *Strate* precludes tribal court jurisdiction over a suit by tribal members against non-Indian officers for false arrest on reservation fee lands that may have been Indian-owned; ownership was held to be irrelevant so long as the defendant officers, who were exercising Public Law 280 jurisdiction, had the right to be there. County of Lewis v. Allen, 1998 WL 191233 (9th Cir.1998). If these actions had been reversed, however, and the tribal members had been the defendants, Williams v. Lee would require the cases to be brought in tribal court. Whether that proposition is threatened by *Strate* remains to be seen.

To summarize the state of civil adjudicatory jurisdiction in Indian country, then, a few general lines can be drawn. When a case involves no tribal members or persons in a consensual relationship with the tribe or its members, and does not affect tribal self-government, the state courts do have jurisdiction. When Indians or Indian interests are involved, at least on trust (non-fee) land, state power is usually excluded unless federal statutes or treaties confer it. For claims arising on fee lands, a tribal member must be sued in tribal court and a non-member perhaps in state court. Any such generalizations are subject, however, to many qualifications that are discussed in Section F, infra.

D. PRESENT DIVISION OF CRIMINAL JURISDICTION IN INDIAN COUNTRY

1. FEDERAL CRIMINAL JURISDICTION

a. Federal Crimes of Nationwide Applicability

There are some general federal criminal statutes that are effective throughout the nation, and they apply in Indian country to all persons, whether or not Indian. Statutes punishing theft from the United States mail or treason are obvious examples. Other examples include the Organized Crime Control Act, see United States v. Funmaker, 10 F.3d 1327 (7th Cir.1993), the Racketeer Influenced and Corrupt Organizations Act (RICO), United States v. Juvenile Male, 118 F.3d 1344 (9th Cir.1997), and the Contraband Cigarette Trafficking Act, United States v. Baker, 63 F.3d 1478 (9th Cir.1995). Such crimes actually have little to do with Indian law, and it need only be noted that federal jurisdiction over them applies in Indian country as it does everywhere else.

In one interesting application of this principle, the Ninth Circuit held that the federal conspiracy statute, 18 U.S.C.A. § 371, was a law of nationwide applicability. United States v. Begay, 42 F.3d 486 (9th Cir.1994), cert. denied, 516 U.S. 826 (1995). The case was interesting because the predicate crimes that were charged as objects of the conspiracy were kidnapping and various assaults punishable under the Major Crimes Act, 18 U.S.C.A. § 1153.

Those predicate crimes were not ones of nationwide applicability; they applied only when the crimes were committed by Indians in Indian country. The court of appeals rejected a contention that linking conspiracy with major crimes impermissibly extended the scope of the Major Crimes Act beyond that intended by Congress. The court also rejected a contention that the government was required to prove that the conspiracy occurred in Indian country. Such proof was unnecessary because the conspiracy statute was of nationwide applicability. On the other hand, the government was required to prove that the objects of the conspiracy-kidnapping and aggravated assault in violation of the Major Crimes Act-occurred in Indian country. 42 F.3d at 501. See also Standing Bear v. United States, 68 F.3d 271 (8th Cir.1995), cert. denied, 116 S.Ct. 1444 (1996), holding that the federal statute proscribing use of a firearm in a crime of violence, 18 U.S.C.A. § 924(c)(1), was one of nationwide applicability, even though the crime in which the firearm was used was murder in violation of the Major Crimes Act.

In United States v. Markiewicz, 978 F.2d 786, 800 (2d Cir.1992), cert. denied, 506 U.S. 1086 (1993), the Second Circuit suggested that crimes of nationwide applicability apply to Indian-against-Indian offenses in Indian country only if the offenses are "peculiarly Federal" crimes and the prosecution "would protect an independent federal interest." This suggestion derived from the Supreme Court's footnote in United States v. Wheeler, 435 U.S. 313,

331 n. 32 (1978), referring to "offenses as to which there is an independent federal interest to be protected." That reference was merely descriptive of federal crimes of nationwide applicability, however; it did not purport to impose an independent requirement. Indeed, *Wheeler* had earlier stated that federal jurisdiction extends "to crimes over which there is federal jurisdiction regardless of whether an Indian is involved, such as assaulting a federal officer * * * *." 435 U.S. at 330 n, 30. No other circuit has imposed the requirement suggested by the Second Circuit. See, e.g., United States v. Begay, 42 F.3d at 500; United States v. Blue, 722 F.2d 383 (8th Cir.1983). Indeed, the requirement would seem to serve little purpose, because virtually any federal criminal statute of nationwide applicability could pass its test. See, e.g., United States v. Boots, 80 F.3d 580, 593–94 (1st Cir.1996), cert. denied, 117 S.Ct. 263 (1996).

b. Crimes Punishable Under the General Crimes Act, 18 U.S.C.A. § 1152

One of the most important federal criminal statutes applicable in Indian country is the General Crimes Act, 18 U.S.C.A. § 1152, sometimes called the Federal Enclaves Act or, more recently, the Indian Country Crimes Act. Its primary present function is to provide for prosecution of crimes by non-Indians against Indians and of non-major crimes by Indians against non-Indians. It was originally passed by Congress in 1817 in order to permit punishment of all crimes committed by non-Indians

in Indian territory, as well as some crimes committed by Indians against non-Indians. At that time, it
was assumed that all such crimes were beyond the
reach of state law and that some of them were
probably also beyond the effective reach of tribal
law. In its present form, the General Crimes Act
provides as follows:

18 U.S.C.A. § 1152:

Except as otherwise expressly provided by law,
the general laws of the United States as to the
punishment of offenses committed in any place
within the sole and exclusive jurisdiction of the
United States, except the District of Columbia,
shall extend to the Indian country.

This section shall not extend to offenses committed by one Indian against the person or property of another Indian, nor to any Indian committing any offense in the Indian country who has
been punished by the local law of the tribe, or to
any case where, by treaty stipulations, the exclusive jurisdiction over such offenses is or may be
secured to the Indian tribes respectively.

The effect of the Act is to import into Indian
country the entire body of criminal law applicable
in areas under exclusive federal jurisdiction. To
understand what has been imported, it is necessary
to know what law governs areas under exclusive
federal jurisdiction and why.

The pattern of criminal law applicable in areas
under exclusive federal jurisdiction reflects certain
problems arising from the nature of federal law. On

a nationwide scale, federal criminal statutes are relatively few in number; Congress has always assumed that the basic, comprehensive body of criminal law would be legislated by the states, as indeed it has been. There are, however, some areas of the country, such as federal forts and arsenals, where federal jurisdiction is exclusive and state law does not apply. In the absence of some sort of special legislation, these areas would have been left with an inadequate criminal law structure. Congress accordingly reacted in two ways to solve the problem. First, it passed statutes from time to time providing for the punishment of specific crimes committed in territory under federal jurisdiction. Thus 18 U.S.C.A. § 1111 provides for the punishment of murder committed within the special maritime and territorial jurisdiction of the United States. Various other crimes were covered in similar fashion, but the result was far from a complete criminal code. Congress consequently took a second approach as early as 1825; it passed what is now known as the Assimilative Crimes Act, 18 U.S.C.A. § 13. That statute provides:

> Whoever within [the special maritime and territorial jurisdiction of the United States] is guilty of any act or omission which, although not made punishable by an enactment of Congress, would be punishable if committed or omitted within the jurisdiction of the State, Territory, Possession, or District in which such place is situated, by the laws thereof in force at the time of such act or

omission, shall be guilty of a like offense and subject to a like punishment.

The effect of this provision is to borrow most of state criminal law and to apply it through federal law to areas under federal jurisdiction. Thus a violator of the Assimilative Crimes Act is charged with a federal offense and is tried in federal court, but the crime is defined and the sentence prescribed by state law.

The relevance of the Assimilative Crimes Act to the subject of Indian Law is that the Assimilative Crimes Act is one of the general laws of the United States that is extended to Indian country by the General Crimes Act, 18 U.S.C.A. § 1152. See Williams v. United States, 327 U.S. 711 (1946). Of course, the other specific federal criminal statutes applicable in areas of exclusive federal jurisdiction, such as 18 U.S.C.A. § 1111 proscribing the crime of murder, are also extended into Indian country by the General Crimes Act.

The primary need filled by the General Crimes Act was that of a body of law to punish non-Indian crime, and it served that purpose. Although the intention of Congress was almost certainly to apply federal law to *all* crimes committed by non-Indians, that intention was eventually frustrated by the Supreme Court. In United States v. McBratney, 104 U.S. 621 (1881), and Draper v. United States, 164 U.S. 240 (1896), the Court held that state courts had jurisdiction over crimes by non-Indians against non-Indians, and that the federal government did not. Later explanations of the *McBratney–Draper* rule place primary emphasis on the point that no Indian interests are involved in wholly non-Indian crimes, so that there is no need to invoke federal jurisdiction as a means of fulfilling the guardianship responsibilities of the United States to the tribe. See Donnelly v. United States, 228 U.S. 243, 271–72 (1913). By the same reasoning, it is probable that victimless crimes by non-Indians are similarly subject to state and not federal law. The result of *McBratney* and *Draper*, therefore, is that the General Crimes Act applies to non-Indians only when they commit crimes against Indians or Indian interests.

The General Crimes Act also applies to Indians, but in a more limited fashion than it does to non-Indians. In the first place, the Act itself enumerates three exceptions; it does not apply to the following:

i.   crimes by Indians against Indians;

ii. crimes by Indians that have been punished by the tribe; and

iii. crimes over which a treaty gives exclusive jurisdiction to the tribe.

The first exception is the largest, and represents a recognition by Congress at the time of the Act's passage that all-Indian crimes were solely the concern of the tribes in the exercise of their powers of self-government. Although Congress later modified its position by asserting federal jurisdiction over "major crimes" by Indians even when the victim was Indian (see subsection c, immediately below), the General Crimes Act exception remained unchanged and leaves the punishment of the majority of all-Indian crimes to the tribes.

While the first exception to the General Crimes Act refers to crimes by Indians *against* Indians, a fair construction of the whole statute seems to require that victimless crimes by Indians also be excluded from federal jurisdiction. A victimless crime by an Indian is just as much an internal tribal matter as a crime by an Indian against an Indian. For that reason the Supreme Court rejected an attempt by federal authorities to prosecute an Indian for the consensual crime of adultery with another Indian in Indian country. The government contended that the crime was not within the first exception to the General Crimes Act because it could not be considered a crime "against" an Indian. The Supreme Court ruled that there was no jurisdiction, and that to hold otherwise would subject Indians "not only to the statute relating to adultery, but also to many others which it seems most reasonable to believe were not intended by Congress to be applied to them." United States v. Quiver, 241 U.S. 602, 606 (1916); see also Ex parte Mayfield, 141 U.S. 107 (1891).

The correctness of the Supreme Court's position in *Quiver* becomes all the more apparent upon examination of the consequences that would follow if the General Crimes Act were applied to victimless crimes by Indians. Because the Assimilative Crimes Act is one of the "general laws of the United States" imported into Indian country by the General Crimes Act, the full panoply of state law governing victimless crimes would be applied to tribal Indians. The result would be an enormous intrusion on tribal authority over Indian affairs. One much-criticized case that supplies an example is United States v. Sosseur, 181 F.2d 873 (7th Cir.1950). There the General Crimes Act and the Assimilative Crimes Act were applied to convict an Indian of operating slot machines for which he had a tribal license. The court relied in part on the fact that the primary users of the machines were non-Indian tourists, and that may be the best explanation for the decision. If, however, the crime is viewed as a victimless one, the decision seems to impose the requirements of state law quite unnecessarily upon an Indian in Indian country whose conduct is more appropriately governed by the contrary provisions of tribal law. In that sense, the *Sosseur* decision seems inconsistent with the Supreme Court's ruling in *Quiver*, supra. It is also inconsistent, in practical effect, with California v. Cabazon Band of Mission Indians, 480 U.S. 202 (1987), which held state law inapplicable to high-stakes bingo and poker games conducted by tribes on their reservations.

In the same vein as *Sosseur* is the recent decision of the Eighth Circuit in United States v. Thunder Hawk, 127 F.3d 705 (8th Cir.1997). There the defendant Indian was convicted in federal court under the Assimilative Crimes Act of driving under the influence of alcohol. The court held that the crime was not within the exception of § 1152 for crimes by an Indian against an Indian, even though the defendant's driving had caused injuries to his Indian daughter, because the offense requires no victim. The victimless crime was held to fall within the terms of the Assimilative Crimes Act. *Quiver* was distinguished on the ground that it involved domestic relations, "an area traditionally left to tribal self-government." 127 F.3d at 709. The court of appeals also viewed driving under the influence as a public crime against both Indians and non-Indians. It is difficult to see, however, why punishment of Indians for driving under the influence does not fall within the tribe's power of self-government. Indeed, the federal authorities prosecuted Thunder Hawk while a charge for the same offense was pending against him in tribal court!

An appealing argument can even be made that the General Crimes Act and its incorporated Assimilative Crimes Act ought *never* to be applied to Indians (in other words, that not only should victimless crimes by Indians be excluded from those Acts, but also crimes by Indians against non-Indians). The Indian who commits a crime in Indian country is subject to the comprehensive criminal jurisdiction of the tribe and, for a few specified crimes, of the federal government under the Major Crimes Act. There is no criminal law vacuum for the Indian (as there was for the non-Indian) and therefore no need to import a body of criminal law by way of the General Crimes Act and Assimilative Crimes Act. To do so merely displaces tribal law that is far more appropriate for governing the conduct of the Indian. See Clinton, *Criminal Jurisdic-*

tion Over Indian Lands: A Journey Through a Jurisdictional Maze, 18 Ariz.L.Rev. 503, 535–36 (1976). A major difficulty with this argument is presented by the second exception to the General Crimes Act, which excludes prosecution of crimes by Indians that have been punished by the tribe. This exception does not appear to be aimed at crimes against Indians, because they are entirely excluded by the first exception. Nor does it seem likely that it applies to victimless crimes by Indians, which are also wholly internal affairs that ought to be left to the tribe whether or not it chooses to punish them. The most sensible meaning that can be attributed to the second exception is that it applies to crimes by Indians against non-Indians, and that Congress intended to apply the General Crimes Act to such crimes unless they had actually been punished by the tribes. Unless Congress later modified that intention by passage or amendment of the Major Crimes Act (and the legislative history is far from conclusive to that effect), it continues to support application of the General Crimes Act to non-major crimes by Indians against non-Indians. In any event, the General Crimes Act and Assimilative Crimes Act have been applied, with varying degrees of attention to their underlying purposes, to such crimes. United States v. John, 587 F.2d 683 (5th Cir.), cert. denied, 441 U.S. 925 (1979); United States v. Burland, 441 F.2d 1199 (9th Cir.), cert. denied, 404 U.S. 842 (1971); cf. United States v. Butler, 541 F.2d 730 (8th Cir.1976). When a crime by an Indian against a non-Indian is one of the enumerated offenses in the Major Crimes Act, however, prosecution must be brought under that Act and not the General Crimes Act. Henry v. United States, 432 F.2d 114 (9th Cir.1970), modified 434 F.2d 1283, cert. denied 400 U.S. 1011 (1971); United States v. John, supra.

The third exception to the General Crimes Act, which excludes crimes over which a treaty gives exclusive jurisdiction to a tribe, is of little significance today. Only a few of the early treaties conferred such jurisdiction, and several of those have been abrogated or have ceased to be enforceable because the tribe no longer exercises governmental functions.

c. Crimes Punishable Under the Major Crimes Act, 18 U.S.C.A. § 1153

The Major Crimes Act was passed by Congress in 1885, in reaction to the Supreme Court's holding in Ex parte Crow Dog, 109 U.S. 556 (1883), that federal courts had no jurisdiction over the murder of an Indian by an Indian in Indian territory. In its present form, the Act provides in part as follows:

18 U.S.C.A. § 1153:

(a) Any Indian who commits against the person or property of another Indian or other person any of the following offenses, namely, murder, manslaughter, kidnapping, maiming, a felony under chapter 109A, incest, assault with intent to commit murder, assault with a dangerous weapon, assault resulting in serious bodily injury (as defined in section 1365 of this title), an assault against an individual who has not attained the age of 16 years, arson, burglary, robbery, and a felony under section 661 of this title within the Indian country, shall be subject to the same law and penalties as all other persons committing any of the above offenses, within the exclusive jurisdiction of the United States.

* * *

Chapter 109A, incorporated in the statute, refers to sexual abuse; section 661 deals with theft.

Even though the primary congressional purpose in passing the Act was to permit punishment of major crimes by Indians against Indians, the Act expressly applies whether the victim is Indian or non-Indian. When the victim is non-Indian, the General Crimes Act also arguably would apply, but it has been held that in those circumstances the Major Crimes Act should control to the exclusion of the General Crimes Act. Henry v. United States, 432 F.2d 114 (9th Cir.1970), modified 434 F.2d 1283, cert. denied, 400 U.S. 1011 (1971).

The principal effect of the Major Crimes Act was to permit prosecution of Indians by reference to selected federal criminal statutes applicable in federal reserves. Seven crimes were originally covered, but the list has been expanded to the present fourteen by a series of amendments. Occasional problems were caused when Congress added to the list crimes for which there was no existing federal definition, but Congress has since amended the Act to provide that the crimes of burglary, incest and any other named major crimes not defined by federal law were to be "defined and punished in accordance with the laws of the State in which such offense was committed." 18 U.S.C.A. § 1153(b). At present only burglary and incest among the fourteen major crimes are undefined by federal law, so those are the only two instances in which state law is incorporated into the federal Act. See United States v. Welch, 822 F.2d 460 (4th Cir.1987).

A split in federal circuits arose over whether the Federal Sentencing Guidelines, which originally applied to anyone convicted of "an offense described in any Federal statute," could be applied to an Indian convicted of burglary or incest under the Major Crimes Act, when those federally-undefined offenses were required by that Act to be "punished in accordance with" state law. Compare United States v. Bear, 932 F.2d 1279 (9th Cir.1990), with United States v. Norquay, 905 F.2d 1157 (8th Cir. 1990). Congress put an end to the conflict by amending 18 U.S.C.A. § 3551 so that it expressly applied the Guidelines to persons convicted under the Major Crimes Act. Federal jurisdiction over a major crime has been treated as including jurisdiction to revoke supervised release imposed as punishment for that crime. United States v. Lomayaoma, 86 F.3d 142 (9th Cir.), cert. denied, 117 S.Ct. 272 (1996).

The Major Crimes Act is supplemented by a jurisdictional statute, 18 U.S.C.A. § 3242, which provides that Indians prosecuted under the Major

Crimes Act "shall be tried in the same courts, and in the same manner, as are all other persons committing such offenses within the exclusive jurisdiction of the United States." For the most part this statute merely emphasizes the fact that Major Crimes Act prosecutions are regular federal criminal trials subject to the same procedures as any others. The statute had controlling effect, however, in one important case determining the extent of federal jurisdiction under the Major Crimes Act. In Keeble v. United States, 412 U.S. 205 (1973), an Indian was charged under the Major Crimes Act with assault with intent to commit serious bodily injury. At the close of his trial, he requested the judge to instruct the jury that they might convict him of the lesser included offense of simple assault. The district court refused the instruction on the ground that the Major Crimes Act did not give it jurisdiction over the crime of simple assault, and the court of appeals affirmed. The Supreme Court reversed, holding that an Indian was entitled to an instruction on a lesser included offense because he was entitled to be tried "in the same manner" as a non-Indian under 18 U.S.C.A. § 3242. It follows that the federal court has jurisdiction to impose punishment on the defendant if he is convicted of the lesser offense. United States v. Demarrias, 876 F.2d 674 (8th Cir.1989).

Although the *Keeble* decision does extend a procedural option to Indian defendants, it also increases the extent to which the Major Crimes Act intrudes on tribal authority. One circuit, for example, has held that a federal court continued to have jurisdiction over lesser-included offenses even after the court ordered a judgment of acquittal on the Major Crime charged. United States v. Walkingeagle, 974 F.2d 551 (4th Cir.1992), cert. denied, 507 U.S. 1019 (1993). As the dissent in that case pointed out, this result raises the possibility that Major Crimes Act prosecutions will be brought as a sham to obtain otherwise-forbidden jurisdiction over lesser included offenses. The danger does not seem great, however. Federal prosecutors are not looking for extra work. Moreover, the right to request an instruction on a lesser included offense can probably be restricted to the defense. See Keeble, 412 U.S. at 214 n.14. As a result, the increase of federal authority at the expense of the tribes will probably be small. *Keeble* also leaves open the question whether an Indian defendant is entitled to plea-bargain and plead guilty in federal court to a reduced charge over which the court would not originally have jurisdiction under the Major Crimes Act. It is possible that such a practice would be viewed as an undue extension of federal authority; on the other hand, forbidding the practice may force an Indian defendant to trial on a Major Crimes charge when he or she otherwise could have bargained for conviction of a lesser offense. A final problem posed by *Keeble* concerns the source to be used by the federal court in defining and punishing the lesser included offense. In Felicia v. United States, 495 F.2d 353 (8th Cir.), cert. denied, 419 U.S. 849 (1974), the court of appeals held that the lesser included offense was to be defined and punished according to state law because the Major Crimes Act mandates such treatment for crimes not defined by federal law. In United States v. John, 587 F.2d 683 (5th Cir.), cert. denied, 441 U.S. 925 (1979), another court of appeals held that the General Crimes Act applied to the lesser included offense. Under the latter approach, the lesser included offense would be defined and punished according to federal statute if there is one and state law if there is not.

Enforcement of the Major Crimes Act (like that of the General Crimes Act) has often been criticized by tribal authorities as being too lax. Overburdened United States Attorneys have often been unenthusiastic about prosecuting the less serious of the major crimes. One solution of the tribes has been to exercise concurrent jurisdiction, which the Major Crimes Act probably permits (see subsection 2, Tribal Criminal Jurisdiction, below). Another has been for the tribe to prosecute for lesser included or collateral minor offenses encompassed in the same act that constituted the major crime. Because the tribes and the federal government are separate sovereigns, the Supreme Court has held that no double jeopardy problem arises even if both prosecute for the same criminal act. United States v. Wheeler, 435 U.S. 313 (1978): see Wetsit v. Stafne, 44 F.3d 823 (9th Cir.1995). *Wheeler* and other cases treating constitutional problems arising from the division of criminal jurisdiction in Indian country are discussed in Chapter XI, infra.

d. Other Federal Statutes

There are innumerable other federal statutes affecting criminal jurisdiction on individual reservations or in specially defined areas of Indian country. See, e.g., Kansas Act, 18 U.S.C.A. § 3243; Negonsott v. Samuels, 507 U.S. 99 (1993). It is neither possible nor desirable to catalog them here. The most that can be said is that an early step in dealing with a particular problem of criminal jurisdiction must be a search to determine the existence and scope of any such statutes.

2. TRIBAL CRIMINAL JURISDICTION

In the absence of federal statutes limiting it, tribal criminal jurisdiction over the Indian in Indian country is complete, inherent and exclusive. Ex parte Crow Dog, 109 U.S. 556 (1883). Although Congress has legislated a number of limitations, much remains of the original jurisdiction of the tribes over Indians. It is exercised primarily by tribal courts, which are described in Chapter IV, Section D, supra.

The tribe has exclusive jurisdiction over non-major crimes committed by Indians against Indians in Indian country. Such crimes are specifically excepted from the jurisdiction conferred upon the federal courts by the General Crimes Act, 18 U.S.C.A. § 1152. Similarly, victimless crimes by Indians are matters wholly internal to the tribes, and they too must be regarded as subject to exclusive tribal jurisdiction. Cf. United States v. Wheeler, 435 U.S. 313 (1978).

Non-major crimes by Indians against non-Indians are also unquestionably subject to the jurisdiction of tribal courts, but here the jurisdiction is not exclusive. Federal courts also have jurisdiction over such crimes by virtue of the General Crimes Act, supra. That Act excludes from its coverage Indians who have been punished by their tribes, thus making it clear that the tribes share jurisdiction over these crimes.

"Major crimes" are the fourteen named crimes made subject to federal jurisdiction by the Major Crimes Act, 18 U.S.C.A. § 1153. That act applies to such crimes when committed by Indians in Indian country, whether the victim is Indian or non-Indian. At least one federal circuit has concluded that tribes have concurrent jurisdiction to punish conduct that also constitutes an offense under the Major Crimes Act. Wetsit v. Stafne, 44 F.3d 823 (9th Cir.1995). The Supreme Court has not decided the question. See Oliphant v. Suquamish Indian Tribe, 435 U.S. 191, 203 n. 14 (1978). The legislative history of the Major Crimes Act strongly supports tribal exercise of concurrent jurisdiction. See Clinton, *Criminal Jurisdiction Over Indian Lands: A Journey Through a Jurisdictional Maze*, 18 Ariz. L.Rev. 503, 559, n. 295 (1976). Moreover, the great majority of tribes for many years have exercised jurisdiction over the crime of theft, which duplicates larceny, a crime rather surprisingly included in the original Major Crimes Act. Congress eliminated much of the overlap in 1984 by deleting larceny from the Act and substituting felony theft under 18 U.S.C.A. § 661.

The issue whether the tribes have concurrent jurisdiction over major crimes by Indians has been rendered less important by the passage of the Civil Rights Act of 1968, which now limits the jurisdiction of the tribal courts to sentences not exceeding one year's imprisonment and a $5,000 fine or both. 25 U.S.C.A. § 1302(7). Even before passage of the Civil Rights Act, most tribes had left major crimes other than larceny entirely to the federal government; with the Act's sentencing limit they have little incentive to change that pattern. Here as elsewhere tribes may choose to exercise less than their maximum jurisdiction.

Because virtually all federal jurisdictional statutes refer to "Indians" and not "tribal members," it generally had been assumed that tribal jurisdiction over crimes by Indians was not limited to members of the tribe asserting jurisdiction. It has been common practice for tribal courts to exercise authority over members of other tribes who commit crimes within the court's geographical jurisdiction. Doubt was first cast upon this practice by language in the Supreme Court decisions of United States v. Wheeler, 435 U.S. 313 (1978), and Washington v. Confederated Tribes of the Colville Indian Reservation, 447 U.S. 134 (1980), both discussed in Section A of this chapter. *Wheeler* continually referred to a tribe's inherent criminal jurisdiction over its *members*, and *Colville* permitted a state to impose a sales tax upon Indians on a reservation other than their own. Then, in 1990, the Supreme Court decided that tribes as domestic dependent sovereigns had no power to exercise criminal jurisdiction over Indians who were not members of the tribe. Duro v. Reina, 495 U.S. 676 (1990). Congress promptly overturned that ruling, however, recognizing and affirming "the inherent power of Indian tribes * * * to exercise criminal jurisdiction over all Indians * * * *" 25 U.S.C.A. § 1301(2). Thus the tribes continue to exercise criminal jurisdiction over nonmember as well as member Indians.

The jurisdiction of a tribe is generally confined to crimes committed within the geographical limits of its reservation and, presumably, any of its dependent Indian communities. One exception to this rule was established in Settler v. Lameer, 507 F.2d 231 (9th Cir.1974), in which the Yakima tribal court was held to have jurisdiction to punish tribal members who committed game violations in exercise of their off-reservation treaty fishing rights. Certain cases of juvenile delinquency also appear to be an exception to the general rule, but in fact are not. When an Indian juvenile domiciled on a reservation commits criminal acts off-reservation, the tribal court generally exercises jurisdiction to adjudicate delinquency. The reason is that the matter in issue is the status of delinquency, with a locus on the reservation, and not the individual acts committed off-reservation.

It now has been authoritatively established that tribes have no general criminal jurisdiction over non-Indians. Oliphant v. Suquamish Indian Tribe, 435 U.S. 191 (1978). As explained in subsection C(1) of this chapter, *Oliphant* arose from attempts by the tribes in the 1970's to solve some of their law enforcement problems by asserting criminal jurisdiction over non-Indians. The Suquamish Tribe argued in *Oliphant* that it had inherent but long-unexercised jurisdiction over non-Indians that had not been limited by treaty or federal statute. The Supreme Court agreed that the tribe's power had not actually been curtailed by treaty or statute, but held that criminal jurisdiction over non-Indians would be inconsistent with the status of tribes as dependent sovereigns. The court also noted that some of the provisions of federal criminal statutes seemed inconsistent with the existence of dormant tribal jurisdiction over non-Indians. For example, the second exception to the General Crimes Act, 18 U.S.C.A. § 1152, precludes federal prosecution of an Indian who has been punished by his tribe. If the tribe had power to punish non-Indians, would they not have been given similar protection against double punishment? The Major Crimes Act, 18 U.S.C.A. § 1153, was passed because Congress did not wish to leave the punishment of serious crimes entirely to the tribes. If the tribes had power to punish both Indians and non-Indians, then why did the Major Crimes Act provide for federal punishment only of Indians? The Court in *Oliphant* did not conclude from these inconsistencies that the General Crimes Act or Major Crimes Act themselves precluded the tribes from exercising criminal jurisdiction over non-Indians. Instead, the Court viewed the Acts as persuasive evidence that no such jurisdiction existed at the times Congress passed them. The Court's reasoning has its force, but it is difficult to evaluate the understanding of Congress during a period when Congress had no reason to focus on the problems that might arise if the tribes elected to exercise jurisdiction over non-Indians. At a much later date, Congress passed the Civil Rights Act of 1968, 25 U.S.C.A. § 1301 et seq., which guaranteed to all persons (not merely Indians) a number of constitutional-type rights against tribal actions that are most likely to occur in the exercise of the tribe's criminal jurisdiction. Federal law accordingly provides opposition as well as support to the decision in *Oliphant*, but the decision in any event is clear: the tribes have no general criminal jurisdiction over non-Indians, and any change in that situation must come from Congress.

One small area of criminal jurisdiction over non-Indians may survive *Oliphant*. It seems likely that a tribal court would still have power to enforce decorum in its courtroom by the use of criminal contempt power against disruptive non-Indians. The exercise of such power may be essential to the very existence of a tribal court, and is therefore not inconsistent with the status of a tribe as a dependent sovereign. The same argument might also be used to support the use of contempt power to enforce subpoenas issued to non-Indians in the course of the tribal court's exercise of its legitimate jurisdiction. Finally, tribes generally retain the power to exclude unwanted persons from their reservations (a power often guaranteed by treaty). The power of exclusion might be viewed as quasi-criminal, and could be exercised against non-Indians at least to the extent that they do not have a federally-conferred right to be on the reservation. See Merrion v. Jicarilla Apache Tribe, 455 U.S. 130, 144–45 (1982); Hardin v. White Mountain Apache Tribe, 779 F.2d 476, 478–79 (9th Cir.1985). The tribe does not have power to exclude federal officials engaged in carrying out their duties. United States v. White Mountain Apache Tribe, 784 F.2d 917 (9th Cir.1986).

3. STATE CRIMINAL JURISDICTION

Outside of Indian country, the state has general criminal jurisdiction over all persons, including Indians. See, e.g., Hagen v. Utah, 510 U.S. 399 (1994). Within Indian country, however, the state's jurisdiction is generally limited to those crimes that do not concern Indians or Indian interests.

The state has exclusive jurisdiction over crimes by non-Indians against non-Indians in Indian country. Even though such crimes would appear to fall within the federal jurisdiction conferred by the General Crimes Act, 18 U.S.C.A. § 1152, the Supreme Court held the state's jurisdiction to be exclusive in United States v. McBratney, 104 U.S. 621 (1881), and Draper v. United States, 164 U.S. 240 (1896). While these cases emphasized the inherent right of the states to jurisdiction within their boundaries, the Supreme Court has subsequently adhered to the results but justified them on the ground that Indians were not directly affected. New York ex rel. Ray v. Martin, 326 U.S. 496 (1946).

Victimless crimes committed by non-Indians in Indian country are also within the exclusive jurisdiction of the state, by reason of the same authority. See Solem v. Bartlett, 465 U.S. 463, 465 n. 2. It should be emphasized, however, that the crimes should be truly victimless. Crimes against Indian property interests are not victimless even though no Indian person is directly assaulted; Indian interests are affected and that fact places the crime within the exclusive jurisdiction of the federal government.

States traditionally have no criminal jurisdiction in Indian country over crimes by Indians against anyone, or crimes by non-Indians against Indians. Crimes by Indians are punishable either by the tribe or the federal government and crimes by non-Indians against Indians are punishable exclusively by the federal government. Williams v. United States, 327 U.S. 711 (1946). The Ninth Circuit has recognized a narrow exception to this principle: the state can prosecute Indians for violation of state laws regarding liquor sales in Indian country. Fort Belknap Indian Community v. Mazurek, 43 F.3d 428 (9th Cir.1994), cert. denied, 516 U.S. 806 (1995). The exception was deemed necessary to effectuate the state power to regulate liquor sales in Indian country, which was recognized in Rice v. Rehner, 463 U.S. 713 (1983). The general rule, however, is that the state is excluded from criminal jurisdiction over crimes involving Indians in Indian country.

In the past this rule held true even when the Indians involved were members of tribes other than the one that governed the reservation where the crime took place. Some doubt was cast upon this application of the rule by United States v. Wheeler, 435 U.S. 313 (1978), and Washington v. Confederated Tribes of the Colville Indian Reservation, 447 U.S. 134 (1980), both discussed in section A of this chapter. Wheeler emphasized tribal criminal jurisdiction over *member* Indians, and *Colville* permitted a state to tax nonmember Indians in Indian country. Then, in 1990, the Supreme Court decided that tribes as domestic dependent sovereigns had no power to exercise criminal jurisdiction over Indians who were not members of the tribe. Duro v. Reina, 495 U.S. 676 (1990). This raised the possibility that there might be a void in enforcement authority over crimes by nonmember Indians, if the states continued to be excluded from jurisdiction in such cases. *Duro* suggested that the states might enforce their laws by agreement with the tribes or that Congress might intervene to correct any void. Congress, however, quickly overturned *Duro* instead, recognizing and affirming "the inherent power of Indian tribes * * * to exercise criminal jurisdiction over all Indians * * * *" 25 U.S.C.A. § 1301(2). This action seems to have removed any possibility that state criminal jurisdiction would be extended to cover crimes by nonmember Indians in Indian country.

4. CHART OF CRIMINAL JURISDICTION IN INDIAN COUNTRY BY PARTIES AND CRIMES

Notes:

i. This chart does not reflect federal crimes applicable to all persons in all places, such as theft from the mails or treason.

ii. This chart does not apply to Indian country over which the state has taken jurisdiction pursuant to Public Law 280, 18 U.S.C.A. § 1162.

Crime by Parties	Jurisdiction	Statutory Authority
a. Crimes by Indians against Indians:		
i. "Major" crimes.	Federal or tribal (concurrent)	18 U.S.C.A. § 1153
ii. Other crimes.	Tribal (exclusive)	
b. Crimes by Indians against non-Indians:		
i. "Major" crimes.	Federal or tribal (concurrent)	18 U.S.C.A. § 1153
ii. Other crimes.	Federal or tribal (concurrent)	18 U.S.C.A. § 1152
c. Crimes by Indians without Victims:	Tribal (exclusive)	
d. Crimes by non-Indians against Indians:	Federal (exclusive)	18 U.S.C.A. § 1152
e. Crimes by non-Indians against non-Indians:	State (exclusive)	
f. Crimes by non-Indians without Victims:	State (exclusive)	

E. ARREST AND EXTRADITION

There is relatively little authority regarding the powers of the federal, state and tribal police in Indian country. In general, powers of policing and arrest follow the criminal jurisdiction of the three governments in the absence of special arrangements or agreements. For example, federal officers enforce the Major Crimes Act against Indians and the General Crimes Act against both Indians and non-Indians in Indian country. Tribal police enforce tribal laws against Indians and also have sufficient power over non-Indians to exercise the tribal power of exclusion. That power has been held to allow tribal police to investigate a crime committed by a non-Indian, and to turn both the results and the offender over to state authorities. State v. Haskins, 269 Mont. 202, 887 P.2d 1189 (1994). In addition to regular tribal police, many reservations utilize Indian police of the Bureau of Indian Affairs, who have authority to arrest for violations of either federal or tribal law. Finally, state police or county sheriffs and similar state personnel have authority to arrest non-Indians committing crimes against non-Indians or victimless crimes. State officers have no jurisdiction over Indians in Indian country, however. A state officer has even been held to lack power to search the reservation residence of an Indian parolee from state prison, even though the parolee as a condition of parole consented to searches. United States v. Anderson, 857 F.Supp. 52 (D.S.D.1994).

The difficulties caused by this division of jurisdiction are obvious. In the absence of special arrangements, a state police officer who stops a speeder on a state highway that passes through Indian country will lack authority to arrest if the speeding driver is an Indian, but will retain authority if the driver is a non-Indian. Needless to say, the officer often cannot know in advance which will be the case. For that reason, one court has held that an officer can briefly stop a moving vehicle to ascertain whether a violator is an Indian and, if so, may turn him or her over to tribal police. United States v. Patch, 114 F.3d 131 (9th Cir.), cert. denied, 118 S.Ct. 445 (1997); see also Duro v. Reina, 495 U.S. 676, 697 (1990). Similarly, tribal police may encounter non-Indians who have committed crimes against non-Indians or victimless crimes, but be without power to arrest them. Those officers, too, have been held to have authority to stop the violator and, if he or she is a non-Indian, to hold the violator for state authorities. State v. Schmuck, 121 Wash.2d 373, 850 P.2d 1332, cert. denied, 510 U.S. 931 (1993).

A more satisfactory solution to these problems is for the tribal and state officers to cross-deputize, so that each is empowered to arrest for the other government. The tribal police officer then can arrest a non-Indian who commits a crime against a non-Indian and may take him or her to state court, because the tribal police officer is acting in the capacity of a deputy of the state. The same advantages apply in reverse for the state police officer, who can arrest Indians on behalf of the tribe.

Provisions for extradition of offenders may be made between tribes and states. One case which exemplifies both the powers of arrest and the nature of extradition is Arizona ex rel. Merrill v. Turtle, 413 F.2d 683 (9th Cir.1969), cert. denied, 396 U.S. 1003 (1970). In that case Oklahoma sought to obtain custody of a Cheyenne Indian whom it had charged with forgery and who was living on the Navajo reservation in Arizona. Oklahoma first applied to the Navajo Tribe for extradition, but the tribal court refused to deliver the accused on the ground that the only extradition provided by the Navajo Tribal Code was to the states of Arizona, Utah and New Mexico. Oklahoma then applied to the Governor of Arizona, and pursuant to his warrant a county sheriff arrested the accused on the Navajo reservation. The United States District Court issued a writ of habeas corpus, ordering release on the ground that the state officer had no power to arrest an Indian in Indian country. The court of appeals affirmed, holding that Arizona's exercise of its extradition authority would interfere with the sovereign power of the tribe to make its own extradition arrangements. As evidence of this tribal power, the court pointed to the treaty between the Navajos and the United States, which contained the common provision by which the tribe agreed to deliver federal offenders to the United States for trial.

The *Turtle* ruling that the state has no power to arrest Indians in Indian country for crimes committed elsewhere has met with some resistance. For example, in State ex rel. Old Elk v. District Court, 170 Mont. 208, 552 P.2d 1394, appeal dismissed,

429 U.S. 1030 (1976), the court held that in the absence of any provision for extradition a county sheriff had authority to arrest an Indian on the Crow Reservation for a homicide committed off-reservation. Courts also have permitted arrests of Indians by state officers when the offense was committed out of Indian country and a fresh pursuit ended in it. State v. Lupe, 181 Ariz. 211, 889 P.2d 4 (Ariz.App.1994); see United States v. Patch, 114 F.3d 131, 134 (9th Cir.1997). On the other hand, where an extradition arrangement existed, it has been held improper for state officers to by-pass it and make an arrest on a reservation. Benally v. Marcum, 89 N.M. 463, 553 P.2d 1270 (1976); State v. Yazzie, 108 N.M. 677, 777 P.2d 916 (N.M.App.), cert. denied, 108 N.M. 681, 777 P.2d 1325 (1989). Even fresh pursuit has been held insufficient to justify the disregard of an extradition agreement. City of Farmington v. Benally, 119 N.M. 496, 892 P.2d 629 (N.M.App.), cert. denied, 119 N.M. 389, 890 P.2d 1321 (1995).

Although the court in *City of Farmington* upheld a dismissal of the charges, that result does not always follow from an unlawful arrest by state officers in Indian country. Some courts hold that, when the charge is valid, the manner in which the defendant is brought from Indian country to the court does not affect the court's jurisdiction. See, e.g., Primeaux v. Leapley, 502 N.W.2d 265 (S.D. 1993).

F. PRESENT DIVISION OF CIVIL JURISDICTION IN INDIAN COUNTRY

1. STATE CIVIL JURISDICTION

a. General Civil Litigation

A description of civil jurisdiction in Indian country is best begun by establishing what the state courts *cannot* do. Williams v. Lee, 358 U.S. 217 (1959), held that state courts had no jurisdiction over a claim by a non-Indian against an Indian when the claim arose in Indian country. The assertion of state jurisdiction in those circumstances would infringe "on the right of reservation Indians to make their own laws and be governed by them." State jurisdiction was permitted only "where essential tribal relations were not involved and where the rights of Indians would not be jeopardized * * *." 358 U.S. at 219–20; see Iowa Mut. Ins. Co. v. LaPlante, 480 U.S. 9, 15 (1987). Moreover, Congress by passing Public Law 280 had provided a method for the states to assume jurisdiction and the state in *Williams* had not availed itself of that method.

It is noteworthy that the discussion in Williams v. Lee drew its jurisdictional line between Indians and non-Indians. The case arose on the Navajo reservation and the defendants were a Navajo Indian and his wife who lived on the reservation, but the Court did not state its rule in terms of tribal membership. It said:

Today the Navajo Courts of Indian Offenses exercise broad criminal and civil jurisdiction which covers suits by outsiders against Indian defendants. No Federal Act has given state courts jurisdiction over such controversies.

358 U.S. at 222. As a consequence of this rationale, courts applying Williams v. Lee for many years thereafter made no distinction between member and nonmember Indians. The Supreme Court, however, first made such a distinction in United States v. Wheeler, 435 U.S. 313 (1978), a criminal double jeopardy case. *Wheeler* continually referred to a tribe's inherent criminal jurisdiction over its *members*, even though nothing in the decision turned on that distinction. Then in Washington v. Confederated Tribes of the Colville Indian Reservation, 447 U.S. 134 (1980), the Court permitted a state to impose a sales tax upon Indians on a reservation other than their own. *Colville* stated that the imposition of the tax would not "contravene the principle of tribal self-government, for the simple reason that nonmembers are not constituents of the governing Tribe." 447 U.S. at 162. That language seemed calculated to avoid the impact of Williams v. Lee, supra, insofar as nonmember Indians are concerned. Then, in 1990, the Supreme Court decided that tribes as domestic dependent sovereigns had no power to exercise criminal jurisdiction over Indians who were not members of the tribe. Duro v. Reina, 495 U.S. 676 (1990). Congress promptly overturned that ruling, however, recognizing and affirming "the inherent power of Indian tribes * * * to exercise criminal jurisdiction over all Indians * * *." 25 U.S.C.A. § 1301(2).

That action of Congress presumably settled the matter for purposes of criminal jurisdiction, but the Supreme Court in its most recent civil case held that tribes had no jurisdiction over a tort action between "nonmembers" arising out of an automobile accident on a state right-of-way through the reservation. Strate v. A–1 Contractors, 117 S.Ct. 1404, 1407–08 (1997). In *Strate*, the distinction was not necessary to the decision, because both parties were non-Indians, but the language of the opinion indicates the Supreme Court's preference for distinguishing between the tribe's power over its own members and its power (or presumptive lack of it) over nonmembers, Indian or not. Although it is not clear how far the Supreme Court will go in applying that distinction when it is crucial to a jurisdictional decision in a civil case, it is no longer safe to assume that a tribe's civil authority over nonmember Indians is the same as its authority over its members. For that reason, much of the following discussion will refer to "members" as the group over which the tribe has indisputable civil authority. The converse term "nonmembers" is not always employed in opposition to it, however, because of the uncertainty over their jurisdictional status in various contexts. (*Strate* is further discussed under Tribal Court Jurisdiction, section 3(a) below).

Strate involved only nonmembers on both sides, but it phrased the question for decision as whether a tribal court could "entertain a civil action against" nonmembers when the claim arose on a state right-of-way. *Strate*, 117 S.Ct. at 1407. It also described tribal interests very narrowly. Consequently, one court of appeals has held that a tribal court could not entertain an action by a *tribal member* against a nonmember when the claim arose on a state highway within the reservation. Wilson v. Marchington, 127 F.3d 805 (9th Cir.1997), cert. denied, 118 S.Ct. 1516 (1998). The state accordingly had jurisdiction. If the tribal member were the defendant, however, Williams v. Lee would require the action to be brought in tribal court. It is not yet clear whether *Strate* forecasts erosion of that rule for non-fee lands and state rights-of-way.

It should be noted that the rule of Williams v. Lee deprives the state courts of *subject matter* jurisdiction; the Court assumed for purposes of its decision that valid service of process had occurred. As a consequence, the parties cannot confer jurisdiction on the state by consent. Even where the tribal council itself consents to the state's exercising concurrent jurisdiction, the state is precluded from doing so in the absence of a formal assumption of jurisdiction pursuant to Public Law 280 (See Chapter VIII). Kennerly v. District Court, 400 U.S. 423 (1971).

Since *Williams* precludes the state courts from assuming jurisdiction when a non-Indian sues a tribal member (or possibly any Indian) over a claim arising in Indian country, it follows even more strongly that the state has no jurisdiction over such claims when both parties are tribal members. E.g., Fisher v. District Court, 424 U.S. 382, 386 (1976); Sigana v. Bailey, 282 Minn. 367, 164 N.W.2d 886

(1969); Gourneau v. Smith, 207 N.W.2d 256 (N.D. 1973).

One might be tempted to conclude from *Williams* that the state is precluded from taking jurisdiction over claims by tribal members against non-Indians, when the claims arise in Indian country. That conclusion would be incorrect; the Supreme Court has said that nothing in Williams v. Lee prevents the maintenance of such actions in state court, and they have traditionally been brought there. Three Affiliated Tribes of the Fort Berthold Reservation v. Wold Engineering, P.C., 467 U.S. 138, 148 (1984) (*Fort Berthold I*); see State v. Zaman, 190 Ariz. 208, 946 P.2d 459 (Ariz. 1997), cert. denied, 118 S.Ct. 1167 (1998). In the *Fort Berthold* litigation, the State of North Dakota attempted to deny jurisdiction over actions brought by tribes or tribal Indians unless the tribe had consented to state jurisdiction over all claims arising on its reservation and had waived its sovereign immunity. The Supreme Court, in an unusual application of preemption doctrine, held that Public Law 280 precluded the state from denying jurisdiction in that manner. Three Affiliated Tribes of the Fort Berthold Reservation v. Wold Engineering, 476 U.S. 877 (1986) (*Fort Berthold II*). See Chapter VIII, Section F, infra. Several state decisions have also guaranteed the access of Indian plaintiffs to state court by invoking the equal protection clause. Paiz v. Hughes, 76 N.M. 562, 417 P.2d 51 (1966); Bonnet v. Seekins, 126 Mont. 24, 243 P.2d 317 (1952). In fact, on some reservations the Indian plaintiff has no alternative; a number of tribal codes provide for civil jurisdiction over non-Indian defendants only when they stipulate to it.

It is not yet clear what effect, if any, Iowa Mut. Ins. Co. v. LaPlante, 480 U.S. 9 (1987), will have on this line of cases. In *LaPlante*, the Supreme Court ruled that a federal court should stay its hand, in a case where it had diversity jurisdiction, in favor of parallel tribal court proceedings against a non-Indian defendant. At least one circuit court has applied *LaPlante* in a situation where there were no parallel proceedings in tribal court; it has required an Indian plaintiff to exhaust tribal court remedies before bringing a diversity case against a non-Indian in federal court. Wellman v. Chevron, U.S.A., Inc., 815 F.2d 577 (9th Cir.1987); see also Crawford v. Genuine Parts Co., 947 F.2d 1405 (9th Cir.1991), cert. denied, 502 U.S. 1096 (1992). If the federal courts in diversity cases must require exhaustion, it is difficult to see why the state courts should not require it as well. There remains a tension, however, between the thrust of *LaPlante*, with its emphasis on deference to tribal court jurisdiction, and *Berthold I*, in which the Supreme Court stated that it failed "to see how the exercise of state-court jurisdiction in this case [brought by an Indian tribe against a non-Indian] would interfere with the right of tribal Indians to govern themselves under their own laws." 467 U.S. at 148. Until that tension is resolved, it is difficult to predict whether the Indian plaintiff will one day be faced with an exhaustion requirement when suing a non-Indian in state court.

One result of the present division of civil jurisdiction is that the court in which a case is heard will often be determined by who sues first. If a tribal member and a non-Indian (or, possibly, a nonmember Indian) have a dispute centered in Indian country (putting aside disputes arising on fee lands, discussed a few paragraphs above), and the non-Indian wishes to sue, his or her sole remedy is in tribal court, under Williams v. Lee. If the tribal member wishes to sue, he or she may sue in state court (and under some tribal codes will be precluded from suing in tribal court). If the tribal member does in fact sue in state court, the question arises whether that court has jurisdiction to entertain a counterclaim against him or her. The issue has not been settled, but the most sensible rule would probably be that "compulsory" counterclaims—those arising from the same transaction or occurrence as the main claim—are within the jurisdiction of the state court. The tribal plaintiff conceded as much in *Fort Berthold II*, 476 U.S. at 891. It is true that under Williams v. Lee the state court seems to lack subject matter jurisdiction for such claims, and that such a deficiency cannot normally be cured by the fiction that a plaintiff in bringing suit "consents" to counterclaims. On the other hand, it seems unacceptably wasteful to litigate the same fact situation twice, and the intrusion upon tribal self-government caused by a counterclaim would seem to be minimal when the controversy is already being litigated in state court. Whether or not the state is allowed to take jurisdiction of compulsory counterclaims, it seems quite clear from Williams v. Lee that it should have no jurisdiction over "permissive" counterclaims against a tribal member that are unrelated to the main claim and that arose in Indian country. The exclusive forum for pursuing the tribal member in regard to those separate matters is tribal court.

State courts have jurisdiction over suits by non-Indians against non-Indians, even though the claim arose in Indian country, so long as Indian interests are not affected. Indeed, as discussed earlier, the Supreme Court has recently held that, when such causes of action between "nonmembers" arise on non-Indian-owned fee lands or state rights-of-way in Indian country, the tribal court has no jurisdiction over the case. Strate v. A–1 Contractors, 117 S.Ct. 1404 (1997). One court of appeals has extended this rule to suits by a tribal member against a nonmember, arising on a state highway. Wilson v. Marchington, 127 F.3d 805 (9th Cir.1997), cert. denied, 118 S.Ct. 1516 (1998). Thus the state court's jurisdiction is exclusive of the tribe in such cases. State court process may be served in Indian country in connection with such a suit. See Langford v. Monteith, 102 U.S. 145 (1880); but see State v. Zaman, 1998 WL 25559 (Ariz.App.1998).

State courts also have jurisdiction over claims against Indian defendants (whether the plaintiff is Indian or non-Indian) that arise outside of Indian country, as when an Indian leaves the reservation and enters a commercial transaction to be performed off-reservation. See Smith Plumbing Co. v. Aetna Casualty & Surety Co., 149 Ariz. 524, 531, 720 P.2d 499, 506, cert. denied, 479 U.S. 987 (1986). Such cases often present the question whether the state may initiate suit by serving process upon the Indian on the reservation. While the traditional view was that state process did not run to Indians in Indian country, modern decisions have split on this point. For example, such service was upheld in State Securities, Inc. v. Anderson, 84 N.M. 629, 506 P.2d 786 (1973), but struck down in Francisco v. State, 113 Ariz. 427, 556 P.2d 1 (1976). Authority is similarly divided over the question whether a valid state judgment against an Indian arising from an off-reservation claim can be directly executed in Indian country. Such enforcement was permitted in Little Horn State Bank v. Stops, 170 Mont. 510, 555 P.2d 211 (1976), cert. denied, 431 U.S. 924 (1977), but denied in Annis v. Dewey County Bank, 335 F.Supp. 133 (D.S.D.1971). Enforcement of such a judgment by garnishing a non-Indian creditor on the reservation was held invalid in Joe v. Marcum, 621 F.2d 358 (10th Cir.1980). See also United States v. Morris, 754 F.Supp. 185 (D.N.M.1991).

An all-or-nothing approach to these issues of service of process and enforcement of judgments presents a dilemma. The state should have some way of initiating a lawsuit over which it has jurisdiction even if the Indian defendant has returned to Indian country. On the other hand, direct execution of a resulting judgment on the reservation does have substantial potential of interfering with tribal self-government. Joe v. Marcum, supra; but see Natewa v. Natewa, 84 N.M. 69, 499 P.2d 691 (1972). The best solution to the problem of service of process in Indian country is to permit the state to exercise long-arm jurisdiction by mail service as it does over defendants located out of state. See Dixon v. Picopa Constr. Co., 160 Ariz. 251, 772 P.2d 1104 (1989). The least intrusive way to enforce a state judgment would be to sue on it in tribal court (or to enforce it by registration if the tribe permits that expeditious approach). While the tribes may not be required by the Constitution or federal statute to give full faith and credit to state court judgments, tribal courts in practice generally do enforce them. Cf. Santa Clara Pueblo v. Martinez, 436 U.S. 49, 65 n. 21 (1978).

b. Divorce

As Williams v. Lee, 358 U.S. 217 (1959), would suggest, state courts have no jurisdiction to grant divorces when both parties are Indians domiciled in Indian country. Whyte v. District Court, 140 Colo. 334, 346 P.2d 1012 (1959), cert. denied, 363 U.S. 829 (1960); State ex rel. Stewart v. District Court, 187 Mont. 209, 609 P.2d 290 (1980); In re Marriage of Limpy, 195 Mont. 314, 636 P.2d 266 (1981). When both parties are Indians domiciled outside of Indian country, however, the state court does have jurisdiction. United States ex rel. Cobell v. Cobell, 503 F.2d 790 (9th Cir.1974), cert. denied, 421 U.S. 999 (1975).

As in other civil cases, state courts have jurisdiction to divorce when both parties are non-Indians, even though they are domiciled in Indian country. There is little chance that such jurisdiction can intrude upon tribal self-government.

The question of jurisdiction over divorces between Indian and non-Indian spouses in Indian country is far from settled. Because the domicile and status of the *plaintiff* was once regarded as the sole basis for state jurisdiction in divorce, the states tended to accept jurisdiction over divorces brought by non-Indians but not by Indians when both were domiciled in Indian country. This tendency may continue even in states that now follow the Uniform Marriage and Divorce Act, which bases jurisdiction on the domicile of either the plaintiff or the defendant. With the option of focusing on the status and domicile of either party, state divorce jurisdiction could follow the pattern of other civil cases. In that event, it could be argued that state courts ought not to accept divorces by non-Indians against Indians in such cases because of the possibility of interfering with the jurisdiction of tribal courts. One court has held that the state lacks jurisdiction in such a case, at least when the tribal court had already exercised jurisdiction. Byzewski v. Byzewski, 429 N.W.2d 394 (N.D.1988). Another court held that the tribe had jurisdiction and expressed no opinion on whether it was exclusive of the state. Sanders v. Robinson, 864 F.2d 630 (9th Cir.1988), cert. denied, 490 U.S. 1110 (1989). It might also be argued by analogy to other civil cases that the Indian has an equal protection right to utilize state court to divorce a non-Indian. There is virtually no authority addressing that question, however. (Further problems arising from divorces between Indians and non-Indians in Indian country are discussed under Tribal Civil Jurisdiction, subsection 2(b), below.)

Because decrees for alimony, child support and child custody pursuant to divorce require *in personam* jurisdiction over the defendant, the jurisdictional rules for such orders are the same as those for general civil litigation, discussed in subsection (a) immediately above.

c. Adoption and Child Custody

Jurisdiction over adoption and custody of Indian children is now governed by the Indian Child Welfare Act of 1978, 25 U.S.C.A. §§ 1901–1963. "Custody" proceedings covered by the Act include foster care placement, termination of parental rights, and pre-adoptive and adoptive placement, but not custody proceedings between parents in connection with divorce. The Act was designed to protect the integrity of the tribes and the heritage of Indian children by inhibiting the practice of removing those children from their families and tribes to raise them as non-Indians. See Mississippi Band of Choctaw Indians v. Holyfield, 490 U.S. 30, 32–37 (1989).

Under the Act, state courts have no jurisdiction over adoption or custody of Indian children who are domiciled or reside within the reservation of their tribe, unless some federal law (such as Public Law 280) confers such jurisdiction. "Domicile" under the Act is a matter of federal law; a legitimate child takes the domicile of its parents and an illegitimate child takes the domicile of its mother. *Holyfield*, 490 U.S. at 43–48. That construction defeats a state rule that children born off-reservation and given up for adoption by their parents were not domiciled on the reservation. The Act also provides that state courts have no jurisdiction over children who are wards of a tribal court, regardless of the domicile or residence of the children. Jurisdiction in these cases lies exclusively with the tribe.

State courts do have jurisdiction over adoption and custody of Indian children not domiciled or residing on their tribe's reservation, but the Act places important qualifications upon that jurisdiction. In any proceeding for foster care placement of such children or for termination of parental rights, the state court, "in the absence of good cause to the contrary" and in the absence of objection by either parent, must transfer the proceeding to tribal court upon the petition of either parent, the child's Indian custodian, or the tribe. The tribe may decline such a transfer. 25 U.S.C.A. § 1911(b). The states are required to give tribal adoption and custody orders full faith and credit. 25 U.S.C.A. § 1911(d).

The Indian Child Welfare Act also provides priorities for state courts to follow in placement of Indian children, with preference first to the child's extended family, then to members of his or her tribe, then to Indian families generally. Preferences are also given to tribally licensed institutions. The tribe may override these preferences by adopting its own list.

25 U.S.C.A. § 1915. The Act also contains numerous other provisions that should be consulted in connection with any adoption or custody proceeding involving Indian children. There is also a large and growing body of precedent applying the Act.

d. Probate

State courts have no jurisdiction over the probate of Indian trust property; such jurisdiction is exclusively federal. In other respects, authority is sparse, but an application of Williams v. Lee, 358 U.S. 217 (1959), would prevent the state from exercising jurisdiction over the probate of non-trust movables of a tribal member (and possibly any Indian) who died domiciled in Indian country.

It also follows that state courts have jurisdiction over non-trust estates of Indians who died domiciled outside of Indian country, and over the estates of non-Indians (and perhaps nonmember Indians) whether or not domiciled in Indian country, at least where the heirs are non-Indian. It might well be argued that where a non-Indian dies domiciled in Indian country and leaves Indian heirs, an exercise of state jurisdiction has the potential of interfering with internal tribal affairs. Many tribes, however, leave such matters to the states (effectively if not legitimately) by providing only for probate of estates of Indian decedents.

State courts also have jurisdiction over probate of any land outside of Indian country, and presumably may exercise ancillary jurisdiction over movables located out of Indian country which are part of the estate of an Indian who died domiciled in Indian country. The state's jurisdiction in the latter case would be ancillary to the primary jurisdiction of the tribe.

2.   TRIBAL CIVIL JURISDICTION

a. General Civil Litigation

The civil jurisdiction of tribal courts, unlike their criminal jurisdiction, is subject to no statutory limit on the relief the courts may grant. When a case calls for it, there is nothing to prevent a tribal court from entering a multi-million dollar judgment. Cf. Burlington Northern R. Co. v. Red Wolf, 106 F.3d 868 (9th Cir.1997), vacated, 118 S.Ct. 37 (1997).

With regard to subject matter, tribal courts have exclusive jurisdiction over a suit by any person against an Indian for a claim arising in Indian country. Williams v. Lee, 358 U.S. 217 (1959). Necessarily, then, the tribe has exclusive jurisdiction over disputes between tribal members arising on the reservation. It also has exclusive jurisdiction over wholly internal tribal subject matter, such as membership disputes. Smith v. Babbitt, 100 F.3d 556 (8th Cir.1996), cert. denied, 118 S.Ct. 46 (1997). The exclusive jurisdiction recognized by Williams v. Lee had always been assumed to extend to suits against Indians from recognized tribes other than the one upon whose reservation the claim arose, but the Supreme Court in recent years has rendered this assumption unsafe. In Duro v. Reina, 495 U.S. 676 (1990), the Court held that tribal courts could not exercise criminal jurisdiction over nonmember Indians. Congress overruled that decision, 25 U.S.C.A. § 1301(2), but that statute did not address civil jurisdiction. In Washington v. Confederated Tribes of the Colville Indian Reservation, 447 U.S. 134 (1980), the Court permitted a state to impose a sales tax on Indians making purchases on a reservation other than their own. The Court stated that "[f]or most practical purposes those Indians stand on the same footing as non-Indians resident on the reservation." 447 U.S. at 161. Then, in Strate v. A–1 Contractors, 117 S.Ct. 1404 (1997), the Court held that a tribal court had no jurisdiction over a dispute between "nonmembers" arising out of a vehicle accident on a state right-of-way within the reservation. In *Strate*, the nonmembers were non-Indians, but the Court talked only of nonmembers and tribal members in drawing a line of adjudicatory jurisdiction.

The line *Strate* drew is not without its problems. The Court stated that "a tribe's adjudicative jurisdiction does not exceed its legislative jurisdiction" and that, apart from the two exceptions set forth in *Montana*, infra, the civil authority of tribes and their courts did not extend to activities of nonmembers on fee lands. *Strate*, 117 S.Ct. at 1413. One difficulty with this formulation is that, because Congress overruled *Duro*, the tribe does have criminal legislative authority over nonmember Indians in Indian country. 25 U.S.C.A. § 1301(2). Indian country includes fee lands and rights-of-way within a reservation. 18 U.S.C.A. § 1151(a). Thus, the tribal court would not be exceeding the tribe's legislative jurisdiction if it entertained litigation between non-member Indians arising from an accident on a right-of-way. If *Strate* was referring only to the tribe's *civil* legislative authority, then the tribe's civil jurisdiction appears to be narrower than its criminal jurisdiction-the opposite of the condition the Court has previously said to prevail. See National Farmers Union Ins. Cos. v. Crow Tribe, 471 U.S. 845, 854–55 & nn. 16 & 17 (1985).

In addition to their exclusive jurisdiction over reservation-based claims against tribal members, tribal courts also probably have the power to adjudicate claims against tribal members domiciled or present within their territory even though those claims arose outside of Indian country. Many tribes, however, have chosen not to exercise such jurisdiction.

Much recent litigation has been concerned with the power of tribal courts to entertain claims against non-Indian (or nonmember) defendants that arise in Indian country. For years the tribes made no attempt to exercise that power by compulsion; some tribal codes still provide for such jurisdiction only when the non-Indian stipulates to it. Recently, however, numbers of tribes have revised their codes to permit their tribal courts generally to exercise jurisdiction over non-Indians for reservation-based claims. A non-Indian defendant contested such jurisdiction in National Farmers Union Ins. Cos. v. Crow Tribe, 471 U.S. 845 (1985). The Supreme Court did not resolve the question, but deferred to the tribal court so that it could determine its own jurisdiction in the first instance. The Court made it clear, however, that Oliphant v. Suquamish Indian Tribe, 435 U.S. 191 (1978), which held that the tribes had no criminal jurisdiction over non-Indians, did not control the question of the tribes' civil jurisdiction.

In Iowa Mut. Ins. Co. v. LaPlante, 480 U.S. 9 (1987), the Supreme Court similarly stayed its diversity jurisdiction to permit a tribal court to determine its own jurisdiction over parallel litigation. Here again, the Supreme Court did not actually decide whether the tribal court had power to entertain a case against a non-Indian defendant, but its language was very affirmative:

Tribal authority over the activities of non-Indians on reservation lands is an important part of tribal sovereignty. * * * Civil jurisdiction over such activities presumptively lies in the tribal courts unless affirmatively limited by a specific treaty provision or federal statute.

Id. at 18.

This passage encouraged many tribes, and numbers of lower courts, to assume that tribal courts could exercise general civil jurisdiction over all reservation-based litigation, particularly if one of the parties was the tribe or a tribal member. The seeds of narrower view had already been planted, however, in Montana v. United States, 450 U.S. 544 (1981). *Montana* held that an Indian tribe had no authority to regulate hunting and fishing by non-

Indians on non-Indian-owned fee land within the reservation. The Court stated that the tribe's domestic dependent sovereignty extended only to self-government and the control of internal relations. Hunting and fishing by non-Indians on non-Indian fee lands was neither. *Montana* at one point went considerably farther, however, and announced a general proposition that "the inherent sovereign powers of an Indian tribe do not extend to the activities of nonmembers of the tribe." The only exceptions were (1) that a tribe could regulate "activities of nonmembers who enter consensual relationships with the tribe or its members," as through commercial dealings, and (2) that a tribe could exercise "civil authority over the conduct of non-Indians on fee lands within its reservation when that conduct threatens or has some direct effect on the political integrity, the economic security, or the health or welfare of the tribe." *Montana*, 450 U.S. at 565–66.

The Supreme Court carried *Montana* a step farther in 1997, when it held that a tribal court had no jurisdiction over litigation between nonmembers arising out of a vehicle accident on a state highway within a reservation. Strate v. A–1 Contractors, 117 S.Ct. 1404 (1997). The Court narrowed the statement in *LaPlante* that civil jurisdiction over non-Indian activities within a reservation "presumptively lies in the tribal courts"; that statement, according to *Strate*, meant nothing more than that the tribal court presumptively had jurisdiction over those non-Indian activities that the tribe could regulate under *Montana*. The right-of-way, which was open to the public, was the equivalent of non-Indian-owned fee land and the tribe therefore lacked jurisdiction. *Montana*'s exceptions did not apply; the nonmembers were not in a consensual relationship with the tribe or its members, and their activity on the highway did not threaten or have a direct effect on the political integrity, economic security, or health or welfare of the tribe. *Strate*, 117 S.Ct. at 1415. The Court also stated that the second *Montana* exception should be read narrowly, in light of *Montana*'s description of tribal authority as the power to punish tribal offenders, to determine membership, and to regulate domestic relations and inheritance for members.

The degree to which *Strate* presages further restrictions on tribal jurisdiction over nonmembers is uncertain. *Strate* stated that it was expressing no view on the governing law or proper forum when such an accident occurs on a tribal road. The major conceptual issue to be resolved is whether *Montana* should be treated as an exception, confined to non-Indian fee lands, to the general sovereignty that a tribe may exercise over its reservation, or whether *Montana* now provides the all-encompassing formula for tribal jurisdiction over nonmembers. Some state courts have already adopted the latter, expansive view of *Montana*. State v. Zaman, 190 Ariz. 208, 946 P.2d 459, 463 (Ariz. 1997), cert. denied, 66 U.S.L.W. 3474 (1998); Harrison v. Boyd Mississippi, Inc., 700 So.2d 247, 250–51 (Miss.1997); but see United States ex rel. Morongo Band of Mission

Indians v. Rose, 34 F.3d 901, 906 (9th Cir.1994). If the second *Montana* exception were broadly interpreted, so that most events within a reservation were deemed to affect tribal interests, the choice would not be a major one. But *Strate* dictates a narrow interpretation of the second *Montana* exception. The first exception does permit tribal regulation of most sizeable reservation businesses and extractive industries, see FMC v. Shoshone–Bannock Tribes, 905 F.2d 1311 (9th Cir.1990), cert. denied, 499 U.S. 943 (1991), which will have leases or other consensual arrangements with the tribe, but still leaves much nonmember activity untouched. If *Montana,* narrowly interpreted, is the only test of tribal authority over nonmembers, the civil authority of the tribes will be considerably diminished from what it was understood to be a decade ago.

The Eighth Circuit, in the decision that the Supreme Court reviewed in *Strate*, and the Ninth Circuit have both stated that the tribe's sovereign powers simply do not permit exercise of jurisdiction over nonmembers unless tribal interests are affected, so as to bring the exercise within one of the two *Montana* exceptions. A–1 Contractors v. Strate, 76 F.3d 930, 939 (8th Cir.1996); Yellowstone County v. Pease, 96 F.3d 1169, 1175–76 (9th Cir.1996). Those cases, however, actually involved non-Indians, and the Supreme Court chose to decide *Strate* on narrower grounds than those relied upon by the Eighth Circuit. The Ninth Circuit, though, has since held that a tribal court has no jurisdiction over a suit by

a *tribal member* against a nonmember arising from
an accident on a state highway through the reservation. Wilson v. Marchington, 127 F.3d 805 (9th
Cir.1997), cert. denied, 118 S.Ct. 1516 (1998). It has
further held that *Strate* precludes tribal court jurisdiction over a suit by tribal members against non-
Indian officers for false arrest on reservation fee
lands that may have been Indian-owned; ownership
was held to be irrelevant so long as the defendant
officers, who were exercising Public Law 280 jurisdiction, had the right to be there. County of Lewis
v. Allen, 1998 WL 191233 (9th Cir.1998). Thus the
ultimate boundaries of tribal civil power over nonmembers remain in some doubt.

If *Strate* is confined to its context and not interpreted as expansively as it has been in *Marchington*
and *Allen*, then there should be little doubt that a
tribal court has jurisdiction when a tribal member
sues a nonmember over a claim arising within the
reservation, at least on non-fee, non-right-of-way
lands. When the tribal member is the defendant in
such a case, Williams v. Lee, 358 U.S. 217 (1959),
requires that tribal jurisdiction be *exclusive*. When
the subject of the litigation is exactly the same, but
the tribal member is the plaintiff instead of being
the defendant, the tribal interest is very nearly as
strong. It is certainly strong enough to support
concurrent jurisdiction. See Stock West, Inc. v. Confederated Tribes of the Colville Reservation, 873
F.2d 1221, 1228 (9th Cir.1989). When the tribe or
its member sues a nonmember for a claim arising
outside of Indian country, tribal jurisdiction is more

doubtful. Cf. Altheimer & Gray v. Sioux Mfg. Corp., 983 F.2d 803 (7th Cir.), cert. denied, 510 U.S. 1019 (1993); Yellowstone County v. Pease, 96 F.3d 1169 (9th Cir.1996), cert. denied, 117 S.Ct. 1691 (1997). The Eighth Circuit has held that the tribal court had no jurisdiction over an action by the estate of Crazy Horse against the brewing company that made and sold "The Original Crazy Horse Malt Liquor." The company did not make or sell its product on the reservation. Hornell Brewing Co. v. Rosebud Sioux Tribal Court, 133 F.3d 1087 (8th Cir.1998). When the subject matter is of great tribal interest and there are substantial contacts with the reservation, the tribal court may have jurisdiction even if both parties are non-Indians. Stock West Corp. v. Taylor, 964 F.2d 912 (9th Cir.1992)(en banc). But when both parties are non-Indian and the litigation does not deal with Indian or tribal property, the tribal interest is very remote and jurisdiction would appear to be lacking. See White Mountain Apache Tribe v. Smith Plumbing Co., 856 F.2d 1301 (9th Cir.1988). It is certainly lacking under *Strate* if the claim arose out of Indian country or on non-Indian fee land (or state right-of-way) within the reservation.

Frequently, when a nonmember (usually a non-Indian) is sued in tribal court, he or she will bring an action in federal court either to challenge the tribal court's jurisdiction or to attempt to litigate the underlying dispute in federal court. In such cases, federal courts have regularly abstained or stayed their proceedings, on the authority of *Na-*

tional Farmers Union and *LaPlante*, supra, to permit the tribal court to determine in the first instance whether it has jurisdiction. Thus a party seeking in federal court to challenge a tribal court's colorable jurisdiction must first exhaust tribal remedies. Stock West Corp. v. Taylor, 964 F.2d 912, 919 (9th Cir.1992); see also Brown v. Washoe Housing Authority, 835 F.2d 1327 (10th Cir.1988); Bruce H. Lien Co. v. Three Affiliated Tribes, 93 F.3d 1412 (8th Cir.1996). Even the United States has been required to exhaust. United States v. Tsosie, 92 F.3d 1037 (10th Cir.1996). Exhaustion must include any tribal appellate remedies. Kerr–McGee Corp. v. Farley, 115 F.3d 1498 (10th Cir.1997), cert. denied, 118 S.Ct. 880 (1998). Tribal courts, therefore, are frequently called upon to decide in the first instance a question of federal Indian law: whether the court has jurisdiction in a case involving nonmembers. If the tribal court decides it has jurisdiction, it proceeds with the case. If the federal court later agrees that the tribe had jurisdiction, it cannot relitigate the merits of the dispute. *LaPlante*, 480 U.S. at 19.

National Farmers Union set forth some exceptions to the requirement of exhaustion of tribal remedies. Exhaustion is not required when (1) the assertion of tribal jurisdiction is motivated by a desire to harass or is otherwise in bad faith; (2) the challenged tribal exercise of authority is patently violative of express jurisdictional prohibitions, or (3) where exhaustion would be futile for lack of an opportunity to challenge the tribal court's jurisdiction. *National Farmers Union*, 471 U.S. at 856 n.21;

see also *Strate*, 117 S. Ct. at 1416 n.14. These exceptions have been interpreted narrowly, however, and have not had much impact. See, e.g., Basil Cook Enterprises v. St. Regis Mohawk Tribe, 117 F.3d 61 (2d Cir.1997). In United States v. Plainbull, 957 F.2d 724 (9th Cir.1992), the court held that a statute giving the federal courts jurisdiction "exclusive of the courts of the States" over certain grazing violations did not preclude tribal court jurisdiction; the United States was required to exhaust. Similarly, the Price–Anderson Act, which grants federal district courts jurisdiction over actions arising from any "nuclear incident," and authorizes removal of such actions from state to federal court, is not an "express prohibition" of tribal jurisdiction. El Paso Natural Gas Co. v. Neztsosie, 136 F.3d 610 (9th Cir.1998); Kerr–McGee Corp. v. Farley, 115 F.3d 1498 (10th Cir.1997), cert. denied, 118 S.Ct. 880 (1998). Tribal courts are therefore entitled to address in the first instance the question of their power to entertain such cases. Id.

At least one federal court of appeals has required exhaustion in diversity cases brought by Indian plaintiffs even though there were no proceedings pending in tribal court. Wellman v. Chevron, U.S.A., Inc., 815 F.2d 577 (9th Cir.1987); Crawford v. Genuine Parts Co., 947 F.2d 1405 (9th Cir.1991), cert. denied, 502 U.S. 1096 (1992). If the federal courts must defer to tribal courts to avoid undue interference with tribal adjudication of claims by tribal members against nonmembers, it is difficult to see why state courts should not be required to do the same. On the other hand, the Supreme Court stated in *Berthold I* that it failed to see how such state court actions interfered with tribal self-government. 467 U.S. at 148. It is likely, therefore, that tribal courts will continue to share any jurisdiction over nonmember defendants with the state courts, with the possibility that some requirement of abstention or exhaustion will one day be imposed on the state courts in favor of the tribes.

Because the tribes until recently have been very cautious in asserting civil jurisdiction, there has been little litigation dealing with service of tribal process. Tribal process is clearly effective when served within tribal territory. Abode service upon absent Indians, and possibly even non-Indians, domiciled within tribal territory should also be permissible. Direct service outside of tribal territory will almost certainly be ineffective to confer jurisdiction by itself. There appears to be no reason, however, why a tribe may not exercise long-arm jurisdiction over absent defendants for claims arising from activities within the tribe's territory. See Red Fox v. Hettich, 494 N.W.2d 638, 645 (S.D. 1993). Service upon the absent defendant can then be effected by mail or some form of substituted service, assuming that the parties or subject matter otherwise qualify for an exercise of tribal jurisdiction.

b. Divorce

The tribal courts have exclusive jurisdiction over divorces between Indians domiciled in Indian coun-

try. Whyte v. District Court, 140 Colo. 334, 346
P.2d 1012 (1959), cert. denied, 363 U.S. 829 (1960);
State ex rel. Stewart v. District Court, 187 Mont.
209, 609 P.2d 290 (1980). They may also have
jurisdiction concurrent with the state over divorces
between Indians domiciled off-reservation who remain tribal members and submit themselves to the
jurisdiction of the tribal court. In other words,
membership as well as domicile might suffice as a
jurisdictional base for a tribal divorce.

Divorce between Indian and non-Indian spouses
domiciled in Indian country presents several unre-
solved jurisdictional problems. Williams v. Lee and
its progeny would suggest that the non-Indian who
seeks to divorce an Indian would have to go to tribal
court, while an Indian who seeks to divorce a non-
Indian would have a right to use the state courts as
well as the tribal courts. The analogy to Williams v.
Lee is difficult to make, however, because states
have traditionally based divorce jurisdiction on the
domicile and status of the *plaintiff*. The plaintiff's
domicile and status remain important even in states
that follow the Uniform Marriage and Divorce Act,
which permits jurisdiction to be based on the domicile of either party. There is accordingly a tendency
for state courts to accept jurisdiction of divorce
cases brought by non-Indians even though they are
domiciled in Indian country and seek a divorce from
an Indian. See Byzewski v. Byzewski, 429 N.W.2d
394 (N.D.1988). Yet such an exercise of jurisdiction
is surely just as much an interference with tribal
self-government as state jurisdiction was in the

ordinary civil case of Williams v. Lee. It would therefore be preferable for such cases to be left to exclusive tribal jurisdiction, but it cannot be said that this preference is presently the law with respect to divorce. The tribe's jurisdiction remains exclusive, however, over the disposition of trust lands in divorce proceedings, In re Marriage of Wellman, 258 Mont. 131, 852 P.2d 559 (Mont. 1993), or orders of custody and support requiring personal jurisdiction over the Indian defendant domiciled in Indian country, *Byzewski*, 429 N.W.2d at 400.

Another problem of jurisdiction arises from the fact that a number of tribal codes do not base jurisdiction, as some states still do, on the domicile and status of the plaintiff, but instead treat divorce the same as other civil cases and provide for jurisdiction only over Indian *defendants*. Jurisdiction under those codes extends to non-Indian defendants only if they consent. The result in such cases is that an Indian wishing to divorce an unconsenting non-Indian cannot do so in tribal court. If the state is one that bases jurisdiction solely on the domicile and status of the plaintiff, the state courts are likely to refuse jurisdiction over the same case on the ground that the plaintiff is an Indian domiciled in Indian country. The Indian plaintiff is then without a forum. The best solution for this problem is for such tribes to modify their codes so that their courts can accept cases brought by Indian plaintiffs domiciled in Indian country whether or not the non-Indian defendant consents to jurisdiction. One court

of appeals has held that the tribal court has jurisdiction in such a case. Sanders v. Robinson, 864
F.2d 630 (9th Cir.1988), cert. denied, 490 U.S. 1110
(1989).

As in other civil cases, tribal courts probably do
not have jurisdiction to divorce when both parties
are non-Indian and no Indian interests are involved,
even though the parties may be domiciled within
the court's geographical territory.

c. Adoption and Child Custody

The Indian Child Welfare Act of 1978, 25
U.S.C.A. §§ 1901–1963, governs adoption and child
custody proceedings involving Indian children. Custody proceedings subject to the Act include foster
care placement, termination of parental rights, and
pre-adoptive and adoptive placement, but not parental custody pursuant to divorce. 25 U.S.C.A.
§ 1903(1); see Comanche Indian Tribe of Okla. v.
Hovis, 53 F.3d 298 (10th Cir.), cert. denied, 516
U.S. 916 (1995). Under the Act, tribal courts have
exclusive jurisdiction over adoption and custody of
Indian children who reside or are domiciled within
the reservation of their tribe, unless some federal
law (such as Public Law 280) provides to the contrary. 25 U.S.C.A. § 1911(a); see also, Fisher v.
District Court, 424 U.S. 382 (1976). "Domicile"
under the Act is a matter of federal law; a legitimate child takes the domicile of its parents and an
illegitimate child takes the domicile of its mother.
Mississippi Band of Choctaw Indians v. Holyfield,
490 U.S. 30, 43–48 (1989). That construction de-

feats a state rule that children born off-reservation and given up for adoption by their parents were not domiciled on the reservation. Tribes also have exclusive jurisdiction over such proceedings involving any Indian child who is a ward of the tribal court, regardless where the child resides or is domiciled. 25 U.S.C.A. § 1911(a).

Tribal courts also have jurisdiction over adoption and custody of Indian children who are tribal members or who are eligible for membership, even though those children reside or are domiciled outside of the tribe's reservation. This jurisdiction is concurrent with that of the state, but in cases of foster care placement or termination of parental rights, the state court must transfer the case to tribal court upon petition of either parent, the child's Indian custodian, or the tribe unless the state court finds "good cause" for retaining the case or unless either parent objects to the transfer. The tribal court may decline to accept such transfers. 25 U.S.C.A. § 1911(b).

d. Probate

Tribal courts have exclusive jurisdiction over the probate of non-trust movable assets of Indians who die domiciled in Indian country, subject only to whatever ancillary jurisdiction state courts may need to exercise to marshall for the tribal court those movables located outside of Indian country. Here again, the principal authority supporting such exclusive jurisdiction is Williams v. Lee, 358 U.S. 217 (1959). Inheritance is perhaps the most traditional and customary aspect of tribal law, and state jurisdiction would probably represent the greatest intrusion imaginable on the right of Indians to manage their internal affairs. Even the narrow description of inherent tribal powers in Montana v. United States, 450 U.S. 544, 564 (1981), includes the power "to prescribe rules of inheritance for members."

Some tribal codes purport to authorize tribal probate jurisdiction over non-trust assets of tribal *members*, even if they die domiciled outside of Indian country. Membership might well support such jurisdiction, but state courts would have concurrent jurisdiction that could cause considerable confusion in the probate of estates. Perhaps for this reason, tribal courts in practice generally confine themselves to probate of estates of Indians who died domiciled on their reservations or restrict their exercise of jurisdiction to movables located on the reservation. Tribal courts generally do not exercise probate jurisdiction over estates of non-Indians. Cf. Hinshaw v. Mahler, 42 F.3d 1178, 1180 (9th Cir.), cert. denied, 513 U.S. 988 (1994).

Tribal courts have no probate jurisdiction over trust property such as land allotments, which are handled exclusively by the federal government. They also have no jurisdiction over land located outside of Indian country, which is subject to the exclusive jurisdiction of the state where the land lies. As a consequence, tribal probate proceedings rarely involve interests in real estate.

3. FEDERAL CIVIL JURISDICTION

a. General Civil Litigation

The federal role in the adjudication of civil disputes in Indian country is far more limited than its role in criminal matters. Unlike the tribal and state courts, the federal courts are not courts of general jurisdiction. There are only two applicable bases of federal jurisdiction in civil suits: federal question and diversity of citizenship.

The federal question jurisdiction of federal courts is the same in Indian country as it is anywhere else. If a claim arises under federal law, then it may be brought under such statutes as 28 U.S.C.A. §§ 1331 or 1343, assuming that the other requirements of those statutes are met. Indian tribes are authorized by U.S.C.A. § 1362 to bring suits as plaintiffs in federal court, but their claims must still arise under federal law. Gila River Indian Community v. Henningson, Durham & Richardson, 626 F.2d 708 (9th Cir.1980), cert. denied, 451 U.S. 911 (1981). A tribe's claim based on pre-Revolutionary British treaties that were implemented by a federal Trade and Intercourse Act was held to arise under federal law. Catawba Indian Tribe v. South Carolina, 865 F.2d 1444 (4th Cir.) (en banc), cert. denied, 491 U.S. 906 (1989). The mere fact that a party to a case is an Indian or an Indian tribe does not turn a civil dispute into a federal question, nor does the fact that the controversy arose in Indian country. Schantz v. White Lightning, 502 F.2d 67 (8th Cir. 1974). A dispute between two Indian residents of the same state over a contract entered and to be performed on an Indian reservation does not, for example, qualify for federal jurisdiction.

Federal question jurisdiction has assumed increased importance in Indian law since the decision of National Farmers Union Ins. Cos. v. Crow Tribe, 471 U.S. 845 (1985). In that case, a non-Indian brought an action in federal court to enjoin tribal court proceedings in which the non-Indian was a defendant. The Supreme Court held:

> Because petitioners contend that federal law has divested the Tribe of this aspect of sovereignty, it is federal law on which they rely as a basis for the asserted right of freedom from Tribal Court interference. They have, therefore, filed an action "arising under" federal law within the meaning of § 1331.

Id. at 853. As a consequence, anyone asserting an absence of tribal power under federal statute, treaty or the "common law" of federal Indian law has an entree into federal court. The potential of this rule for permitting undue federal interference in the tribal courts was largely removed, however, by the other holding in *National Farmers Union*: that the federal court must stay its hand and permit the tribal court to rule in the first instance upon the question of its own jurisdiction. Id. at 856. The only exceptions to this requirement occur when tribal jurisdiction is asserted to harass or in bad faith, or the tribal act is patently violative of express jurisdictional prohibitions, or exhaustion would be futile because of lack of opportunity to challenge tribal court jurisdiction. *National Farmers Union*, 471 U.S. at 856 n.21.

The rule of exhaustion is regularly enforced. See Duncan Energy Co. v. Three Affiliated Tribes of the Fort Berthold Reservation, 27 F.3d 1294, 1300 (8th Cir.1994), cert. denied, 513 U.S. 1103 (1995). It applies even when no tribal court proceedings are pending. Smith v. Moffett, 947 F.2d 442 (10th Cir. 1991). It applies in favor of Courts of Indian Offenses as well as tribal courts. Tillett v. Lujan, 931 F.2d 636 (10th Cir.1991). The rule applies to tribal members. Kerr–McGee Corp. v. Farley, 115 F.3d 1498 (10th Cir.1997), cert. denied, 118 S.Ct. 880 (1998). Even the United States has been forced to exhaust when it sued tribal members for grazing violation penalties. United States v. Plainbull, 957 F.2d 724 (9th Cir.1992). One court of appeals, however, excused a tribe from having to exhaust when it sought to characterize the action as arising off-reservation and no tribal court proceedings were pending. Altheimer & Gray v. Sioux Mfg. Corp., 983 F.2d 803 (7th Cir.), cert. denied, 510 U.S. 1019 (1993). A plaintiff also is not required to exhaust when no tribal court was in existence at the time suit was filed. Krempel v. Prairie Island Indian Community, 125 F.3d 621 (8th Cir.1997). Exhaustion includes exhaustion of tribal appellate remedies. Kerr–McGee Corp. v. Farley, 115 F.3d 1498 (10th Cir.1997), cert. denied, 118 S.Ct. 880 (1998).

If, during exhaustion, the tribal court decides that it has jurisdiction, it presumably will proceed to decide the merits of the case. The objecting party may then return to federal court, where the federal court will review de novo the federal question of the tribe's jurisdiction, being "guided" but not controlled by the tribal court's views. It will review the tribe's jurisdictional factual findings only for clear error. FMC v. Shoshone–Bannock Tribes, 905 F.2d 1311 (9th Cir.1990), cert. denied, 499 U.S. 943 (1991). If the federal court decides that the tribal court had jurisdiction, it will not re-litigate the tribal decision on the merits. See Iowa Mut. Ins. Co. v. LaPlante, 480 U.S. 9, 19 (1987).

Several federal statutes confer jurisdiction on the federal courts to adjudicate disputes involving beneficial rights in trust property. See, e.g., 25 U.S.C.A. §§ 345–346, 28 U.S.C.A. § 1353. This jurisdiction is exclusive.

Diversity of citizenship is a basis for federal jurisdiction under 28 U.S.C.A. § 1332 when the amount in controversy exceeds $75,000. Because Indians are citizens of the states where they reside whether or not the residence is in Indian country, the requisite diversity does not exist between a reservation Indian and a non-Indian domiciled in the same state. An Indian tribe that is not incorporated is not a citizen of any state and cannot be sued in federal court on the basis of diversity. A tribe may, however, incorporate and thereby become a citizen of the state of its principal place of business for purposes of diversity jurisdiction. See Gaines v. Ski Apache, 8 F.3d 726 (10th Cir.1993).

For a number of years it was assumed that the diversity jurisdiction of federal courts was more limited in Indian country than it was elsewhere. The limitation was thought to arise from the fact that a federal court in diversity cases sat as an alternative to the state courts and applied state law. It therefore could not hear any case that the state courts could not entertain (such as a reservation-based claim against an Indian) under the doctrine of Williams v. Lee, even if diversity of citizenship existed. E.g., Hot Oil Service, Inc. v. Hall, 366 F.2d 295 (9th Cir.1966); Littell v. Nakai, 344 F.2d 486 (9th Cir.1965), cert. denied, 382 U.S. 986 (1966); but see Poitra v. Demarrias, 502 F.2d 23 (8th Cir. 1974), cert. denied, 421 U.S. 934 (1975). The Supreme Court changed this rule in Iowa Mut. Ins. Co. v. LaPlante, 480 U.S. 9 (1987). In that case, an insurance company that was being sued in tribal court brought a diversity action in federal court, seeking a declaration that its policy did not cover the disputed claim. As the defendant in the federal action was an Indian, the Supreme Court assumed that the state courts would have no jurisdiction over the case, and the insurance company did not contend otherwise. Id. at 13 n.4. The Supreme Court held that the technical requisites of diversity jurisdiction were present, but that the federal court should stay its hand until the tribal court determined its own jurisdiction. If the tribal court ruled that it had jurisdiction and decided the merits of the insurance dispute, the jurisdictional ruling could be challenged in federal court, but "proper deference to the tribal court system precludes relitigation" of the merits as resolved in tribal court. Id. at 19. Thus diversity jurisdiction may exist in suits against Indians, but its exercise may not interfere with pending tribal court proceedings. One circuit court has even held, in a case where no tribal proceedings were pending, that an Indian plaintiff must exhaust tribal court remedies before bringing a diversity case against a non-Indian in federal court. Wellman v. Chevron, U.S.A., Inc., 815 F.2d 577 (9th Cir.1987).

b. Divorce; Adoption and Child Custody; Probate

Federal courts exercise no divorce, adoption or child custody jurisdiction. They also exercise no probate jurisdiction, but probate of Indian trust properties is the sole responsibility of the federal government and is administered by the Department of Interior. 25 U.S.C.A. § 372. The decisions of the Secretary are "final and conclusive," but may be judicially reviewed for conformity with the Constitution. Kicking Woman v. Hodel, 878 F.2d 1203 (9th Cir.1989).

4. CHART OF CIVIL JURISDICTION IN INDIAN COUNTRY BY PARTIES AND SUBJECT MATTER

Notes:

i. This chart does not apply to Indian country over which the state has assumed jurisdiction pursuant to Public Law 280, 25 U.S.C.A. § 1322, 28 U.S.C.A. § 1360.

ii.   In all instances where state jurisdiction is shown, federal jurisdiction may be acquired if the parties meet requirements of diversity of citizenship and amount.

iii.   Where subject matter of claim particularly affects Indian interests, normal state jurisdiction may be precluded.

———

a.   *General Civil Litigation:*

Plaint.	Defend.	Source of Claim	Jurisdiction
Indian	Indian	Indian country	Tribal (exclus.)
		Non–Indian country	Tribal or state (concurr.)
Non–Indian	Indian	Indian country	Tribal (exclus.)
		Non–Indian country	State; possibly tribal (concurr.)
Indian	Non–Indian	Indian country exc. non-Indian fee lands	Tribal (if code allows); State (concurr.)
		Indian country non-Indian fee lands	State; possibly tribal (concurr.)
		Non–Indian country	State (exclus.)
Non–Indian	Non–Indian	Indian country	State; possibly tribal (concurr.)
		Non–Indian country and Indian country fee lands	State (exclus.)

b.   *Divorce:*

Plaint.	Defend.	Domicile of Parties	Jurisdiction
Indian	Indian	Indian country	Tribal (exclus.)

Plaint.	Defend.	Domicile of Parties	Jurisdiction
		Non–Indian country	State; Tribal if code allows (concurr.)
Non–Indian	Indian	Indian country	State (probable); Tribal (concurr.)
		Non–Indian country	State (exclus.)
Indian	Non–Indian	Indian country	Tribal (exclus.)
		Non–Indian country	State (exclus.)
Non–Indian	Non–Indian	Anywhere	State (exclus.)

c. *Adoption and Child Custody (non-Divorce)* (Consult 25 U.S.C.A. § 1911):

Proceeding	Domicile or Residence of child	Jurisdiction
Adoption and all custody	Indian country	Tribal (exclus.)
Adoption or adoptive placement	Non–Indian country	Tribal or State (concurr.)
Foster care or termination of parental rights	Non–Indian country	Tribal preferred; State (concurr.)

d. *Probate*

Decedent	Decedent's Domicile	Property	Jurisdiction
Indian	Indian country	Trust assets	Federal (exclus.)
		Land out of Indian country	State (exclus.)
		Movables	Tribal (primary)
	Non–Indian country	Trust assets	Federal (exclus.)
		Land out of Indian country	State (exclus.)
		Movables	State (primary); Possibly Tribal (concurr.)
Non–Indian	Anywhere	All assets	State (exclus.)

G. RECOGNITION OF JUDGMENTS; FULL FAITH AND CREDIT

The division of civil jurisdiction among the tribes, the states and the federal government occasionally gives rise to questions of the enforceability of tribal judgments in state and federal courts and the enforceability of state judgments in tribal courts (federal judgments can be enforced on their own authority in Indian country or out). The Constitution requires each state to give full faith and credit to the judgments of other *states*, U.S.Const., Art. IV, § 1, but this clause in terms does not apply to the judgments of tribes. The Supreme Court has noted however, that tribal court judgments have "in some circumstances" been regarded as entitled to full faith and credit. Santa Clara Pueblo v. Martinez, 436 U.S. 49, 65, n. 21 (1978). Some state courts have simply given full faith and credit. E.g., In re Buehl, 87 Wash.2d 649, 555 P.2d 1334 (1976). Others, while denying the applicability of the full faith and credit clause, have nevertheless given full effect to tribal judgments or decrees as a matter of "comity". E.g., In re Lynch's Estate, 92 Ariz. 354, 377 P.2d 199 (1962); Matter of Marriage of Red Fox, 23 Or.App. 393, 542 P.2d 918 (1975); Wippert v. Blackfeet Tribe, 201 Mont. 299, 654 P.2d 512 (1982). A few states have legislated or adopted court rules on the subject; South Dakota, for example, permits recognition of tribal judgments as a matter of comity if a list of conditions is met, including impartiality of the tribal proceedings. S.D. Cod. Laws 1–1–25; see Red Fox v. Hettich, 494 N.W.2d 638 (S.D.1993).

Other state statutes or rules vary greatly in the degree to which they condition recognition of tribal court judgments.

The federal statute implementing the full faith and credit clause, 28 U.S.C.A. § 1738, requires all courts within the United States to honor the judgments of courts of "territories." Despite some argument over the matter, it is probable that tribal court judgments do not fall within that terminology. See Ragsdale, *Problems in the Application of Full Faith and Credit for Indian Tribes*, 7 N.Mex.L.Rev. 133 (1977); but see Jim v. CIT Financial Services Corp., 87 N.M. 362, 533 P.2d 751 (1975). One state court, however, has held that the Navajo Nation qualifies as a "territory" for purposes of the Uniform Act to Secure the Attendance of Witnesses from Without a State. Tracy v. Superior Court of Maricopa County, 168 Ariz. 23, 810 P.2d 1030 (1991).

The Indian Child Welfare Act of 1978 requires every tribal, state and federal court to give full faith and credit to tribal judgments in Indian child custody proceedings, as defined by the Act. 25 U.S.C.A. § 1911(d).

Neither the Constitution nor federal statutes appear to require tribal courts to give full faith and credit to state court judgments. As a matter of practice, however, many tribal courts regularly give full effect to state court judgments, presumably also as a matter of "comity."

H. CHOICE OF LAW

Disputes over civil jurisdiction often presume that the law to be applied to the case will differ with the court that decides it. The presumption is often but not always correct. Many tribal codes require the tribal courts to apply, in order: (1) federal law, (2) tribal ordinances and customs not in conflict with federal law and, in matters not covered by the first two categories, (3) state law. Because very few tribes have comprehensive codes or bodies of common law dealing with civil matters, state law is likely to govern a large proportion of the civil cases, particularly those of a nature likely to involve non-Indian parties.

State courts applying normal choice of law principles should frequently apply tribal law to issues arising in Indian country. As indicated in the preceding paragraph, this practice may result in the ultimate application of state law anyway. There are important cases, however, where tribal law leads to a different result from state law, and all too often the tribal law is overlooked. On the other hand, there have been rare but notable instances where state courts have been sensitive to possible application of tribal law. E.g., Jim v. CIT Fin. Serv. Corp., 87 N.M. 362, 533 P.2d 751 (1975).

Federal statutes also impose choice of law requirements on state courts in special circumstances. The Indian Child Welfare Act specifies preferences for placement of Indian children for foster care or adoption and provides that if the child's tribe chooses to establish a different order of preferences they will apply in state court, with certain qualifications. 25 U.S.C.A. § 1915. In addition, Public Law 280 requires state courts exercising jurisdiction over Indian country to apply tribal ordinances and customs "if not inconsistent with any applicable civil law of the State." 28 U.S.C.A. § 1360(c).

In two large areas of jurisdictional dispute—criminal law and divorce—choice of law plays no part. Tribal and state courts alike follow the general rule that the forum applies its own substantive law in each of these fields.

CHAPTER VIII

PUBLIC LAW 280: A FEDERAL GRANT OF JURISDICTION TO THE STATES

A. INTRODUCTION

Congress has the power to change the division of jurisdiction among the federal, tribal and state governments. On many occasions it has passed statutes affecting jurisdiction over specific tribes or even over all tribes within a given state. In 1953, however, Congress adopted a more general approach. In what is commonly known as Public Law 280, 67 Stat. 588, Congress gave five (later six) states extensive criminal and civil jurisdiction over Indian country, and permitted all other states to acquire it at their option. In the states where Public Law 280 applies, then, it radically shifts the balance of jurisdictional power toward the states and away from the federal government and the tribes. It does not, however, confer total jurisdiction on the states, nor does it alter the trust status of Indian lands or terminate the trust relationship between the tribes and the federal government. It does not end the sovereign immunity of the tribes. California v. Quechan Tribe of Indians, 595 F.2d 1153 (9th Cir.1979).

From its inception Public Law 280 engendered criticism from both the states and the tribes. State governments resented the fact that they were given the duty of law enforcement without the means to pay for it; Congress neither appropriated funds for that purpose nor rendered Indian lands taxable by the states. The tribes, on the other hand, resented the fact that state jurisdiction was thrust upon them without their consent and they particularly objected to the provision that additional states could acquire jurisdiction without even consulting the concerned tribes. The ultimate result of these criticisms was a group of amendments to Public Law 280 which was passed as part of the Indian Civil Rights Act of 1968. These amendments permitted states to retrocede jurisdiction to the federal government, and also provided that no states in the future could assume jurisdiction without tribal consent. As a consequence, there has been almost no expansion of Public Law 280 jurisdiction since 1968. In the number of states where it is still in effect, however, Public Law 280 presents jurisdictional questions of considerable complexity.

B. CRIMINAL JURISDICTION

The basic outlines of Public Law 280 are established in those sections that confer jurisdiction on six named states—the "mandatory" states—by operation of the Law itself. Variations that occurred in other states which later elected to assume Public Law 280 jurisdiction—the "optional" states—will be discussed below (Section F).

While Public Law 280 conferred both criminal and civil jurisdiction on the mandatory states, the criminal provision was clearly the most important to Congress. Non–Indians living on or near reservations believed that law enforcement in Indian country had broken down, and urged state jurisdiction as a remedy. See Goldberg, *Public Law 280: The Limits of State Jurisdiction Over Reservation Indians*, 22 U.C.L.A.L.Rev. 535, 541 (1975). That jurisdiction was provided by the following section of Public Law 280:

18 U.S.C.A. § 1162(a):

Each of the States or Territories listed in the following table shall have jurisdiction over offenses committed by or against Indians in the areas of Indian country listed opposite the name of the State or Territory to the same extent that such State or Territory has jurisdiction over offenses committed elsewhere within the State or Territory, and the criminal laws of such State or Territory shall have the same force and effect within such Indian country as they have elsewhere within the State or Territory:

State or Territory of	Indian country affected
Alaska [added in 1958]	All Indian country within the State except [the Annette Islands with regard to the Metlakatla Indians]
California	All Indian country within the State
Minnesota	All Indian country within the State, except Red Lake Reservation
Nebraska	All Indian country within the State
Oregon	All Indian country within the State, except the Warm Springs Reservation
Wisconsin	All Indian country within the State

The effect of this section is clear from its wording; it gives the named states the same power to enforce their regular criminal laws inside Indian country that they had always exercised outside of it. The states already possessed jurisdiction over wholly non-Indian crimes within Indian country, see Chapter VII, Section D3, supra; Public Law 280 filled in all the remaining gaps by extending state power to crimes "by or against Indians."

At the same time that Public Law 280 extended the authority of the six listed states into Indian country, it provided that the General Crimes Act (18 U.S.C.A. § 1152) and the Major Crimes Act (18 U.S.C.A. § 1153) no longer applied in those areas.

18 U.S.C.A. § 1162(c). Federal authority to enforce those two statutes was therefore wholly supplanted by that of the mandatory states in the areas over which they were granted jurisdiction. (Federal power to enforce federal laws of national applicability remained, of course. United States v. Stone, 112 F.3d 971 (8th Cir.1997)). The repeal of the Major Crimes Act and General Crimes Act did not, however, extend to the optional states that later assumed jurisdiction. See United States v. High Elk, 902 F.2d 660 (8th Cir.1990); cf. Negonsott v. Samuels, 507 U.S. 99 (1993); United States v. Cook, 922 F.2d 1026 (2d Cir.), cert. denied, 500 U.S. 941 (1991). In those states, the federal government and the states may both punish conduct that falls within the scope of the Major Crimes or General Crimes Acts. Cf. *Negonsott*, 507 U.S. at 105; State v. Hoffman, 116 Wash.2d 51, 68, 804 P.2d 577, 586 (1991).

The effect of Public Law 280 on tribal criminal law was less clear; the Act made no mention of it. One court of appeals upheld a tribe's exercise of criminal jurisdiction over a member, even though Public Law 280 had granted criminal jurisdiction for such a crime (vehicular homicide) to the state. Walker v. Rushing, 898 F.2d 672 (8th Cir.1990). The court reasoned that a tribe enjoys inherent sovereignty over its members unless clearly limited by Congress, and that Public Law 280 contained no such clear limitation. An amendment to Public Law 280 referred to the criminal jurisdiction earlier given to the mandatory states as "exclusive," but the legislative history is unclear and that term may simply mean exclusive of federal, not tribal, jurisdiction. See 18 U.S.C. § 1162(c). In any event, implementation of Public Law 280 usually has marked the end of tribal criminal jurisdiction, either because of a lack of need or a lack of resources to maintain a tribal criminal justice system parallel to that of the state. Tribes may, however, choose to exercise authority in those areas from which Public Law 280 excludes the states, notably the regulation of hunting and fishing guaranteed by treaty or statute. 78 Interior Dec. 101, 103 (1971).

Public Law 280 expressly declines to authorize states to interfere with hunting and fishing rights, or to take certain actions affecting Indian trust lands. See Section E, below. States also have been held to lack general powers of taxation and regulation in Indian country. See Bryan v. Itasca County, 426 U.S. 373 (1976). The latter limitation, which affects both the civil and criminal jurisdiction of the states, is of considerable importance and is discussed in Section D, below.

C. CIVIL JURISDICTION

The grant of civil jurisdiction was added to Public Law 280 as an afterthought, and there is consequently little legislative history concerning it. See Goldberg, supra, at 542–543. The grant covered the same areas of Indian country within the same six mandatory states as did the grant of criminal jurisdiction: California, Minnesota (except the Red Lake Reservation), Nebraska, Oregon (except the Warm

Springs Reservation), Wisconsin (except the Menominee Reservation), and, as added in 1958, Alaska (except the Annette Islands). The civil grant was in the following terms:

28 U.S.C.A. § 1360(a):

Each of the States listed * * * shall have jurisdiction over civil causes of action between Indians or to which Indians are parties which arise in the areas of Indian country listed * * * to the same extent that such State has jurisdiction over other civil causes of action, and those civil laws of such State that are of general application to private persons or private property shall have the same force and effect within such Indian country as they have elsewhere within the State * * *.

Like the parallel grant of criminal jurisdiction, this civil section filled in the greatest existing gap in state jurisdiction. Williams v. Lee, 358 U.S. 217 (1959), had denied the state power to adjudicate civil actions against Indians that arose in Indian country; Public Law 280 expressly conferred that power. The state's adjudicatory power was not made total, however. 28 U.S.C.A. § 1360(b) expressly provided that nothing in the grant should confer jurisdiction upon the states "to adjudicate, in probate proceedings or otherwise, the ownership or right to possession of [trust] property or any interest therein." The same section declined to grant the state power to encumber trust property or to interfere with treaty rights—a disclaimer that is common to both the civil and criminal grants and that is discussed in Section E below.

The grant of civil jurisdiction to the states in § 1360 did not deprive tribal courts of concurrent jurisdiction if they choose to exercise it. Native Village of Venetie I.R.A. Council v. Alaska, 944 F.2d 548, 559–62 (9th Cir.1991); Confederated Tribes of the Colville Reservation v. Superior Court, 945 F.2d 1138 (9th Cir.1991). In *Venetie*, the state argued that state jurisdiction under Public Law 280 must be exclusive, or Congress would not have provided in the Indian Child Welfare Act that tribes subject to Public Law 280 could petition the Secretary to "reassume" jurisdiction over child custody proceedings pursuant to the Act. See 25 U.S.C.A. § 1918(a). The court of appeals held, however, that § 1918(a) was not rendered unnecessary or meaningless if the tribes already had general concurrent jurisdiction; the grant of jurisdiction under the Indian Child Welfare Act was broader than concurrent-it could give the tribe exclusive or primary jurisdiction. See § 1918(b)(2); see also Chapter VII, Section F(1)(c), F(2)(c), supra. Thus the Village of Venetie was held to have concurrent jurisdiction over child custody even though it had not petitioned for broader jurisdiction under the Indian Child Welfare Act. *Venetie*, 944 F.2d at 561–62.

One court of appeals, applying Strate v. A–1 Contractors, 117 S.Ct. 1404 (1997), held that a tribal court had no jurisdiction over a civil suit by tribal members against state officers for a false arrest on reservation fee lands that may have been Indian-owned; ownership was held to be irrelevant because the state officers, who were exercising Public Law 280 criminal jurisdiction, had a right to be there. County v. Allen, 1998 WL 191233 (9th Cir.1998). If this decision endures, it means that grants of criminal jurisdiction to the state under Public Law 280 (and quite possibly other grants of permission to enter the reservation) diminish the tribal court's civil jurisdiction.

One controversy that arose from the language of the grant of civil jurisdiction to the states in 28 U.S.C.A. § 1360 concerned the applicability of local law. The question was whether a county or city ordinance qualifies as one of the "civil laws of [the] State that are of general application to private persons or private property" and that are to have the same force and effect in Indian country as they have "elsewhere within the State." The Ninth Circuit took the view that the statute refers only to the generally applicable laws of the *state*, and not those of the state's local subdivisions; Congress could not have intended the severe interference with tribal self-government that would result from imposing detailed local regulations upon Indians in Indian country. Santa Rosa Band of Indians v. Kings County, 532 F.2d 655 (9th Cir.1975), cert. denied, 429 U.S. 1038 (1977); Segundo v. City of Rancho Mirage, 813 F.2d 1387, 1390 (9th Cir.1987). The Supreme Court has not ruled squarely on this issue, but has expressed doubt that Public Law 280 authorizes the application of local laws to the reservations. California v. Cabazon Band of Mission Indians, 480 U.S. 202, 212 n. 11 n. 11 (1987).

D. EXCEPTION FOR TAXATION AND REGULATION

One further issue that arose from Public Law 280's grant of civil jurisdiction overshadows all others and has important implications for criminal jurisdiction as well. The civil grant is one of power over "civil causes of action." This language would appear to mean that the state simply acquired adjudicatory jurisdiction—the power to decide cases—and not the entire power to legislate and regulate in Indian country. On the other hand, the statutory grant also provides that the "civil laws of [the] State shall have the same force and effect within such Indian country as they have elsewhere within the State." That language might arguably confer full legislative jurisdiction on the state. The true meaning of the statute was vigorously disputed until the Supreme Court resolved the matter adversely to the states in Bryan v. Itasca County, 426 U.S. 373 (1976).

Bryan involved the attempt of a Minnesota county to assess a state and local property tax against personal property owned by an Indian in Indian country over which the state had been granted jurisdiction by Public Law 280. The personal property involved was not trust property, and the state argued that it therefore became subject to the general "civil laws" of the state, including its tax laws.

The Supreme Court examined the legislative history and concluded that the primary purpose of the civil provisions of Public Law 280 was to provide a state forum for the resolution of disputes. Viewed in that light, the provision that the civil laws of the state should have effect in Indian country simply "authorizes application by the state courts of their rules of decision to decide such disputes." 426 U.S. at 384.

The effect of the Court's decision is to confine the civil grant of Public Law 280 to adjudicatory jurisdiction only. State "civil laws" are applicable only in the sense that state courts can apply the state law of torts or contracts, for example, to decide disputes involving Indians in Indian country. The Court in *Bryan* was quite explicit in rejecting any notion that Public Law 280 conferred general legislative jurisdiction upon the states:

[N]othing in its legislative history remotely suggests that Congress meant the Act's extension of civil jurisdiction to the States should result in the undermining or destruction of such tribal governments as did exist and a conversion of the affected tribes into little more than " 'private, voluntary organizations,' " * * *—a possible result if tribal governments and reservation Indians were subordinated to the full panoply of civil regulatory powers, including taxation, of state and local governments.

426 U.S. at 388. It followed that Minnesota's attempted taxation was not authorized by Public Law 280. Whatever powers of taxation or regulation

states have in Indian country, see Chapter IX, must be derived from some other source; Public Law 280 confers no such authority.

The *Bryan* principle was applied to the area of criminal law in California v. Cabazon Band of Mission Indians, 480 U.S. 202 (1987). In that case, tribes were operating high-stakes bingo and poker games on their reservations. California sought to apply its penal law prohibiting bingo games unless they were conducted by charitable organizations and offered prizes not exceeding $250 per game. Riverside County sought to apply its ordinance forbidding gambling on card games, with exceptions if municipalities licensed them. A major issue was whether the state and county laws were "criminal laws" applicable to Indian country under Public Law 280, or were "regulations" excepted from Public Law 280 by the rule of *Bryan*. The Supreme Court, in ruling for the tribes, accepted the distinction made by the court of appeals between state "criminal/prohibitory" laws and state "civil/regulatory" laws:

> [I]f the intent of a state law is generally to prohibit certain conduct, it falls within Pub. L. 280's grant of criminal jurisdiction, but if the state law generally permits the conduct at issue, subject to regulation, it must be classified as civil/regulatory and Pub. L. 280 does not authorize its enforcement on an Indian reservation. The shorthand test is whether the conduct at issue violates the State's public policy.

480 U.S. at 209. The Court then held that, although there were weighty arguments both ways, it would accept the view of the court of appeals that the statute and ordinance were regulatory. The Supreme Court pointed out that the circuit court's view was supported by the fact that California allowed or, in the case of its lottery, encouraged various forms of gambling, and that the County permitted card gambling if municipalities authorized it. 480 U.S. at 210–11. The Supreme Court also said that the fact "that an otherwise regulatory law is enforceable by criminal as well as civil means does not necessarily convert it into a criminal law within the meaning of Pub.L. 280." Id. at 211. *Bryan*, therefore, significantly narrows the criminal as well as the civil effect of Public Law 280.

The distinction between criminal/prohibitory and civil/regulatory laws continues to arise in a variety of settings, with results not entirely predictable. The distinction is subject to manipulation by the manner in which the issue is presented. For example, a state law prohibiting driving after the suspension of a license could be viewed as a mere regulation of driving, an activity that is regulated rather than prohibited, or as a criminal, public-policy-driven prohibition against driving after suspension of a license. The latter view was adopted (at least for a repeat offender) and the state law enforced against a tribal member in St. Germaine v. Circuit Court of Vilas County, 938 F.2d 75 (7th Cir.1991), cert. denied, 503 U.S. 997 (1992). On the other hand, where a state had reduced speeding from a criminal offense to a "traffic infraction," the law was held to be regulatory. Confederated Tribes of the Colville Reservation v. Washington, 938 F.2d 146 (9th Cir. 1991), cert. denied, 503 U.S. 997 (1992). Some cases seem to turn on the strength of a state's interest, even though it remains difficult to determine whether that interest lies in regulation or prohibition. A state fireworks law regulating classes of fireworks, and prohibiting dangerous fireworks except in the hands of licensed and trained persons, with violation a misdemeanor, was held to be criminal/prohibitory in Quechan Indian Tribe v. McMullen, 984 F.2d 304 (9th Cir.1993). One state appellate court even ruled that state hunting regulations were criminal/prohibitory. Jones v. State, 936 P.2d 1263, 1266–67 (Alaska App.1997).

In larger perspective, however, *Bryan's* restriction of state legislative and regulatory authority helped to preserve the vitality of tribes' law-making powers. Public Law 280 had expressly provided that tribal ordinances or customs were to be given full force and effect in the decision of civil controversies by state courts, 28 U.S.C.A. § 1360(c), but this provision was limited to ordinances or customs "not inconsistent with any applicable civil law of the State." Since most states have relatively complete bodies of civil law, the statute did not leave much room for tribal law to operate. The *Bryan* case leaves open to the tribe a much larger legislative role dealing with regulation and taxation.

E. OTHER EXCEPTIONS TO STATE JURISDICTION UNDER PUBLIC LAW 280

Both the grant of criminal jurisdiction and that of civil jurisdiction in Public Law 280 contain the following exceptions:

Nothing in this section shall authorize the alienation, encumbrance, or taxation of any real or personal property, including water rights, belonging to any Indian or any Indian tribe, band, or community that is held in trust by the United States or is subject to a restriction against alienation imposed by the United States; or shall authorize regulation of the use of such property in a manner inconsistent with any Federal treaty, agreement, or statute or with any regulation made pursuant thereto * * *.

18 U.S.C.A. § 1162(b); 28 U.S.C.A. § 1360(b). The two principal effects of these limitations are to preserve the trust status of Indian property and to protect Indian treaty rights.

The provisions negating any grant of power to the states to alienate or tax trust property are reinforced by a provision in the civil grant that nothing therein "shall confer jurisdiction upon the State to adjudicate, in probate proceedings or otherwise, the ownership or right to possession of such property or any interest therein." 28 U.S.C.A. § 1360(b). These provisions have not in themselves been the source of much litigation; the states were previously excluded from such actions and the statute merely maintained the status quo. There has been controversy, however, over what kinds of state activity may constitute an "encumbrance" of Indian lands. If the term is read very broadly, it may preclude the state from enforcing any of its laws that would diminish the value of Indian lands. See Snohomish County v. Seattle Disposal Co., 70 Wash.2d 668, 425 P.2d 22, cert. denied, 389 U.S. 1016 (1967). Carried to its extreme, that definition would even prevent the states from enforcing much of their criminal law. At the other extreme, "encumbrance" can be interpreted to refer only to matters that directly threaten the Indians' land title. See Rincon Band of Mission Indians v. County of San Diego, 324 F.Supp. 371 (S.D.Cal.1971), aff'd on other grounds, 495 F.2d 1 (9th Cir.), cert. denied, 419 U.S. 1008 (1974).

The most reasonable definition of "encumbrance" probably lies between the two extreme views. The term cannot include all criminal legislation that might directly or indirectly affect the utility value of Indian lands, but it also ought not to be restricted to traditional liens upon the land. State zoning laws, for example, have been held to be encumbrances within the meaning of Public Law 280. Santa Rosa Band of Indians v. Kings County, 532 F.2d 655, 667 (9th Cir.1975), cert. denied, 429 U.S. 1038 (1977). In the end, it may be impossible to give a general definition of "encumbrance" in Public Law 280; each challenged state action must be weighed for the degree and directness of its adverse effect upon trust lands. The controversy over the meaning of the term may tend to decline in importance because Public Law 280 can no longer be viewed as authorizing general state regulation of tribes or tribal members in Indian country, whether or not the regulation constitutes an encumbrance of trust lands. Bryan v. Itasca County, 426 U.S. 373 (1976).

State and local land use regulation is also inhibited by the limitation that nothing in the criminal or civil grants of jurisdiction "shall authorize regulation of the use of [trust] property in a manner inconsistent with any Federal treaty, agreement, or statute or with any regulation made pursuant thereto * * *." 18 U.S.C.A. § 1162(b); 28 U.S.C.A. § 1360(b). The Secretary of Interior has issued a regulation excluding state and local land use regulation of any trust land leased from Indians or Indian tribes, except insofar as the Secretary specifically adopts such regulations. 25 C.F.R. § 1.4. The regulation was attacked as unauthorized, but a court of appeals upheld it as applied to lands purchased by the Secretary for Indians under 25 U.S.C.A. § 465, and suggested that the regulation generally may be authorized by the congressional grant to the Secretary of broad authority over Indian affairs in 25 U.S.C.A. § 2. Santa Rosa Band of Indians v. Kings County, 532 F.2d 655, 665–67 and n. 19 (9th Cir. 1975), cert. denied, 429 U.S. 1038 (1977).

A clause in Public Law 280's grant of civil jurisdiction provides that the grant does not authorize regulation of the use of trust property in a manner inconsistent with any federal treaty or statute. 28

U.S.C.A. § 1360(b). A more specific provision in the grant of criminal jurisdiction in Public Law 280 provides that nothing in the grant "shall deprive any Indian or any Indian tribe, band, or community of any right, privilege, or immunity afforded under Federal treaty, agreement, or statute with respect to hunting, trapping, or fishing or the control, licensing, or regulation thereof." 18 U.S.C.A. § 1162(b). This restriction simply leaves the states in the same position with regard to treaty hunting and fishing rights that they occupy in the absence of Public Law 280. That position is the subject of much litigation and is discussed in Chapter XV, below.

In at least two cases dealing with termination of the federal trust relationship, however, the language of Public Law 280 has assumed special significance with respect to hunting and fishing. In Menominee Tribe v. United States, 391 U.S. 404 (1968), the Supreme Court was confronted with the question whether the federal statute terminating the trust relationship between the federal government and the Menominee Tribe subjected tribal members to state regulation of hunting and fishing rights arising (by implication) from a treaty. The Termination Act applying to the Menominee and certain other tribes provided that after federal supervision ended, "the laws of the several States shall apply to the tribe and its members in the same manner as they apply to other citizens or persons within their jurisdiction." 25 U.S.C.A. § 899, repealed, P.L. 93–197, § 3(b), 87 Stat. 770 (1973).

Despite this apparently unequivocal language, the Supreme Court held that tribal treaty hunting and fishing rights survived termination and that Wisconsin could not apply its game and fish laws to the Menominees exercising such rights. The Court relied heavily on the fact that Public Law 280, which came from the same committees of Congress and was amended at about the same time as the Termination Act, expressly excluded any grant of power to the states to interfere with treaty hunting and fishing rights. Reading the two statutes in pari materia, the Supreme Court concluded that Congress could not have intended termination to cause the loss of the Menominees' treaty rights. The same reasoning subsequently was employed to preserve the treaty hunting and fishing rights of the terminated Klamath Tribe. Kimball v. Callahan, 493 F.2d 564 (9th Cir.), cert. denied, 419 U.S. 1019 (1974), and Kimball v. Callahan, 590 F.2d 768 (9th Cir.), cert. denied, 444 U.S. 826 (1979).

F. ASSUMPTION OF JURISDICTION BY THE OPTIONAL STATES

In addition to conferring criminal and civil jurisdiction on six named states, Public Law 280 authorized all other states to assume such jurisdiction over Indian country if they chose. P.L. 280, § 7, 67 Stat. 588, 590 (1953). Under this provision there have been total or partial assumptions of jurisdiction by the following states: Arizona, Florida, Idaho, Iowa, Montana, Nevada, North Dakota, Utah and

Washington. The manner in which these optional states assumed jurisdiction varied greatly, ranging from total assumptions of both criminal and civil jurisdiction, Fla. Stat. Ann. § 285.16, to a very limited assumption for the purposes of regulating only air pollution, Ariz.Rev.Stat.Ann. § 49–561. Other states assumed jurisdiction only over certain reservations, e.g., Mont.Code Ann. §§ 2–1–301 to 306, or over certain offenses, Wash.Rev.Code §§ 37.12.010–.070. In some cases, the assuming state required consent of the tribes, but Public Law 280 did not require it.

There was considerable doubt about the validity of partial assumptions of jurisdiction under Public Law 280 as it was originally passed, because it authorized the optional states to assume jurisdiction "as provided for in this act." Because the mandatory states were given total jurisdiction, an argument could be made that optional states had to assume all civil or criminal jurisdiction or none. Otherwise the states might simply assume advantageous portions of jurisdiction and leave the most expensive or difficult enforcement problems to the tribes or the federal government. See Goldberg, Public Law 280: *The Limits of State Jurisdiction Over Reservation Indians*, 22 U.C.L.A.L.Rev. 535, 548–49, 553–55 (1975). In 1968 Congress eliminated all doubt about the validity of partial assumptions of jurisdiction made after that date; it amended Public Law 280 to permit the states to assume "such measure of jurisdiction over any or all of such offenses committed within such Indian country or any part thereof" and "such measure of jurisdiction over any or all such civil causes of action arising within such Indian country or any part thereof" as the state might choose to acquire with the consent of the tribes. 25 U.S.C.A. §§ 1321(a), 1322(a). There still remained a question whether partial assumptions of jurisdiction occurring before 1968 were valid, but the Supreme Court largely settled the issue in Washington v. Confederated Bands and Tribes of the Yakima Indian Nation, 439 U.S. 463 (1979). In that case the Court upheld an incredibly complicated partial assumption of jurisdiction by the State of Washington that had occurred in 1963. The Court reasoned that the selective assumption was authorized by § 7 of Public Law 280, which permitted the optional states to assume jurisdiction "in such manner" as the people of the State, by legislative action, bound themselves to assume. P.L. 280, § 7, 67 Stat. 588, 590 (1953). Subsequently, however, the Eighth Circuit held that South Dakota's narrow assumption in 1961 of jurisdiction only over highways was invalid as inconsistent with the purposes of Public Law 280. Rosebud Sioux Tribe v. South Dakota, 900 F.2d 1164 (8th Cir.1990), cert. denied, 500 U.S. 915 (1991). *Rosebud* is probably unique, however, because of South Dakota's long and involved history of abortive attempts to assume Public Law 280 jurisdiction. See id. at 1166–68.

The *Yakima* case also settled another major controversy that had surrounded the assumption of jurisdiction by some of the western states. These states had clauses in their constitutions disclaiming all title to Indian lands and providing that such lands should "remain under the absolute jurisdiction and control of the congress of the United States * * *." E.g., Wash.Const. Art. XXVI. These disclaimers had been required by the relevant congressional enabling acts as conditions of admission to the Union. As a consequence, they could not be amended without the consent of Congress. Congress expressly gave its consent in § 6 of Public Law 280 "to the people of any State to amend, where necessary, their State constitution or existing statutes, as the case may be, to remove any legal impediment to the assumption of civil and criminal jurisdiction in accordance with the provisions of this Act." P.L. 280, § 6, 67 Stat. 588, 590 (1953). Several of the disclaimer states, however, simply assumed jurisdiction under Public Law 280 by statute, without bothering to amend their constitutions. This omission raised substantial questions about the validity of the assumptions of jurisdiction. In the *Yakima* case, the Supreme Court had to face these questions because Washington had enacted its assumption of jurisdiction without modifying the disclaimer in its state constitution. After extensive analysis, the Supreme Court concluded that Congress had not intended to require such an amendment if state law itself did not require it. Washington's assumption of jurisdiction was therefore upheld.

Perhaps the greatest criticism of Public Law 280 was that it permitted the states to assume jurisdiction without the consent of the concerned tribes. Congress reacted to this criticism in the Indian

Civil Rights Act of 1968 by amending Public Law 280 to provide that no states could assume jurisdiction thereafter without the consent of the tribe or tribes concerned. 25 U.S.C.A. §§ 1321(a), 1322(a). This consent may only be obtained by a majority vote of the adult Indians of the tribe in a special election. 25 U.S.C.A. § 1326. As a result of this provision, there has been only one assumption of jurisdiction under Public Law 280 since 1968—that of Utah—and Utah bound itself to retrocede that jurisdiction whenever a tribe requests it by a majority vote at a special election. Utah Code Ann. § 63–36–15. It is not likely that many states will agree to such a provision, and the result is that the 1968 amendments have largely halted further expansion of Public Law 280 jurisdiction. The 1968 amendments are not retroactive, however; they do not invalidate those assumptions of jurisdiction made without Indian consent prior to 1968 nor do they affect the jurisdiction originally conferred on the mandatory states. United States v. Hoodie, 588 F.2d 292 (9th Cir.1978).

The existence of the optional provisions of Public Law 280 has had an important collateral effect. The Supreme Court has held that Public Law 280 provides the exclusive method by which states may acquire jurisdiction over Indian country, and that conclusion has resulted in the invalidation of less formal acquisitions of state power. In Kennerly v. District Court, 400 U.S. 423 (1971), a tribal council had by resolution provided that civil jurisdiction over suits against Indians should be concurrent in the state and the tribe. The state court exercised jurisdiction in such a case, but the Supreme Court reversed, holding that the state could not acquire jurisdiction without following the requirements of Public Law 280 as amended by the 1968 Indian Civil Rights Act. See also *Fort Berthold I* and *II*, 467 U.S. 138 (1984) and 476 U.S. 877 (1986). Subsequently, the failure of the State of Arizona to assume general Public Law 280 jurisdiction was used by the Supreme Court to reinforce its conclusion that the state had no power to tax income earned by an Indian in Indian country. McClanahan v. Arizona State Tax Com'n, 411 U.S. 164 (1973).

G. RETROCESSION OF JURISDIC- TION BY A STATE TO THE FED- ERAL GOVERNMENT

In further response to criticism of Public Law 280 by both tribes and states, Congress in its 1968 amendments provided a method for states to return Public Law 280 jurisdiction to the federal government. The United States was authorized "to accept a retrocession by any State of all or any measure of the criminal or civil jurisdiction" acquired by that state pursuant to the mandatory or optional provisions of Public Law 280. 25 U.S.C.A. § 1323(a). The President thereupon designated the Secretary of the Interior to exercise the discretionary power of the United States to accept retrocessions of jurisdiction. Exec. Order 11435, 33 Fed.Reg. 17339 (1968).

Notably absent from the retrocession provision is any mechanism for requiring tribal consent or permitting tribal initiative for retrocession. The original option is entirely that of the retroceding state, although the Secretary of the Interior may exercise discretion in accepting or rejecting the proposed retrocession. If the affected tribes wish to influence the process, they must do so by political means directed at the state or the Secretary.

The few questions that have arisen over retrocession have concerned the state's method of retroceding and the effect of the Secretary's acceptance. For example, the Governor of Washington retroceded jurisdiction over the Suquamish Port Madison Reservation by proclamation, without any action by the state legislature. The Secretary accepted it, and the courts examining it have held that the validity of the retrocession is a question of federal law and that validity was established by the Secretary's acceptance. Oliphant v. Schlie, 544 F.2d 1007 (9th Cir.1976), rev'd on other grounds, 435 U.S. 191; United States v. Lawrence, 595 F.2d 1149 (9th Cir.), cert. denied, 444 U.S. 853 (1979). A different question arose when Nebraska by legislative act offered to retrocede jurisdiction over the Omaha and Winnebago Reservations. The Secretary accepted the retrocession of the Omaha Reservation, but not the Winnebago. Nebraska contended that the retrocession was invalid because the Secretary's acceptance deviated from the state's offer. That contention was rejected and the retrocession of jurisdiction over the Omaha Reservation was held valid. Omaha Tribe of Nebraska v. Village of Walthill, 460 F.2d 1327 (8th Cir.1972), cert. denied, 409 U.S. 1107 (1973).

The provisions of Public Law 280 for assumption and retrocession of jurisdiction played what can only be described as a bizarre part in Three Affiliated Tribes of the Fort Berthold Reservation v. Wold Engineering, 467 U.S. 138 (1984) and Three Affiliated Tribes of Fort Berthold Reservation v. Wold Engineering, 476 U.S. 877 (1986) (*Fort Berthold I* and *II*). In that case the State of North Dakota, apparently in reliance on Public Law 280, attempted to disclaim jurisdiction over actions brought in state court by tribes or tribal Indians, unless the tribe consented generally to state jurisdiction. In *Fort Berthold I*, the Supreme Court understandably held that state courts had jurisdiction over such cases before Public Law 280 was passed and that, in essence, Public Law 280 simply had nothing to do with the case. 467 U.S. at 150. The Court nevertheless remanded to the state supreme court because that court's jurisdictional ruling might have been based on an erroneous view that Public Law 280 governed.

On remand, the Supreme Court of North Dakota adhered to the view that the state courts had no jurisdiction. It held that, under state law, such cases could only be brought if the tribe consented to full state jurisdiction on its reservation, and if the tribe waived its sovereign immunity. The United States Supreme Court then reversed. *Fort Berthold II*, 476 U.S. 877 (1986). It held that the scheme provided by Public Law 280 for the assumption of civil jurisdiction (which did not include the assumption of the jurisdiction the state courts already had over suits by Indians against non-Indians), and for the retrocession of only that jurisdiction assumed pursuant to Public Law 280, preempted the state from disclaiming jurisdiction in the manner it had. Thus Public Law 280, which had no effect one way or another on jurisdiction over cases brought in state court by Indians against non-Indians, was held to preempt the state's denial of such jurisdiction. Whatever the analytical difficulties, the result in *Berthold II* is clear: Indian plaintiffs are guaranteed access to state courts for suits against non-Indians. See also State v. Zaman, 190 Ariz. 208, 946 P.2d 459 (1997), cert. denied, 118 S.Ct. 1167 (1998). That outcome is consistent with that reached by several state courts on equal protection grounds. E.g., Paiz v. Hughes, 76 N.M. 562, 417 P.2d 51 (1966); Bonnet v. Seekins, 126 Mont. 24, 243 P.2d 317 (1952).

CHAPTER IX

TAXATION AND REGULATION
IN INDIAN COUNTRY

A. INTRODUCTION

A distinction is drawn in the field of Indian Law between governmental power to tax or regulate and the power to adjudicate. This division is significant because the two kinds of jurisdiction are not always coextensive. Public Law 280, for example, gives certain states the power to adjudicate civil controversies arising in Indian country but does not authorize those states to exercise their full powers of taxation or regulation there. Bryan v. Itasca County, 426 U.S. 373 (1976); California v. Cabazon Band of Mission Indians, 480 U.S. 202 (1987).

Even when Public Law 280 does not apply, the Supreme Court tends to treat issues of taxation and regulation somewhat differently from questions of adjudicatory jurisdiction. At least until recently, state exercise of adjudicatory jurisdiction has been subjected to a rigorous application of the test of Williams v. Lee, 358 U.S. 217 (1959): absent governing acts of Congress, the state may not exercise jurisdiction if it would interfere with the "right of reservation Indians to make their own laws and be ruled by them." Id. at 220. In theory, at least, this test precludes state interference with tribal self-government no matter how important the state's interest may be. The adjudicatory jurisdiction of the tribal courts thus has been vigorously protected from state encroachment. See Iowa Mut. Ins. Co. v. LaPlante, 480 U.S. 9 (1987). Although this protection has been removed for cases involving nonmembers on non-Indian fee lands or state rights-of-way in Indian country, see Strate v. A–1 Contractors, 117 S.Ct. 1404 (1997), it remains strong when tribal members and trust lands are involved.

When the state seeks to extend its power of taxation or regulation to Indian country, however, the emphasis changes. While the Supreme Court has stated that the rule of Williams v. Lee still applies, e.g., White Mountain Apache Tribe v. Bracker, 448 U.S. 136, 142 (1980), the *Williams* test tends to be subordinated. The Supreme Court is likely "to avoid reliance on platonic notions of Indian sovereignty and to look instead to the applicable treaties and statutes" to determine whether they preempt state law. McClanahan v. Arizona State Tax Comm'n, 411 U.S. 164, 172 (1973). This preemption test is more fully discussed in Chapter III, Section B, and Chapter VII, Section C(2), above. It appears to presume that state law applies unless federal law or policy excludes it. Preemption analysis also injects both flexibility and unpredictability into questions of taxation and regulation because the result in each case depends upon a fact-specific balancing of the competing interests. See, e.g., New

Mexico v. Mescalero Apache Tribe, 462 U.S. 324, 334 (1983).

Despite the uncertainties inherent in the preemption analysis now being applied, there have been enough decisions in the area of taxation to permit a fairly complete description of the taxing powers of the federal government, the states, and the tribes. Fish and game regulation has also been the subject of extensive litigation, and the topic is sufficiently complex and distinctive that it is treated separately in Chapter XV, below. The law governing other kinds of regulation is less complete, but is growing rapidly as issues of environmental and economic regulation increasingly find their way to court.

B. FEDERAL TAXATION IN INDIAN COUNTRY

The federal taxing power does not depend on geography, and it is fully effective in Indian country with regard to both Indians and non-Indians. Contrary to a common misconception, Indians are not exempt from federal income tax by reason of being Indians or because their income is earned in Indian country. Superintendent of Five Civilized Tribes v. Commissioner, 295 U.S. 418 (1935).

There are, however, certain kinds of income of Indians that Congress has elected not to tax. Perhaps the most important is income from individually allotted land that remains in trust. The General Allotment Act of 1887 provided for tribal lands to be allotted to individual Indians in trust for a period of years, after which the lands were to be conveyed to the allottees in fee "free of all charge or incumbrance whatsoever." 25 U.S.C.A. § 348. This provision has been interpreted to prevent taxation of income or capital gains "derived directly" from allotted land while it remains in trust. Squire v. Capoeman, 351 U.S. 1 (1956). This exemption applies to rents and royalties as well as income from sale of crops or minerals from the land. Rev.Rul. 56–342, 1956–2 Cum.Bull. 20. Gain from the sale of livestock raised and grazed on allotted trust land has also been ruled exempt. Rev.Rul. 62–16, 1962–1 Cum.Bull. 7. On the other hand, income from the operation of a motel or a smokeshop on allotted land has been held to derive from labor and the use of capital improvements rather than directly from the land itself, and has accordingly been held taxable. Critzer v. United States, 597 F.2d 708 (Ct.Cl.), cert. denied, 444 U.S. 920 (1979); Dillon v. United States, 792 F.2d 849 (9th Cir.1986), cert. denied, 480 U.S. 930 (1987). Similarly, when exempt income is reinvested, the reinvestment income is subject to taxation. Superintendent of Five Civilized Tribes v. Commissioner, 295 U.S. 418 (1935).

Income from trust lands allotted under other allotment acts is exempt from federal taxation even though those acts do not contain the same protective language as the General Allotment Act. Stevens v. Commissioner, 452 F.2d 741 (9th Cir.1971). When allotted land is removed from trust and a fee patent is issued to the allottee, income from the land (like the land itself) becomes fully taxable.

Choteau v. Burnet, 283 U.S. 691 (1931). Income of an Indian from trust land leased from the tribe has been held taxable on the ground that the individual Indian had no present or potential ownership interest and the tax could not therefore be a charge or burden on the land. Holt v. Commissioner, 364 F.2d 38 (8th Cir.1966), cert. denied, 386 U.S. 931 (1967); United States v. Anderson, 625 F.2d 910 (9th Cir. 1980), cert. denied, 450 U.S. 920 (1981).

C. STATE TAXATION IN INDIAN COUNTRY

1. STATE TAXATION OF TRIBES AND TRIBAL MEMBERS

State powers of taxation are severely limited in Indian country, particularly where Indian interests are affected. It has long been settled that the states have no power to tax Indian trust lands, whether held tribally or in allotments. The Kansas Indians, 72 U.S. (5 Wall.) 737 (1866). This exclusion was required by Congress to be written into the constitutions of several western states as conditions of their admission into the Union. The states are also without power to tax other kinds of Indian trust property. Congress may change these rules, and on rare occasion has done so. In 1924, Congress authorized the states to tax royalties from mineral leases of Indian trust lands. 25 U.S.C.A. § 398. In the absence of an explicit provision, however, the usual rule controls, and the state may not tax such receipts. Thus tribal royalties from leases entered after 1938 are not taxable by the states, because the 1939 Indian Mineral Leasing Act contained no such authorization. Montana v. Blackfeet Tribe, 471 U.S. 759 (1985).

At times the immunity of tribes from state taxation in Indian country has been thought to arise from the general doctrine of federal-state intergovernmental immunity—a doctrine that has enjoyed an unstable career. In truth, however, Indian immunities from state taxation arise from federal policies quite distinct from those relating to traditional intergovernmental immunity, and the Supreme Court effectively has recognized that the Indian policy must be evaluated on its own merits. McClanahan v. Arizona State Tax Com'n, 411 U.S. 164, 169–170 (1973). In fact, the exclusion of the states from taxation of Indian property does not even depend on federal trust status of the property; in the absence of congressional authorization, states lack the power to tax even non-trust property when it is owned by a tribal member and has its situs on that tribe's reservation. Bryan v. Itasca County, 426 U.S. 373 (1976); Moe v. Confederated Salish & Kootenai Tribes, 425 U.S. 463 (1976). Thus a state may not impose vehicle excise and registration fees upon Indians who live and garage their vehicles in Indian country. Oklahoma Tax Comm'n v. Sac and Fox Nation, 508 U.S. 114 (1993). The General Allotment Act, however, has been held to authorize the states to tax fee land within a reservation, whether owned by Indians or non-Indians; the congressional intent was to permit the land to become alienable and taxable when a fee patent was issued. County of Yakima v. Confederated Tribes and Bands of the Yakima Indian Nation, 502 U.S. 251 (1992); cf. Yellowstone County v. Pease, 96 F.3d 1169 (9th Cir.1996), cert. denied, 117 S.Ct. 1691 (1997). Thus, when a tribe reacquires in fee simple land that was formerly allotted and patented under that provision of the Allotment Act, the state may tax the lands. Leech Lake Band of Chippewa Indians v. Cass County, 108 F.3d 820 (8th Cir.), cert. granted, 118 S.Ct. 361 (1997). It may not tax other reservation land that the tribe or its members acquired in fee when that land originally had been patented under other statutes containing no clear permission for the state to tax. Id; United States on behalf of Saginaw Chippewa Indian Tribe v. Michigan, 106 F.3d 130 (6th Cir.), pet. for cert. filed, 66 U.S.L.W. 3085 (1997). Moreover, the permission to tax in the Allotment Act is limited to taxation of the patented allotted land only; it does not authorize taxation in Indian country of other activities such as the *sale* of those lands by the tribe or its members. *Yakima*, 502 U.S. at 268–70. Similarly, a state may not impose motor fuel excise taxes in Indian country when their legal incidence falls upon the tribe or its members. Oklahoma Tax Comm'n v. Chickasaw Nation, 515 U.S. 450 (1995).

States are also without power to tax the reservation income of tribal members domiciled on the tribe's reservation, as the Supreme Court held in the pivotal decision of McClanahan v. Arizona State Tax Com'n, 411 U.S. 164 (1973); see also Oklahoma

Tax Comm'n v. Sac and Fox Nation, 508 U.S. 114 (1993). Reading the relevant statutes and treaties in the light of a history of Indian sovereignty and self-government, the Court in *McClanahan* ruled that the state's power to tax was preempted by federal law and policy. Among the statutes that the Court relied upon was the Buck Act, 4 U.S.C.A. § 105 et seq., which extended state taxing power into federal reserves but provided that nothing in the applicable sections of the Act should "be deemed to authorize the levy or collection of any tax on or from any Indian not otherwise taxed." 4 U.S.C.A. § 109. The Court also pointed out that it was very difficult to see how the state could impose or collect its tax when it lacked civil and criminal adjudicatory jurisdiction over Indians in Indian country. The Court has subsequently observed that the policies in favor of immunity of tribes and members from state taxation are so strong, and the corresponding state interest so weak, that they need not be rebalanced in each new case; a *per se* rule against such taxation is applied. California v. Cabazon Band of Mission Indians, 480 U.S. 202, 215 n. 17 (1987); see also Oklahoma Tax Comm'n v. Chickasaw Nation, 515 U.S. 450, 457 (1995).

At the time *McClanahan* and prior cases restricting state taxation were decided, it was assumed that the restriction imposed upon the state was against taxing *any* Indian in Indian country, regardless of the tribal affiliation of that Indian. This assumption seemed justified both by the language of the decisions and the fact that for the purposes of civil and criminal jurisdiction the crucial fact has always been status as an Indian and not status as a tribal member. In 1980, however, the Supreme Court drew a sharp distinction between members of the tribe that governed a given reservation and other Indians not members of that tribe. In Washington v. Confederated Tribes of Colville Indian Reservation, 447 U.S. 134 (1980), the Court held that the State of Washington could impose cigarette and sales taxes on sales made to nonmember Indians in Indian country. The Court stated:

Federal statutes, even given the broadest reading to which they are reasonably susceptible, cannot be said to pre-empt Washington's power to impose its taxes on Indians not members of the Tribe. We do not so read the Major Crimes Act, * * * which at most provides for federal-court jurisdiction over crimes committed by Indians on another Tribe's reservation. * * * Similarly, the mere fact that nonmembers resident on the reservation come within the definition of "Indian" for purposes of the Indian Reorganization Act of 1934 * * * does not demonstrate a congressional intent to exempt such Indians from state taxation.

Nor would the imposition of Washington's tax on these purchasers contravene the principle of tribal self-government, for the simple reason that nonmembers are not constituents of the governing Tribe. For most practical purposes those Indians stand on the same footing as non-Indians resident on the reservation.

447 U.S. at 160–61. The Court repeated this ruling in Oklahoma Tax Comm'n v. Citizen Band Potawatomi Indian Tribe, 498 U.S. 505, 512–13 (1991). It seems likely, therefore, that the Court will treat nonmember Indians the same as non-Indians for most or all tax purposes.

Outside of Indian country, every Indian is subject to state jurisdiction and if he or she engages in taxable activity there, the state can impose its tax. The state can tax income of a tribal member domiciled outside of Indian country even if the income is earned from employment by the tribe on the reservation. Oklahoma Tax Comm'n v. Chickasaw Nation, 515 U.S. 450 (1995). Even an Indian tribe is subject to state taxation if it undertakes to operate a business outside of Indian country. Mescalero Apache Tribe v. Jones, 411 U.S. 145 (1973).

2. STATE TAXATION OF NONMEMBERS

The state has long been allowed to impose taxes on the property of non-Indians located within Indian country. Utah & Northern Ry. v. Fisher, 116 U.S. 28 (1885); Thomas v. Gay, 169 U.S. 264 (1898). It has also been permitted to tax reservation income of non-Indians domiciled on Indian reservations. Kahn v. Arizona State Tax Com'n, 16 Ariz.App. 17, 490 P.2d 846 (1971), appeal dismissed, 411 U.S. 941 (1973); see Oklahoma Tax Comm'n v. Chickasaw Nation, 515 U.S. 450, 467 (1995). There are, however, important limitations on the general power of states to levy taxes in Indian country. The primary

limitation is that the state may not tax when the
subject matter is preempted by federal law. The
application of that standard is usually not difficult
when the tax falls directly on Indians. "When on-
reservation conduct involving only Indians is at
issue, state law is generally inapplicable, for the
State's regulatory interest is likely to be minimal
and the federal interest in encouraging tribal self-
government is at its strongest." White Mountain
Apache Tribe v. Bracker, 448 U.S. 136, 144 (1980).
Most recent litigation, however, has concerned state
taxes imposed upon non-Indians or, stated more
broadly, on nonmembers in Indian country. Such
taxes are sometimes preempted because they interfere with the regulatory activities of the federal
government itself. More often the state tax is
preempted because, although imposed on non-Indians, it has an indirect effect on the tribe that
frustrates federal policies of tribal self-determination. At other times, the tax is deemed not to
interfere with either federal policy or tribal self-
government, and is not preempted.

The seminal preemption case is Warren Trading
Post Co. v. Arizona Tax Com'n, 380 U.S. 685
(1965). There the Supreme Court held that Arizona
could not tax the gross receipts of a non-Indian
trading post on the Navajo Reservation. The Court
pointed out that Indian traders had to be federally
licensed and were subject to extensive federal regulation. These regulations took the business of Indian trading "so fully in hand that no room remains
for state laws imposing additional burdens upon

traders." 380 U.S. at 690. Although this expansive
language suggests that no state regulation of any
kind could be imposed on Indian traders, the Supreme Court has since rejected that implication in
holding that Indian traders could be required to
collect and remit state sales taxes collected from
nonmember purchasers of cigarettes. Dep't of Taxation and Finance v. Milhelm Attea & Bros., Inc.,
512 U.S. 61 (1994).

The Supreme Court has quite regularly invalidated state taxes imposed on non-Indian contractors
engaged in sales or services to the tribes in Indian
country. In White Mountain Apache Tribe v. Bracker, 448 U.S. 136 (1980), the Court struck down
state taxes on non-Indians cutting timber on a
reservation and delivering it to the tribal sawmill.
The taxes were a motor carrier license tax based on
gross receipts and a fuel use tax. They were held to
be preempted by extensive federal regulations applying to timber operations in Indian country. See
also Hoopa Valley Tribe v. Nevins, 881 F.2d 657
(9th Cir.1989), cert. denied, 494 U.S. 1055 (1990).
The Court in *Bracker* made it clear that preemption
did not require an express congressional declaration
invalidating state taxes, and observed that "[t]he
unique historical origins of tribal sovereignty make
it generally unhelpful to apply to federal enact-
ments regulating Indian tribes those standards of
pre-emption that have emerged in other areas of the
law." 448 U.S. at 143. In a contemporaneous case,
the Supreme Court held invalid a state gross receipts tax applied to the sale of machinery in Indian

country by a non-Indian dealer whose permanent place of business was off-reservation. The Court ruled that the sale was preempted by federal statutes regulating Indian trading, which applied to the sale. Central Machinery Co. v. Arizona State Tax Com'n, 448 U.S. 160 (1980). Similarly, the Court has struck down a gross receipts tax imposed on a non-Indian contractor building a school for an Indian school board on the reservation. Ramah Navajo School Board v. Bureau of Revenue, 458 U.S. 832 (1982). In so holding, the Court reiterated its view that traditional notions of tribal sovereignty, as well as federal policies favoring tribal self-development, must inform the preemption analysis. "As a result, ambiguities in federal law should be construed generously, and federal pre-emption is not limited to those situations where Congress has explicitly announced an intention to pre-empt state activity." Id. at 838.

This line of cases seems to be at odds with the Supreme Court's later statement in Cotton Petroleum Corp. v. New Mexico, 490 U.S. 163, 175 (1989), that "[u]nder current doctrine, * * * a State can impose a nondiscriminatory tax on private parties with whom the United States or an Indian tribe does business, even though the financial burden of the tax may fall on the United States or tribe." This statement must be taken in context, however. It concludes a discussion of the rise and fall of the intergovernmental immunity doctrine, and points out that all that remains of that doctrine is a prohibition against state taxes imposed directly on the federal government or the tribes. The quoted statement does not purport to describe preemption, which often defeats a state tax imposed on a non-Indian dealing with a tribe. Indeed, *Cotton Petroleum* undertakes a preemption analysis after its discussion of intergovernmental immunities. It concludes that New Mexico may impose a severance tax on a non-Indian corporation producing oil and gas on a reservation, even though the tribe also imposes a severance tax. In so holding, *Cotton Petroleum* does weigh the competing interests in a manner more favorable to the state than was the case in *Bracker* and *Ramah*, but it does not overrule those cases. It distinguishes them partly on the grounds that federal policies were more pronounced in *Bracker* and *Ramah*, that the state in those cases provided virtually no services except taxation, and that the burden of the tax fell directly on the tribes. *Cotton Petroleum*, 490 U.S. at 183–87. *Cotton Petroleum* also distinguished its summary affirmance of the Ninth Circuit's decision holding the Montana coal severance tax preempted, see Crow Tribe of Indians v. Montana, 819 F.2d 895 (9th Cir.1987), aff'd, 484 U.S. 997 (1988), by pointing out that the Montana tax was extraordinarily high. *Cotton Petroleum*, 490 U.S. at 186 n.17.

Thus, although *Cotton Petroleum* tilts more toward the states than the Supreme Court's earlier preemption cases, it does not represent a total change in direction. It does re-emphasize some propositions that were already manifest in prior Supreme Court or lower court decisions. For example, some indirect burden on the tribe has often been permitted. A state has been allowed to impose a "possessory interest" tax on non-Indian lessees of Indian trust lands, even though the effect may be to reduce the amount of rental the Indians are able to obtain for their land. Agua Caliente Band of Mission Indians v. County of Riverside, 442 F.2d 1184 (9th Cir.1971), cert. denied, 405 U.S. 933 (1972); Fort Mojave Tribe v. County of San Bernardino, 543 F.2d 1253 (9th Cir.1976), cert. denied, 430 U.S. 983 (1977).

In permitting dual taxation, *Cotton Petroleum* echoed Washington v. Confederated Tribes of the Colville Reservation, 447 U.S. 134 (1980), in which both the tribe and the state imposed a tax on cigarettes sold by tribal shops in Indian country. The Court in *Colville* stated:

> There is no direct conflict between the state and tribal schemes, since each government is free to impose its taxes without ousting the other. Although taxes can be used for distributive or regulatory purposes, as well as for raising revenue, we see no nonrevenue purposes to the tribal taxes at issue in these cases, and, as already noted, we perceive no intent on the part of Congress to authorize the Tribes to pre-empt otherwise valid state taxes.

447 U.S. at 159. It is therefore clear that the mere existence of a tribal tax does not preempt a state tax even when the result is double taxation that places those who deal with tribes at a disadvantage.

See also Fort Mojave Tribe v. County of San Bernardino, 543 F.2d 1253 (9th Cir.1976), cert. denied, 430 U.S. 983 (1977). *Colville's* language does suggest, however, that when the tribal tax has regulatory purposes that are hindered by a state tax, the state tax may be invalid for interfering with tribal self-government.

Cases like *Colville* involving state cigarette taxes probably go farthest in permitting imposition of state taxes. *Colville* held that sales by a tribe to non-Indians and nonmember Indians were taxable by the state, but that sales to tribal members were not. The state could require the tribal organization to affix state tax stamps to packages of cigarettes and to keep records of exempt and non-exempt sales. None of these provisions was found to interfere with tribal self-government or to be federally preempted. A major reason for the result was that the Court viewed tribal cigarette sales to nonmembers as a "magnet" operation, in which the tribe adds no reservation-based value to the product but markets its tax exemption to purchasers who would otherwise buy elsewhere. *Colville*, 447 U.S. at 155. See also Moe v. Confederated Salish and Kootenai Tribes, 425 U.S. 463 (1976). The same taxes were upheld in Oklahoma Tax Comm'n v. Citizen Band Potawatomi Indian Tribe, 498 U.S. 505 (1991), but the Court also held that the tribe retained its sovereign immunity from suit to collect the taxes. The states are therefore left with a substantial remedy problem when the cigarette seller is the tribe. The Court stated that it has never held individual tribal officers immune from damage suits by the tribe, id. at 514, but those officers sued in their individual capacities are unlikely to have deep pockets. The officers may not be sued in their official capacities; they share the immunity of the tribe when acting within the scope of their official duties. Hardin v. White Mountain Apache Tribe, 779 F.2d 476, 479 (9th Cir.1985). The most effective solution for the states is to enforce the tax against those who supply the cigarettes to the tribes. See *Powatomi*, 498 U.S. at 514; Department of Taxation and Finance v. Milhelm Attea & Bros., Inc., 512 U.S. 61 (1994).

The principle of the cigarette cases has been applied to permit states to impose sales and rental taxes on sales and rentals by non-Indian businesses to non-Indians at a shopping mall on a reservation. Salt River Pima–Maricopa Indian Community v. Arizona, 50 F.3d 734 (9th Cir.), cert. denied, 516 U.S. 868 (1995). The court permitted the tax because "the Community's activities did not contribute to the value of the goods sold, and * * * Arizona provides most of the governmental services used by the non-Indian taxpayers." Id. at 736. Similarly, Arizona was permitted to impose a transaction tax on ticket sales for entertainment events conducted by non-Indians for non-Indians at a reservation lake and concert site. Gila River Indian Community v. Waddell, 91 F.3d 1232 (9th Cir.1996). State services and activities connected with the events predominated over those of the tribe. On the other hand, where a tribe had invested significant funds and effort in constructing and operating off-track betting facilities (and the federal government had regulated gaming in the tribe's interest), a state tax was held to be preempted; the tribe was not "merely serving as a conduit for the products of others." Cabazon Band of Mission Indians v. Wilson, 37 F.3d 430, 435 (9th Cir.1994).

Although all of these cases depend upon preemption analysis, the rule of Williams v. Lee, 358 U.S. 217 (1959)—that the states may not interfere with the right of reservation Indians to make their own laws and be governed by them—has been held to be an additional, independent limitation on the states' power to tax. E.g., White Mountain Apache Tribe v. Bracker, 448 U.S. 136, 142 (1980); Ramah Navajo School Board v. Bureau of Revenue, 458 U.S. 832, 837 (1982). So stated, the rule would doubtless curb any attempt of the states to tax the sovereign functions of the tribes. Where the tax is upon non-Indians, however, the absolute prohibition of Williams v. Lee tends to recede into the background while the courts engage in the balancing of interests called for by the preemption approach that they prefer. Id. When that process results in the preemption of the state tax, the rule of Williams v. Lee is sometimes then invoked as additional support for the result. E.g., Crow Tribe v. Montana, 819 F.2d at 902–03.

D. TRIBAL TAXATION

Even though taxation is one of the most basic powers of self-government, the tribes have only recently begun to exercise it. Tribes always have been assumed to have power to tax their own members, but traditional Indian hostility to taxation and the obvious poverty of a large part of the tribal population forestalled attempts to tax. It is still true that there are few tribal taxes aimed primarily at the member population.

Some of the tribes have imposed taxes on business activity within Indian country, and those taxes have fallen largely upon non-Indian enterprises. Morris v. Hitchcock, 194 U.S. 384 (1904). A tribe has been held to retain a sufficient property interest in a railroad right-of-way to support a tribal property tax on that right-of-way. Burlington Northern R. Co. v. Blackfeet Tribe, 924 F.2d 899 (9th Cir.1991), cert. denied, 505 U.S. 1212 (1992). It is uncertain whether that result would be different after Strate v. A–1 Contractors, 117 S.Ct. 1404, 1413–14 (1997), which held that a tribe's underlying property interest was insufficient to support adjudicatory jurisdiction over nonmembers on a state highway right-of-way.

There has recently been a sharp increase in tribal taxes on non-Indian businesses, arising from a new awareness of the governmental powers of the tribes, along with heightened revenue needs. In some cases there is also a conviction that non-Indian enterprises have been granted leases or licenses that are unduly advantageous to them and disadvantageous to the tribes. Taxation is seen as one means of recouping the loss.

Attempts by the tribes to tax non-Indians have been met with the contention that the tribes lacked the requisite power, particularly in view of the decision in Oliphant v. Suquamish Indian Tribe, 435 U.S. 191 (1978), which held that tribal courts had no criminal jurisdiction over non-Indians. The Supreme Court, however, has made it abundantly clear that the tribes may tax non-Indians. In Washington v. Confederated Tribes of the Colville Reservation, 447 U.S. 134 (1980), the Court upheld the imposition of a tribal cigarette tax on non-tribal purchasers, indicating that federal courts had long acknowledged the power of tribes to tax non-Indians entering the reservation to engage in economic activity. That power was not inconsistent with the tribes' domestic dependent status. No federal statute had taken the power away. Indeed, where the tribe had a significant interest in the subject matter, its power to tax was probably confirmed by the Indian Reorganization Act of 1934, 25 U.S.C.A. § 476. *Colville* also indicated that a legitimate tribal tax is not preempted by a state tax on the same subject matter: "[E]ven if the State's interests were implicated by the tribal taxes, * * * it must be remembered that tribal sovereignty is dependent on and subordinate to only the Federal Government, not the States." 447 U.S. at 154.

This broad view of tribal taxing power was reaffirmed in Merrion v. Jicarilla Apache Tribe, 455 U.S. 130 (1982), which upheld a tribal severance tax applied to non-Indian lessees who mined oil and gas on the reservation. The lessees contended that the

tribal power to tax was based entirely on the right
of the tribe to exclude nonmembers from the reservation, and that the power could not be exercised
against lessees whose leases conferred a right of
entry. The Supreme Court held that the power of
exclusion was sufficiently broad to support the tax,
but it also rejected the lessees' limited view of the
tribal taxing power.

> The power does not derive solely from the Indian
> tribe's power to exclude non-Indians from tribal
> lands. Instead, it derives from the tribe's general
> authority, as sovereign, to control economic activ-
> ity within its jurisdiction, and to defray the cost
> of providing governmental services. * * *

455 U.S. at 137. The Court also held that neither
federal statutes nor the Interstate Commerce
Clause, assuming that it applied to Indian tribes,
divested the tribe of the power to tax.

The Jicarilla Apache Tribe's Constitution,
adopted pursuant to the Indian Reorganization Act,
required the approval of the Secretary of the Interi-
or to adopt a tax. *Merrion*, 455 U.S. at 155. Such
constitutional clauses are not required by the Indian Reorganization Act, however, and there is no
general rule of law that requires secretarial approval for a tribal tax to be effective. The Supreme
Court has held that the Navajo Tribe, which rejected application of the Indian Reorganization Act, and
which had adopted no internal requirement of secretarial approval, could impose a possessory interest

tax and a business activity tax without it. Kerr–McGee Corp. v. Navajo Tribe, 471 U.S. 195 (1985).

A tribe's power to tax non-Indian business activity is not confined to its reservation, but also extends to trust allotments of tribal members, which are also Indian country. Thus a tribe may impose a severance tax on non-Indian oil and gas producers operating on trust allotments outside of the tribe's reservation. Mustang Production Co. v. Harrison, 94 F.3d 1382 (10th Cir.1996), cert. denied, 117 S.Ct. 1288 (1997).

Non–Indian businesses seeking to challenge in federal court a tribe's power of taxation regularly have been required first to exhaust tribal court remedies. See, e.g., Reservation Telephone Cooperative v. Three Affiliated Tribes of the Fort Berthold Reservation, 76 F.3d 181 (8th Cir.1996). Exhaustion has been required even when the challenge is to imposition of a business activity tax off-reservation, but on trust land. Texaco, Inc. v. Hale, 81 F.3d 934 (10th Cir.1996).

E. FEDERAL REGULATION IN INDIAN COUNTRY

The federal power to regulate Indian affairs is plenary; it is limited only by the constitutional restraints applicable to all federal activity. In the exercise of this power, the federal government may wholly preempt the regulatory power of both the states and the tribes.

No attempt will be made here to canvass the numerous federal statutes and regulations operative in Indian country. Land use is probably the area most thoroughly regulated by the federal government, but many other subjects are affected as well.

Because federal power over Indian affairs is plenary, questions of the applicability of general federal legislation in Indian country depend upon the intention rather than the power of Congress. In most cases, Congress does not state whether it intends its legislation to apply to tribes or Indians or Indian country, and courts are consequently called upon to decide that question. Generalizations are particularly suspect in this area because each piece of legislation has its own subject matter that affects Indian interests in its own particular way. The process is or ought to be one of balancing tribal interests in exemption against the federal interest in applicability. The most widely accepted rule is that set forth in Donovan v. Coeur d'Alene Tribal Farm, 751 F.2d 1113, 1116 (9th Cir.1985):

A federal statute of general applicability that is silent on the issue of applicability to Indian tribes will not apply to them if: (1) the law touches "exclusive rights of self-governance in purely intramural matters"; (2) the application of the law to the tribe would "abrogate rights guaranteed by Indian treaties"; or (3) there is proof "by legislative history or some other means that Congress intended [the law] not to apply to Indians on their reservations. . . . "

Results under this test and its predecessors have varied. A provision of the Federal Power Act authorizing power companies to condemn lands was held to permit condemnation of fee lands owned by the Tuscarora Tribe. Federal Power Com'n v. Tuscarora Indian Nation, 362 U.S. 99 (1960). No implied requirement of tribal consent is read into the licensing provisions of that Act. Escondido Mut. Water Co. v. La Jolla Band of Mission Indians, 466 U.S. 765 (1984). The National Labor Relations Act has been held applicable to a non-Indian employer in Indian country even though the tribe opposed it. Navajo Tribe v. NLRB, 288 F.2d 162 (D.C.Cir.), cert. denied, 366 U.S. 928 (1961). The Employee Retirement Income Security Act (ERISA) has been held to apply to tribes. Lumber Industry Pension Fund v. Warm Springs Forest Products Industries, 939 F.2d 683 (9th Cir.1991); Smart v. State Farm Ins. Co., 868 F.2d 929 (7th Cir.1989). The National Environmental Protection Act has been held applicable to Indian country. Davis v. Morton, 469 F.2d 593 (10th Cir.1972).

The Resource Conservation and Recovery Act (RCRA) expressly provides for application to Indian tribes, and consequently applies to them and even abrogates tribal sovereign immunity. Blue Legs v. U.S. BIA, 867 F.2d 1094 (8th Cir.1989); Backcountry Against Dumps, Inc. v. EPA, 100 F.3d 147 (D.C.Cir.1996).

On the other hand, statutes (other than ERISA) that would regulate the relation between tribes and their employees have generally been ruled inappli-

cable. The National Labor Relations Act has been
held not to apply to an Indian tribe itself as an
employer. Fort Apache Timber Co., 226 N.L.R.B.
503, 93 L.R.R.M. 1296 (1976). Title VII of the Civil
Rights Act of 1964 expressly excepts Indian tribes
from coverage. 42 U.S.C. § 2000e(b). The Age Discrimination in Employment Act (ADEA), which has
no such exception, has been ruled to be inapplicable
as an undue interference, respectively, with treaty
or inherent rights of tribal self-government. EEOC
v. Cherokee Nation, 871 F.2d 937 (10th Cir.1989);
EEOC v. Fond du Lac Heavy Equip. & Constr. Co.,
986 F.2d 246 (8th Cir.1993). One federal circuit has
held that the Occupational Safety and Health Act
(OSHA) does not apply to a tribal business, because
it would conflict with treaty-secured rights to exercise sovereignty and exclude nonmembers. Donovan
v. Navajo Forest Products Industries, 692 F.2d 709
(10th Cir.1982). Two other circuits, however, concluded that OSHA did apply and was not an undue
abrogation of the tribe's right of exclusion, whether
founded in treaty or inherent sovereignty. U.S.
Dep't of Labor v. OSHA, 935 F.2d 182 (9th Cir.
1991); Donovan v. Coeur d'Alene Tribal Farm, 751
F.2d 1113 (9th Cir.1985); Reich v. Mashantucket
Sand & Gravel, 95 F.3d 174 (2d Cir.1996). Even
when a treaty expressly conflicts with a federal
statute of general application, the statute will apply
if Congress appears to have intended to override
treaty rights. Thus the Bald Eagle Protection Act
applies to Indians and abrogates their treaty rights

to take bald eagles. United States v. Dion, 476 U.S. 734 (1986).

When a federal regulation rather than a statute is involved, its validity depends upon its being within the statutory authority Congress conferred upon the regulating agency. For example, controversy has arisen over the authority of the Secretary of Interior to issue the regulation in 25 C.F.R. § 1.4, which purports to exclude all state and local zoning or land use regulations from being applied to trust lands leased from any tribe. The regulation was held beyond the Secretary's authority in Norvell v. Sangre de Cristo Dev. Co., 372 F.Supp. 348 (D.N.M. 1974), rev'd for lack of jurisdiction, 519 F.2d 370 (10th Cir.1975), and Rincon Band of Mission Indians v. County of San Diego, 324 F.Supp. 371 (S.D.Cal.1971), aff'd on other grounds, 495 F.2d 1 (9th Cir.), cert. denied, 419 U.S. 1008 (1974). It was upheld as to lands purchased by the Secretary for Indians under 25 U.S.C.A. § 465 in Santa Rosa Band of Indians v. Kings County, 532 F.2d 655, 665–67 (9th Cir.1975), cert. denied, 429 U.S. 1038 (1977), and it was also suggested there that the regulation may be within the Secretary's general authority over Indian affairs granted by 25 U.S.C.A. § 2. Id. at 667 n. 2.

F.   STATE REGULATION IN INDIAN COUNTRY

Questions of state power to regulate in Indian country, like questions of state power to tax, are generally treated as issues of preemption:

> State jurisdiction is pre-empted by the operation
> of federal law if it interferes or is incompatible
> with federal and tribal interests reflected in fed-
> eral law, unless the state interests at stake are
> sufficient to justify the assertion of state authori-
> ty.

New Mexico v. Mescalero Apache Tribe, 462 U.S.
324, 334 (1983). This test, with its fact-specific
weighing and balancing, probably yields even more
unpredictable results in the field of regulation than
it does in that of taxation. As in tax cases, preemption analysis is sometimes buttressed by reference
to the rule of Williams v. Lee, 358 U.S. 217 (1959),
that state law may not interfere with the right of
reservation Indians to make their own laws and be
governed by them. The primary tool, however, is
preemption analysis, perhaps because the standard
of Williams v. Lee does not lend itself to a balancing
process.

Until quite recently, it was assumed that the
states were utterly without power to regulate Indians in Indian country. The Supreme Court even
cautioned against applying the test of Williams v.
Lee in such situations because that test, now viewed
as highly protective of tribal sovereignty, might
permit undue extension of state power. McClanahan
v. Arizona State Tax Com'n, 411 U.S. 164, 179–80
(1973). The state fared no better under a preemption analysis. "When on-reservation conduct involving only Indians is at issue, state law is generally
inapplicable, for the State's regulatory interest is
likely to be minimal and the federal interest in

encouraging tribal self-government is at its strongest." White Mountain Apache Tribe v. Bracker, 448 U.S. 136, 144 (1980). It is not surprising, then, that state traffic safety laws and motor vehicle safety responsibility laws have been held inapplicable to Indians in Indian country, even though the Indians may be using state highways there. United States v. Harvey, 701 F.2d 800, 805 (9th Cir.1983); Wauneka v. Campbell, 22 Ariz.App. 287, 526 P.2d 1085 (1974). State hazardous waste regulations are similarly inapplicable to Indians in Indian country. Washington v. United States EPA, 752 F.2d 1465, 1467–68 (9th Cir.1985).

The usual absence of state power to regulate tribal members in Indian country is clearly emphasized in Bryan v. Itasca County, 426 U.S. 373 (1976). There the Supreme Court held that even when state civil jurisdiction had been extended into Indian country by Public Law 280, the state lacked power to tax property held by a tribal member there. The Court pointed to the destruction of tribal governments likely to result "if tribal governments and reservation Indians were subordinated to the full panoply of civil regulatory powers including taxation, of state and local governments." 426 U.S. at 388.

A few small cracks have begun to appear, however, in the barrier that precludes the states from regulating Indians in Indian country. One is that the states may be as free to regulate "nonmember Indians"—Indians of tribes other than that which beneficially owns the reservation—as they are to regulate non-Indians. "For most practical purposes those [nonmember] Indians stand on the same footing as non-Indians resident on the reservation." Washington v. Confederated Tribes of the Colville Indian Reservation, 447 U.S. 134, 161 (1980). In civil cases, the Supreme Court now draws its jurisdictional lines between tribal members and nonmembers, rather than between Indians and non-Indians. See Strate v. A–1 Contractors, 117 S.Ct. 1404 (1997).

The Supreme Court has acknowledged "that in exceptional circumstances a State may assert jurisdiction over the on-reservation activities of tribal members." New Mexico v. Mescalero Apache Tribe, 462 U.S. 324, 331–32 (1983). In that sense, the preemption test for state regulation is more lenient toward the states than the test for state taxation; the states are subject to a virtually *per se* rule against taxation of tribes or Indians in Indian country. California v. Cabazon Band of Mission Indians, 480 U.S. 202, 215 n. 17 (1987). It should be emphasized, however, that the occasions when states have been permitted to regulate Indians in Indian country indeed have been rare and truly exceptional. In one instance the State of Washington was allowed to regulate on-reservation fishing of salmon and steelhead trout. Puyallup Tribe, Inc. v. Department of Game, 433 U.S. 165 (1977) (*Puyallup III*). That case is more fully described in Chapter XV; it is enough to note here that the decision was one in a series that dealt with the sharing of off-reservation fishing between Indian treaty fishermen and non-

Indians. It was unexpectedly discovered late in the litigation that some of the fishing stations were actually on-reservation. Another instance in which state regulations may reach tribal members on the reservation occurs when the state taxes sales of cigarettes to non-Indians; the state may require the tribal seller to collect and remit the tax. Washington v. Confederated Tribes of the Colville Indian Reservation, 447 U.S. 134 (1980).

The other significant area in which states can regulate tribal members on the reservation is that of liquor sales. In Rice v. Rehner, 463 U.S. 713 (1983), the Supreme Court upheld a state licensing requirement as applied to a tribal Indian who sold liquor pursuant to a license from the tribe. Part of the Court's rationale was based upon 18 U.S.C.A. § 1161, which permits sales of liquor in Indian country only "in conformity both with the laws of the State * * * and with an ordinance duly adopted by the tribe * * *." The Court also engaged, however, in a most unusual preemption analysis. It held that extensive federal regulation for more than a century, with no tradition of tribal authority over liquor sales, preempted the *tribe* from any ability to exclude the operation of state law. This approach is the reverse of the usual preemption analysis. Ordinarily, a long history of federal regulation will preempt the *state* from exercising regulatory power over a tribe. Nor is this unusual preemption analysis the only surprising facet of Rice v. Rehner; the opinion even goes so far as to hold that the tribes lost their inherent power to regulate liquor as a

consequence of their domestic dependent status!
463 U.S. at 726. Despite its expansive approach,
Rice probably does not represent a significant modification of the usual rule that states may not regulate tribal members in Indian country. The long
history of federal prohibition of liquor in Indian
country almost certainly confines the *Rice* ruling to
its subject matter. See also Fort Belknap Indian
Community v. Mazurek, 43 F.3d 428 (9th Cir.1994),
cert. denied, 516 U.S. 806 (1995); Citizen Bank
Potawatomi Indian Tribe v. Oklahoma Tax
Comm'n, 975 F.2d 1459 (10th Cir.1992).

Fears that tribes would be unable to escape state
regulation of non-traditional activities were significantly allayed in California v. Cabazon Band of
Mission Indians, 480 U.S. 202 (1987). That case
involved high-stakes bingo and poker games conducted by tribes on their reservations. The state
and one of its counties sought to impose their more
restrictive regulations on the games, which catered
entirely to non-Indian players. After holding that
the state laws were regulatory, and thus not extended into California Indian country by Public Law
280, the Supreme Court held that the state laws
were preempted. Although it rejected any *per se*
rule that state law could not apply to tribal operations, the Court held that federal and tribal interests in tribal self-development and self-sufficiency
outweighed any state interest in discouraging organized crime. The Court placed heavy emphasis on
the encouragement and approval of the gambling
enterprises by federal authorities.

Two federal statutes may permit the application of state law to tribal members in narrow areas. One authorizes states to apply workers' compensation laws to all lands owned or held by the United States. 40 U.S.C. § 290. One state court has relied on this statute in applying its compensation laws to a tribal member operating a business on a reservation. Idaho ex rel. Industrial Comm'n v. Indian Country Enterprises, Inc., 130 Idaho 520, 944 P.2d 117 (1997). Another, unusual federal statute provides that the Secretary of Interior, under such rules as he may prescribe, shall permit the states to enforce sanitation and quarantine regulations and, if the tribe consents, compulsory educational laws in Indian country. 25 U.S.C.A. § 231. The Secretary has never issued regulations so permitting, and the state power has accordingly been unexercised except where the tribe has approved application of school attendance laws.

Despite these actual or potential exceptions, the opportunities for state law to apply to tribal members in Indian country are extremely limited. Accordingly, much current controversy between the states and the tribes centers on regulation of activities of non-Indians on the reservation. In these cases, preemption analysis is applied in its conventional form. The more the federal government and the tribe have taken control of an activity, the more likely is the state to be preempted.

The prime example is New Mexico v. Mescalero Apache Tribe, 462 U.S. 324 (1983), which concerned non-Indian hunting and fishing on the reservation.

The tribe, in conjunction with the federal government, had undertaken substantial development of game and fish resources, to provide a source of tribal income from non-Indian hunters and fishermen. The state had not contributed to game and fish development on the reservation, so its stake was correspondingly low. The Supreme Court held that the state was preempted from applying its regulations to the non-Indian hunting and fishing. The loss of state license revenues was insufficient to overcome the interests in tribal self-development, which would be impaired by the state's strict bag and creel limits. Game and fish regulation, which is more fully discussed in Chapter XV, is perhaps especially likely to be preemptive because dual regulation is impracticable; the more restrictive regulation necessarily governs. Nevertheless, *Mescalero*'s weighing and balancing process is typical of that which will govern other cases involving a clash of state and tribal regulation of non-Indians.

State regulation of nonmembers in Indian country is least likely to be preempted when the activity takes place on, or involves, fee lands owned by nonmembers. In Montana v. United States, 450 U.S. 544 (1981), the Supreme Court held that a tribe could not regulate hunting and fishing by non-Indians on non-Indian-owned fee land. The tribe lacked inherent sovereign power to regulate non-Indian activities on fee land unless the non-Indian had entered a consensual relationship with the tribe or the activity threatened or had a direct effect on the political integrity, economic security, health or welfare of the tribe. To the extent that the tribe is excluded, state regulation is in little danger of being preempted. The same principle applies to state highway rights-of-way as to fee lands. See Strate v. A–1 Contractors, 117 S.Ct. 1404 (1997). It also applies to land condemned for a dam and reservoir project that remained within the reservation but had been broadly opened to the public. South Dakota v. Bourland, 508 U.S. 679 (1993).

With regard to zoning of nonmember fee lands within a reservation, the Supreme Court reached an unusual compromise in Brendale v. Confederated Tribes and Bands of the Yakima Indian Nation, 492 U.S. 408 (1989). The compromise resulted from a split vote of the Justices and the lack of a majority position. The state was permitted to zone fee lands within an "open" part of the reservation, which had largely passed into nonmember ownership, and the tribe was permitted to zone the smaller proportion of fee lands within the "closed" part of the reservation that retained its primarily tribal flavor. The distinction between "open" and "closed" portions of Indian country had not previously been accorded jurisdictional significance.

G. TRIBAL REGULATION

The power of the tribes to regulate parallels their power to tax, both in its general scope and in the fact that it has been sparingly exercised (except for application of ordinary criminal laws to Indians). Like tribal taxation, tribal regulation is certain to increase with the growing economic development of the reservations. The tribe clearly has power to regulate tribal members in Indian country, and may even regulate them outside of Indian country when important tribal interests are at stake. Thus a tribe may regulate off-reservation treaty fishing by its members. Settler v. Lameer, 507 F.2d 231 (9th Cir.1974). The Navajo Tribe was held to have authority to order its members to remove structures they had erected on Hopi lands, in a case arising out of the Hopi–Navajo partition. Sidney v. Zah, 718 F.2d 1453 (9th Cir.1983).

Tribes also have substantial power to regulate nonmembers engaged in activity in Indian country that affects Indian interests. See Washington v. Confederated Tribes of the Colville Indian Reservation, 447 U.S. 134, 152 (1980). For example, a tribe has been permitted to regulate on-reservation repossession of motor vehicles by off-reservation dealers. Babbitt Ford, Inc. v. Navajo Indian Tribe, 710 F.2d 587 (9th Cir.1983). Recently, however, the Supreme Court has held that tribes in most cases lack regulatory power over nonmembers' activities on non-Indian owned fee lands. In Montana v. United States, 450 U.S. 544 (1981), the Court held that a tribe could not regulate hunting and fishing by non-Indians on non-Indian-owned fee land. The tribe lacked inherent sovereign power to regulate non-Indian activities on fee land with but two exceptions noted. "A tribe may regulate, through taxation, licensing, or other means, the activities of nonmembers who enter consensual relationships with the tribe or its members, through commercial dealings, contracts, leases, or other arrangements." Id. at 565. And a tribe may retain power to regulate conduct that "threatens or has some direct effect on the political integrity, the economic security, or the health or welfare of the tribe." Id. at 566. For purposes of applying *Montana*, state highway rights-of-way are equivalent to non-Indian-owned fee lands. Strate v. A–1 Contractors, 117 S.Ct. 1404 (1997). So is land condemned for a dam and reservoir project that remained within the reservation but had been broadly opened to the public. South Dakota v. Bourland, 508 U.S. 679 (1993).

Montana's first exception for consensual activity undoubtedly permits regulation of many major non-Indian industries in Indian country; they are almost certain to be engaged in consensual activity with the tribe or its members. Thus a tribe was held to have power to regulate a bingo enterprise because its non-Indian operator had entered a joint venture with a tribal member. United States ex rel. Morongo Band of Mission Indians v. Rose, 34 F.3d 901 (9th Cir.1994). There are many more modest activities of nonmembers, however, that may not be consensual. *Montana*'s second exception could be interpreted to permit tribal regulation of all activity significantly affecting tribal interests, but that exception was given a narrow interpretation in Strate v. A–1 Contractors, 117 S.Ct. 1404 (1997). *Strate* stated that the exception must be read with *Montana*'s description of inherent tribal powers in mind: the power to determine membership, to regulate domestic relations among members, and to prescribe rules of inheritance for members. That is an exceptionally limited description of tribal self-government, however; the area that the tribe is entitled to protect almost certainly must encompass other functions. Tribal health and safety regulations come to mind. See Cardin v. De La Cruz, 671 F.2d 363 (9th Cir.1982). There is no doubt, however, that the Supreme Court currently interprets tribal self-government narrowly for purposes of the second *Montana* exception. The Eighth Circuit also did so, before *Strate*, in upholding a finding that non-Indian hunting did not have a "direct effect on the political integrity, the economic security, or the health or welfare of the Tribe as a whole," even though non-Indians may have harassed cattle grazing on tribal lands, failed to close pasture gates or let down wires on fences, and had taken deer that reduced the numbers available to tribal members. South Dakota v. Bourland, 39 F.3d 868 (8th Cir. 1994).

Even after *Montana*, tribes were able to enforce zoning regulations against non-Indian fee owners within a reservation. Knight v. Shoshone and Arapahoe Indian Tribes, 670 F.2d 900 (10th Cir.1982). The Supreme Court subsequently addressed the zoning issue, however, in Brendale v. Confederated Tribes and Bands of the Yakima Indian Nation, 492 U.S. 408 (1989), and reached a mixed result, because of the Court's lack of a majority position. The state was permitted to zone fee lands within an "open" part of the reservation, which had largely passed into nonmember ownership, and the tribe was permitted to zone the smaller proportion of fee lands within the "closed" part of the reservation that retained its primarily tribal flavor.

Even after *Brendale* and *Strate*, however, tribes retain considerable power to regulate non-Indians on fee lands with regard to water pollution. In 1987, Congress amended the Clean Water Act to permit the Environmental Protection Agency to treat tribes as states for purposes of establishing water quality standards. The Agency approves tribal standards only after a determination that the potential impact of regulated activities on the health and welfare of the tribe is serious and substantial. Under this system, a tribe's regulation of non-Indians on fee land was upheld as falling within *Montana*'s second exception. Montana v. U.S. Environmental Protection Agency, 137 F.3d 1135 (9th Cir.1998); see also City of Albuquerque v. Browner, 97 F.3d 415 (10th Cir.1996), cert. denied, 118 S.Ct. 410 (1997).

Tribes have power to regulate, concurrently with the states, non-Indian liquor sales by reason of a federal statute, § 18 U.S.C. 1161. United States v. Mazurie, 419 U.S. 544 (1975); Rice v. Rehner, 463 U.S. 713, 730–31 (1983). This authority is more expansive than the inherent regulatory authority limited in Montana v. United States, 450 U.S. 544 (1981), because it extends without qualification to non-Indian liquor transactions on non-Indian-owned fee lands within the reservation. City of Timber Lake v. Cheyenne River Sioux Tribe, 10

F.3d 554 (8th Cir.1993), cert. denied, 512 U.S. 1236 (1994).

One limitation upon tribal regulation of non-Indians is a practical one; tribal courts have no criminal jurisdiction over non-Indians. Oliphant v. Suquamish Indian Tribe, 435 U.S. 191 (1978). This fact apparently deprives the tribes of one of the most common methods of enforcing regulatory measures. As a result, tribes are attempting to enforce their regulatory ordinances by the use of civil recoveries or, when nonmember fee lands or rights-of-way are not involved, by the power of exclusion.

An ultimate limitation of tribal power to regulate either Indians or non-Indians is federal preemption; Congress clearly has the power to oust the jurisdiction of the tribe or to condition its exercise, as it has done in the Indian Civil Rights Act of 1968 (see Chapter XI).

CHAPTER X

INDIAN GAMING

A. INTRODUCTION

Indian gaming is a startling economic phenomenon. In the space of a few years, it has become the largest single revenue-producing activity for the Indian tribes. That is not to say that every tribe is able to share in the economic benefits; a great many tribes are not geographically situated to conduct a profitable gaming operation. Other tribes have declined to engage in gaming for moral or traditional reasons. For those who are engaged in large commercial gaming operations, however, the returns have been enormous. Those tribes are quite aware that this favorable economic condition could change. Indian gaming might reach a saturation point. Competition from non-Indian gaming could increase as pressure builds on the states to authorize more statewide gaming. For at least the near future, however, those tribes with substantial gaming operations are understandably inclined to view gaming as the first tribal economic program that has really worked.

The present system of regulation of Indian gaming grew out of the division of jurisdiction among

the federal government, the states, and the tribes
that has been described in Chapters VII–IX, but
from those fundamental materials Congress fashioned a structure that is unique. The governing
federal statute, the Indian Gaming Regulatory Act
of 1988, 25 U.S.C.A. §§ 2701–2721, occupies the
field of Indian gaming regulation, but also provides
for the application of state law to a significant
degree. The Act requires compacts between the
tribes and states to govern the scope and conduct of
Indian casino-type gaming, and those compacts may
further allocate jurisdiction between tribe and state.
The Act requires states that meet certain criteria to
bargain in good faith to arrive at such compacts. In
order to enforce that duty, the Act authorized tribes
to bring an action in federal court against states
that failed to comply. That key provision for the
enforcement of the duty to bargain was struck
down, however, by the Supreme Court in Seminole
Tribe of Florida v. Florida, 517 U.S. 44 (1996).
Seminole held that Congress lacked the power under the Indian Commerce Clause to abrogate the
states' Eleventh Amendment immunity from suit in
federal court. Thus the complex scheme devised by
Congress became substantially skewed. To understand where the law of Indian gaming now stands,
it is necessary first to review its initial status, and
then to examine the changes wrought by the Regulatory Act and, finally, to gauge the impact of *Seminole* on the Act's operation.

B. CALIFORNIA v. CABAZON BAND OF MISSION INDIANS

During the late 1970's and early 1980's, a number of tribes began operating commercial bingo or poker games on their reservations, in a manner that did not conform to state law. In most cases, such operations required the enactment of a tribal authorizing ordinance which, under the tribal constitution adopted pursuant to the Indian Reorganization Act, required the approval of the Secretary of the Interior. The Secretary approved several such ordinances. States in which these operations took place attempted to enforce their laws regulating or prohibiting the tribal bingo or card operations. Such an attempt by California and one of its counties reached the Supreme Court in California v. Cabazon Band of Mission Indians, 480 U.S. 202 (1987).

California was (and is) a Public Law 280 state, with the consequence that its criminal laws had been extended to Indians in Indian country, but its regulatory and legislative authority had not. See Chapter VIII, Section D. The primary issue in *Cabazon Band*, therefore, was whether California's law prohibiting bingo games unless they were conducted by charitable organizations and limited pots to $250, and the county's ordinance prohibiting poker games, were "criminal/prohibitory" or "civil/regulatory" in nature. The Supreme Court described the distinction made by the court of appeals as follows:

[I]f the intent of a state law is generally to prohibit certain conduct, it falls within Pub. L.

280's grant of criminal jurisdiction, but if the state law generally permits the conduct at issue, subject to regulation, it must be classified as civil/regulatory and Pub. L. 280 does not authorize its enforcement on an Indian reservation. The shorthand test is whether the conduct at issue violates the State's public policy.

480 U.S. at 209. Although the Supreme Court deemed it a close question, it agreed with the court of appeals that the state laws were civil/regulatory. California's public policy did not forbid gambling: the state operated its own lottery, authorized pari-mutual betting on horse races, and permitted many organizations to conduct bingo and card games. The county, too, permitted municipalities to authorize card games otherwise prohibited by the county ordinance. The fact that California's regulations were enforced by misdemeanor penalties did not change their nature. "[T]hat an otherwise regulatory law is enforceable by criminal as well as civil means does not convert it into a criminal law within the meaning of Pub. L. 280." 480 U.S. at 211.

Having concluded that the law was regulatory and therefore not made applicable to Indian country by Public Law 280, the Supreme Court in *Cabazon Band* then determined whether the case presented the "exceptional circumstances" permitting a state to regulate Indians in Indian country absent congressional authorization. The Court took account of the strong federal support for Indian gaming operations, in the form of the Secretary's approval of tribal ordinances, approval of gaming management contracts under 25 U.S.C. § 81, and the granting of various federal development loans. The Court rejected the state's argument that the tribes were marketing a tax exemption as they did in the case of cigarette sales. The tribes did not simply resell a product; they built facilities and provided services to their patrons. The only significant state interest, that of preventing organized crime from infiltrating gaming, was not real or substantial enough to overcome the strong federal interest in the promotion of tribal economic activity in the form of gaming.

Finally, the Supreme Court held that California could not invoke the federal Organized Crime Control Act, which prohibited operation of gambling businesses in violation of state law. Because that Act was federal, the state could not enforce it. Federal authorities had not applied the Act to Indian bingo operations. 480 U.S. at 213–14.

After this decision in *Cabazon Band*, tribal bingo and card operations grew apace. Some of the tribes undertook to branch out into other forms of gaming. In states that were not subject to Public Law 280, the tribes believed themselves to be in a particularly strong position; even if state law were deemed to be criminal/prohibitory, it could not be applied against the tribe or its members. On the other hand, the states were not without their weapons. State criminal law presumably could be applied against the nonmember customers, so long as gambling was viewed as a victimless crime. See State ex rel. Poll v. Montana Ninth Judicial Dist. Ct., 257 Mont. 512, 851 P.2d 405 (Mont. 1993). Immunity from state law would do the tribes little good if the states stood ready to arrest their customers. Also lurking in the background were the federal Organized Crime Control Act, 18 U.S.C. § 1955, which prohibits gambling operations in violation of state law, see United States v. Farris, 624 F.2d 890 (9th Cir.1980), cert. denied, 449 U.S. 1111 (1981), and the Johnson Act, 15 U.S.C. §§ 1171–1178, which prohibits gambling machines within Indian country. See Citizen Band Potawatomi Indian Tribe v. Green, 995 F.2d 179 (10th Cir.1993).

Even prior to the decision in *Cabazon Band*, Congress had responded to pressures arising primarily from the states and had considered several federal Indian gaming bills. After *Cabazon Band*, the impetus toward federal legislation increased. The ultimate result was the enactment of the Indian Gaming Regulatory Act of 1988. Although that Act built upon some of the reasoning of *Cabazon Band*, it also provided novel responses to the competing regulatory claims of the federal government, the states, and the tribes.

C. THE INDIAN GAMING REGULATORY ACT OF 1988

The Indian Gaming Regulatory Act (IGRA), 25 U.S.C.A. §§ 2701–2721, 18 U.S.C.A. § 1166, divides Indian gaming into three classes, with different regulatory results for each class. Class I gaming consists of social games for prizes of minimal value or traditional forms of Indian gaming connected with tribal ceremonies or celebrations. § 2703(6). Class I gaming is within the exclusive jurisdiction of the tribes and is not regulated by the Act. § 2710(a). Class I gaming is not of legal or economic significance.

Class II gaming consists first of bingo, "whether or not electronic, computer, or other technologic aids are used in connection therewith," including "pull tabs, lotto, punch boards, tip jars, instant bingo, and other games similar to bingo." "Lotto" in that application means a board game played with counters, similar to bingo, and not a lottery operation like that conducted by several states under the name of "Lotto." Oneida Tribe of Indians v. Wisconsin, 951 F.2d 757 (7th Cir.1991). The Commission's view that keno is not "similar to bingo" has been upheld. Shakopee Mdewakanton Sioux Community v. Hope, 16 F.3d 261 (8th Cir.1994). Also included in Class II are card games either explicitly authorized by state law, or not prohibited by state law and played anywhere within the state, but only if the card games are played in conformity with state regulations regarding hours of play and limits on wagers or pot sizes. Explicitly excluded from Class II gaming are banked card games, such as baccarat, chemin de fer, and blackjack, as well as "electronic or electromechanical facsimiles of any game of chance or slot machines of any kind." § 2703(7). (Card games already in operation in Michigan, the Dakotas, and Washington were grandfathered, but only for the existing "nature and scope" of those games. § 2703(7)(C); see United States v. Sisseton–Wahpeton Sioux Tribe, 897 F.2d 358 (8th Cir.1990)). Class II gaming is within the jurisdiction of the tribes, but is subject to other restrictions of the Act. Notably, a tribe may engage in Class II gaming "within a State that permits such gaming for any purpose by any person, organization or entity * * * " but it must be authorized by a tribal ordinance. This restriction is reflective of the rationale in *Cabazon Band*; if a state permits bingo or unbanked card games for any purpose, its public policy cannot be offended by this type of gambling.

Class II gaming is subject to regulation and oversight by a National Indian Gaming Commission of three members, established by the Act. §§ 2704–2708. Tribal gaming ordinances for both Class II and III gaming are subject to approval by the Commission Chairman, according to certain criteria set by the Act. The Commission also has certain duties of inspection and oversight of Class II gaming, unless it has granted the tribe a certificate of self-regulation. The Act specifies the purposes for which Class II gaming revenues may be used, and requires approval of the Secretary for any plan to distribute per capita payments to tribal members. § 2710(b)(3). The latter requirement apparently is made applicable to Class III revenues by § 2710(d)(1)(A)(ii) and (2)(A). Ross v. Flandreau Santee Sioux Tribe, 809 F.Supp. 738, 741 n. 2 (D.S.D.1992).

290 INDIAN GAMING Ch. 10

Class III gaming is defined as "all forms of gaming that are not class I gaming or class II gaming." § 2703(8). In practice, Class III includes the staples of the typical casino, such as slot machines, craps, roulette, and banked card games such as blackjack. In order to conduct Class III gaming, a tribe must first meet the two requirements for Class II gaming-that it has an approved authorizing ordinance, and is "located in a State that permits such gaming for any purpose by any person, organization, or entity." It then must meet the additional requirement that its Class III gaming be "conducted in accordance with a Tribal–State compact entered into by the Indian tribe and the State * * * * that is in effect." § 2710(d)(1). A compact takes effect when notice of its approval by the Secretary is published in the Federal Register. § 2710(d)(3)(B). The Act specifies that the Johnson Act, forbidding the use or possession of gambling devices in Indian country, does not apply to gaming under a compact that is in effect in a state in which gambling devices are legal. § 2710(d)(6). Signing of a compact does not avoid the effect of the Johnson Act if the state otherwise prohibits gambling devices entirely. Citizen Band of Potawatomi Indian Tribe v. Green, 995 F.2d 179 (10th Cir.1993).

The Act provides that compacts may include provisions relating to "the application of the criminal and civil laws and regulations of the Indian tribe or the State" concerning the gaming activity, "the allocation of criminal and civil jurisdiction between the State and the Indian tribe" necessary to enforce such laws and regulations, remedies for breach of contract, and other matters concerning the gaming operation. § 2710(d)(3)(B). There is accordingly an unprecedented degree of freedom on the part of the parties to allocate jurisdiction over Class III gaming under the umbrella of the federal Act.

The Act provides that, upon request of a tribe, a state shall negotiate in good faith with the tribe to enter such a compact. § 2710(d)(3). If the state fails to bargain in good faith, the tribe has a cause of action in federal court. (This latter provision is the one rendered largely ineffectual by the decision in *Seminole Tribe*, discussed in Section D, below). If the court finds that the state failed to bargain in good faith, it can order the state and tribe to conclude a compact within 60 days. § 2710(d)(6)(B)(iii). If the parties do not reach agreement within 60 days, they submit their last best offers to a court-appointed mediator, who chooses one of the two proposed compacts. If the state does not consent to that proposal, it is submitted to the Secretary, who then issues regulations consistent with the selected proposal for the conduct of Class III gaming on the reservation in question. Once a compact is entered, the tribe cannot immediately enforce bargaining to revise a term that it finds unsatisfactory. Wisconsin Winnebago Nation v. Thompson, 22 F.3d 719 (7th Cir.1994). Although no provision of the Act expressly grants a cause of action to enforce a compact, such a claim has been held to arise under the Act and therefore may be brought in federal court under federal question jurisdiction. Cabazon Band of Mission Indians v. Wilson, 124 F.3d 1050 (9th Cir.1997).

Finally, the Act forbids gaming on lands away from the tribe's reservation and acquired by the Secretary for the tribe after 1988. § 2719. There are exceptions to this prohibition for new reservations of newly recognized tribes or restored lands of restored tribes, and for lands acquired in settlement of land claims. There is a further exception: the Secretary, after consultation with appropriate tribal, state and local officials, may approve such gaming on newly-acquired lands if he or she determines that it would be in the best interest of the tribe and its members, and would not be detrimental to the surrounding community, but only if the governor of the state concurs. This provision has been the subject of a rather celebrated claim that improper political influence led to the denial of the request of three small Wisconsin tribes to come within the exception. See Sokaogon Chippewa Community (Mole Lake Band of Lake Superior Chippewa) v. Babbitt, 961 F.Supp. 1276 (W.D.Wis.1997). The Act's provision for a "governor's veto" with regard to this exception has been upheld against claims by a tribe that such interference with the Secretary's power was unconstitutional as a violation of the Appointments Clause or of the principle of separation of powers. Confederated Tribes of Siletz Indians v. United States, 110 F.3d 688 (9th Cir.), cert. denied, 118 S.Ct. 625 (1997). Approval of the Secretary for gaming on newly acquired lands is required under § 2719 even if the tribe and state have entered an approved compact governing Class III gaming there. Keweenaw Bay Indian Community v. United States, 136 F.3d 469 (6th Cir.1998).

Much of the contention over Class III gaming has centered on the tribal-state compact process. Major difficulties have ensued because the governors of some states entered such compacts and were later held to have lacked authority under state law to contract. Several compacts in New Mexico were held invalid for that reason, despite Secretarial approval, in Pueblo of Santa Ana v. Kelly, 104 F.3d 1546 (10th Cir.), cert. denied, 118 S.Ct. 45 (1997). Although the contracts had been "entered into," they were signed by the state governor without authority and therefore were not "in effect" as required by § 2710(d)(1)(C) for legalized Class III gaming. See also Narragansett Indian Tribe v. State, 667 A.2d 280 (R.I.1995); cf. Kickapoo Tribe of Indians v. Babbitt, 43 F.3d 1491 (D.C. Cir. 1995).

Another controversial issue concerns the requirement that Class II and Class III gaming be located in a state that "permits such gaming" by anyone. § 2710(b)(1)(A), (d)(1)(B). This requirement means that if a state chooses, as Utah has, to allow no gambling at all for any purpose anywhere within the state, then the tribes in that state may not conduct either Class II or Class III gaming. Almost no other states are that pure, however; most permit some form of gambling by some persons. The issue then arises whether the state's permission of some gambling that falls within Class II or Class III satisfies the entire condition for *all* kinds of tribal gambling within that class. Answers have varied. In Sycuan Band of Mission Indians v. Roache, 54 F.3d 535, 539 (9th Cir.1994), cert. denied, 516 U.S. 912 (1995), the Ninth Circuit, relying on the rationale of *Cabazon Band*, asserted that, if California permits any type of Class II gaming, the tribe may conduct Class II gaming. The Second Circuit made a similar ruling with regard to Class III gaming: if the state permits some types of Class III gaming, it has a duty to negotiate with a tribe a Class III compact that is not limited to the games the state otherwise permits. Mashantucket Pequot Tribe v. Connecticut, 913 F.2d 1024 (2d Cir.1990), cert. denied, 499 U.S. 975 (1991); see also Lac du Flambeau Band of Lake Superior Chippewa Indians v. Wisconsin, 770 F.Supp. 480 (W.D.Wis.1991), app. dism., 957 F.2d 515 (7th Cir.), cert. denied, 506 U.S. 829 (1992). Otherwise, the state could impose unilaterally its full system of regulation, by negotiating only for games it permits. The Eighth and Ninth Circuits, however, have ruled that the state has no duty to negotiate with the tribe over particular types of Class III games that state law prohibits. Cheyenne River Sioux Tribe v. South Dakota, 3 F.3d 273 (8th Cir.1993); Rumsey Indian Rancheria of Wintun Indians v. Wilson, 64 F.3d 1250 (9th Cir.1994), amended, 99 F.3d 321 (1996), cert. denied, 117 S.Ct. 2508 (1997). The state must actually prohibit the game, however; if it permits and regulates it, then the state must bargain even if the form of the game the tribe seeks to operate would not fall within the state's permissive regulation. *Rumsey*, 64 F.3d at

1259 n.5; cf. United States v. Sisseton–Wahpeton Sioux Tribe, 897 F.2d 358 (8th Cir.1990). Nothing prevents a state from changing its public policy to prohibit a particular type of gaming, thereby eliminating its duty to negotiate. Coeur d'Alene Tribe v. State, 842 F.Supp. 1268 (D.Idaho 1994), aff'd, 51 F.3d 876 (9th Cir.), cert. denied, 516 U.S. 916 (1995).

There has been a considerable amount of litigation over whether particular games fall within Class II or Class III. One source of ambiguity is the provision allowing as a Class II game bingo including punch boards, pull-tabs and certain other games "whether or not electronic, computer, or other technologic aids are used in connection therewith." It is to be contrasted with the exclusion from Class II of any "electronic or electromechanical facsimiles of any game of chance or slot machines of any kind." § 2703(7). An issue arose whether a game of pull-tab, played in a coin machine with a computer program limiting choices to the specified number of chances on the pre-determined board, was simply a pull-tab or punchboard game using a permissible electronic or computer "aid," or was an "electronic facsimile" of a game of chance or "slot machine" excluded from Class II. The District of Columbia and Ninth Circuits held that the games were Class III facsimiles of games of chance. Cabazon Band of Mission Indians v. National Indian Gaming Comm'n, 14 F.3d 633 (D.C.Cir.), cert. denied, 512 U.S. 1221 (1994); Sycuan Band of Mission Indians v. Roache, 54 F.3d 535 (9th Cir.1994), cert. denied,

516 U.S. 912 (1995); see also 25 C.F.R. § 502.7. A video "Pick 6" lotto game met the same fate in Spokane Indian Tribe v. United States, 972 F.2d 1090 (9th Cir.1992).

The Act provides that nothing in the section governing Class III gaming shall be interpreted to permit a state or any of its subdivisions to impose "any tax, fee, charge, or other assessment upon any Indian tribe or upon any other person or entity authorized by an Indian tribe to engage in a class III activity." § 2710(d)(4). No state may refuse to negotiate because of inability to tax. Id. In addition, a demand by a state for direct taxation of a tribe or Indian land is evidence of the state's refusal to bargain in good faith. § 2710(d)(7)(B)(iii)(II). Although these provisions do not directly *prohibit* the state from taxing Indian gaming, the Act has been held to preempt California from collecting a business license tax on the portion of off-track wagers placed in tribal gaming facilities on-reservation. Cabazon Band of Mission Indians v. Wilson, 37 F.3d 430 (9th Cir.1994). Although the tax fell on the non-Indian racing association, it clearly burdened the Bands and was inconsistent with the Act's goal of promoting the tribes' economic welfare. Id.; cf. Indian Country, U.S.A. v. Oklahoma Tax Comm'n, 829 F.2d 967 (10th Cir.1987), cert. denied, 487 U.S. 1218 (1988).

A central feature of the Act is its unique criminal jurisdictional provision, 18 U.S.C.A. § 1166. That section extends all state laws pertaining to gambling, including but not limited to criminal provisions, into Indian country. "State laws" include state decisional law authorizing injunctive relief against illegal gaming enterprises. United States v. Santee Sioux Tribe, 135 F.3d 558 (8th Cir.1998). The statute excepts from the definition of "gambling" any Class I gaming, any Class II gaming regulated by the Commission, and any Class III gaming under a compact approved by the Secretary that is in effect. Finally, § 1166 provides that the United States has exclusive jurisdiction to enforce those state gambling laws extended to Indian country unless the tribe, by compact, consents to the state's exercise of that jurisdiction.

The fact that the federal government's criminal jurisdiction is exclusive in the absence of a compact providing otherwise has been of great practical importance in certain instances. In some states where there has been a standoff between tribe and state, either because compacts are invalid for lack of the governor's authority to enter them, or because the state has determined that it has no duty to negotiate the kind of games the tribes seek to operate, the state has not prevailed automatically or instantaneously. Although § 1166 extends state gambling laws to Class III gambling in the absence of a compact, the state cannot prosecute because the right to prosecute is exclusively federal. Sycuan Band of Mission Indians v. Roache, 54 F.3d 535 (9th Cir.1994), cert. denied, 516 U.S. 912 (1995). Numbers of tribes have continued to operate Class III games for substantial periods of time without a compact, because federal authorities have been reluctant to shut the operations down. See, e.g., Cabazon Band of Mission Indians v. Wilson, 124 F.3d 1050 (9th Cir.1997). That tolerant attitude has not prevailed at all times and places, however. Operation of casinos in Indian country without a compact has resulted in convictions under the Organized Crime Control Act, 18 U.S.C. § 1955, which prohibits operation of a gambling business in violation of state law, and the Johnson Act, 18 U.S.C. § 1175, which prohibits use of a gambling device in Indian country. United States v. E.C. Investments, Inc., 77 F.3d 327 (9th Cir.1996); United States v. Cook, 922 F.2d 1026 (2d Cir.), cert. denied, 500 U.S. 941 (1991).

The Regulatory Act authorizes the Chairman of the Gaming Commission to issue orders of temporary closure of gaming activities for substantial violations of the Act, and the Commission may make such orders permanent. 25 U.S.C. §§ 2705(a)(1), 2713(b)(1), 2706(a)(5). The Eighth Circuit held that a closure order against a tribe conducting Class III gaming without a compact may be enforced by injunction in federal court, in an action brought by a United States Attorney under the Justice Department's general authority to represent the Government, 28 U.S.C.A. § 516. United States v. Santee Sioux Tribe, 135 F.3d 558 (8th Cir.1998). The court also held that an injunction was a proper remedy under Nebraska decisional law, imported into the Regulatory Act by 18 U.S.C.A. § 1166(a). Id. A district court in California has held that the United States may maintain a suit for injunction of non-compact gaming without a Commission order, but has required a showing that the state bargained in good faith. United States v. Santa Ynez Band of Chumash Mission Indians, 983 F.Supp. 1317 (C.D.Cal.1997). In the absence of such a showing, the Ninth Circuit has held that a temporary injunction against Class III gaming is improper. United States v. Spokane Tribe, ___ F.3d ___, 1998 WL 136213 (9th Cir.1998).

The Regulatory Act provides a cause of action for a tribe or state to enjoin Class III gaming carried on in violation of any tribal-state compact. § 2710(d)(7)(A). This provision waives tribal sovereign immunity for such suits. See Mescalero Apache Tribe v. State of N.M., 131 F.3d 1379 (10th Cir. 1997). This provision does not, however, give a state a right to enjoin gaming conducted *without* a compact; such a construction would improperly extend all of state regulatory enforcement into Indian country. See Cabazon Band of Mission Indians v. Wilson, 124 F.3d 1050, 1059–60 (9th Cir.1997). Thus, when a compact permits only simulcast horse race gaming, and says nothing of slot machines or other Class III gaming, the state cannot obtain an injunction against slot machines under § 2710(d)(7)(A) on the theory that the Class III gaming is "in violation" of a compact. Id. Section 2710(d)(7)(A) also has the effect of preempting the jurisdiction of a tribal gaming commission to determine whether a particular form of gaming violates the compact; the state is not required to exhaust that tribal remedy and is not bound by the tribal commission's ruling that slot machines were permitted by a compact. Crow Tribe of Indians v. Racicot, 87 F.3d 1039 (9th Cir.1996).

When private parties seek to sue a tribe or its officials for violation of the Regulatory Act, the results are mixed. Some lower courts have permitted suit by individuals challenging a distribution of per capita payments for failure to comply with the Act's requirement of secretarial approval. Those courts have held that the tribe, by engaging in gaming under the Act, waived its immunity for suits seeking only injunctive or declaratory relief requiring compliance with the Act. They also have held that the plaintiffs had standing, and assumed or decided that the Act provides a private right of action to persons claiming improper distribution. See Ross v. Flandreau Santee Sioux Tribe, 809 F.Supp. 738 (D.S.D.1992); Maxam v. Lower Sioux Indian Community of Minnesota, 829 F.Supp. 277 (D.Minn.1993); but see Davids v. Coyhis, 869 F.Supp. 1401 (E.D.Wis.1994); Montgomery v. Flandreau Santee Sioux Tribe, 905 F.Supp. 740 (D.S.D. 1995). On the other hand, when a challenge to distribution was actually a challenge to a tribe's decisions regarding membership, the tribal court had exclusive jurisdiction. Smith v. Babbitt, 100 F.3d 556 (8th Cir.1996), cert. denied, 118 S.Ct. 46 (1997). One group of tribal members, however, was able to challenge in federal court under the Administrative Procedure Act the approval of a tribal adoption ordinance by the Interior Board of Indian Appeals; the ordinance diluted the members' right to gaming proceeds. Feezor v. Babbitt, 953 F.Supp. 1 (D.D.C.1996).

Others seeking to sue on an implied right of action for violations of the Regulatory Act have had little success. A management contractor has been held to have no private right of action under the Act to compel the tribe to license the contractor's employees. Tamiami Partners, Ltd. v. Miccosukee Tribe of Indians of Florida, 63 F.3d 1030, 1049 (11th Cir.1995). A tribal member who opposed gaming has also been held to have no standing to challenge a gaming compact properly entered between a tribe and the state. Willis v. Fordice, 850 F.Supp. 523 (S.D.Miss.1994), aff'd, 55 F.3d 633 (5th Cir.1995). One gambler was successful in raising violation of a gaming compact as a matter of defense; the compact prohibited credit gambling, so the gambler's debt was held illegal and void. CBA Credit Services v. Azar, 551 N.W.2d 787 (N.D.1996).

The Regulatory Act provides for Commission approval of gaming management contracts, which are defined to include all collateral contracts relating to gaming. § 2711(a)(3). Management contracts previously had been held to require Secretarial approval as contracts "in consideration of services for said Indians relative to their lands" under 25 U.S.C. § 81, see United States ex rel. Morongo Band of Mission Indians v. Rose, 34 F.3d 901 (9th Cir.1994), but other related agreements such as slot machine leases did not require such approval. United States ex rel. Mosay v. Buffalo Bros. Mgt., Inc., 20 F.3d 739 (7th Cir.), cert. denied, 513 U.S. 866 (1994).

The Commission did not begin to function for several years after passage of the Act; contracts entered during the interim continued to be governed by 15 U.S.C. § 81, not by the Regulatory Act. Id. The Commission's review of such contracts is limited to ensuring that they comply with the provisions of IGRA; it does not extend to the question whether the tribal chairman had authority to contract-a matter for the tribal court to decide in the first instance. Bruce H. Lien Co. v. Three Affiliated Tribes of the Fort Berthold Reservation, 93 F.3d 1412 (8th Cir.1996). The tribe may waive its sovereign immunity in such contracts, as by an arbitration clause. Calvello v. Yankton Sioux Tribe, 899 F.Supp. 431 (D.S.D.1995). A management contractor has been required, however, to exhaust tribal court remedies governing the capacity of the tribal signatories to enter a valid arbitration agreement, before compelling arbitration pursuant to the agreement. Bruce H. Lien Co. v. Three Affiliated Tribes, 93 F.3d 1412 (8th Cir.1996); see also Basil Cook Enterpr. v. St. Regis Mohawk Tribe, 117 F.3d 61 (2d Cir.1997).

The Regulatory Act is sufficiently pervasive that it occupies the field of regulation of Indian gaming. There is accordingly no room for the Assimilative Crimes Act to be applied to an Indian gaming operation. United Keetoowah Band of Cherokee Indians v. Oklahoma, 927 F.2d 1170 (10th Cir.1991). The Regulatory Act preempts the field of licensing of Indian gaming to the degree that a complaint raising issues concerning denial of a tribal gaming license may be removed to federal court; if the claim is properly pleaded, it raises a federal question. Gaming Corp. of America v. Dorsey & Whitney, 88 F.3d 536 (8th Cir.1996). Although the Act occupies the field everywhere it applies, it has been held not to apply to Maine Indian lands governed by the Maine Indian Claims Settlement Act, Passamaquoddy Tribe v. Maine, 75 F.3d 784 (1st Cir.1996), or the Ysleta Del Sur Pueblo in Texas, which is governed by a special restoration act. Ysleta del Sur Pueblo v. Texas, 36 F.3d 1325 (5th Cir.1994). The Catawba Tribe Restoration Act similarly exempts the Catawbas of South Carolina from the Regulatory Act. 25 U.S.C.A. § 941*l*. The Regulatory Act does, however, override pro tanto provisions of the Rhode Island Indian Claims Settlement Act giving the state criminal and civil jurisdiction over settlement lands. Rhode Island v. Narragansett Indian Tribe, 19 F.3d 685, 704–05 (1st Cir.), cert. denied, 513 U.S. 919 (1994).

It was against the background of this entire pervasive and operating scheme of regulation under the Act that the Supreme Court decided *Seminole Tribe*. That case had a profound effect on the Act's operation, the full extent of which is yet to be felt.

D. SEMINOLE TRIBE OF FLORIDA v. FLORIDA

The provision of the Indian Gaming Regulatory Act that was at issue in *Seminole Tribe*, 517 U.S. 44 (1996), was § 2710(d)(7), which authorized a tribe to bring an action in federal court against a state that refused to bargain in good faith for a state-tribal gaming compact. The Supreme Court had earlier held that the Eleventh Amendment immunity of states from unconsented suit in federal court extended to actions brought by tribal sovereigns. Blatchford v. Native Village of Noatak, 501 U.S. 775 (1991). In § 2710(d)(7) of the Regulatory Act, however, Congress had clearly indicated its intention to waive the states' Eleventh Amendment immunity, and Congress had been held to have that power under the Interstate Commerce Clause in Pennsylvania v. Union Gas Co., 491 U.S. 1 (1989). In a decision having ramifications far beyond the field of Indian law, the Supreme Court in *Seminole* held 5–4 that Congress lacked the power under the Indian Commerce Clause to abrogate the states' Eleventh Amendment immunity from unconsented suit in federal court.

The Court in *Seminole* rejected Florida's contention that Congress's power to abrogate state immunity was narrower under the Indian Commerce Clause than it was under the Interstate Commerce Clause. Indeed, the constitutional grant of power to the federal government was greater under the Indian Commerce Clause, because the states there yielded *all* authority over Indian affairs, while they retained some jurisdiction over commerce under the Interstate Commerce Clause. 517 U.S. at 60. But Congress lacked the power, the Court held, to abrogate state Eleventh Amendment immunity under *either* the Indian or the Interstate Commerce

Clause. *Union Gas* was overruled. The Eleventh
Amendment restricted the judicial power granted to
the federal courts under Article III of the Constitution. Congress could not enlarge that restricted
judicial power by statute enacted pursuant to the
Commerce Clauses. The provision of the Indian
Gaming Regulatory Act that authorized tribes to
sue unconsenting states for failure to bargain in
good faith was therefore unconstitutional.

The Court in *Seminole* then addressed the argument that, even if the state could not be sued, a suit
for injunctive relief could be maintained against the
governor or other state officials, under the doctrine
of Ex Parte Young, 209 U.S. 123 (1908). *Young*
employs the fiction that a state officer acting in
violation of federal law does not really act for the
state, and therefore can be enjoined. The Supreme
Court in *Seminole*, however, held that it would be
inappropriate to assume that Congress intended to
permit the *Young* alternative, because it had set out
a complex set of remedial procedures in the Regulatory Act that included no such option. The Court
pointed out that it was not holding that Congress
was without power to authorize a *Young* remedy; it
was merely holding that Congress had not so intended in the Regulatory Act. 517 U.S.at 75 n.17.
(The Court in a later case again resisted easy invo-
cation of the *Young* remedy. Idaho v. Coeur d'Alene
Tribe, 117 S.Ct. 2028 (1997)). One court of appeals,
however, has permitted suit under *Young* when the
plaintiff seeks prospective relief against a continuing violation of federal law. Mille Lacs Band of

Chippewa Indians v. Minnesota, 124 F.3d 904, 913–
14 (8th Cir.1997).

Seminole presents debatable issues far beyond
Indian law; the extensive dissents argued that the
Eleventh Amendment should not be read to bar
suits against a state by its citizens when the claim
arises under federal question jurisdiction. For present purposes, however, it is enough to emphasize
that *Seminole* opened a gaping hole in the system
established by Congress in the Regulatory Act. The
Act gave the states regulatory authority that they
otherwise did not have; state law relating to gambling was extended into Indian country. The compensation for the tribes was that they could force
the states to bargain for a compact permitting Class
III gaming. After *Seminole*, the tribes could force
the states no longer. Although some states might
continue to bargain, and one or two might even
waive their Eleventh Amendment immunity, many
states are likely simply to hold the line and refuse
to bargain. The fact that a state may have bargained in the past does not waive its Eleventh
Amendment immunity. Ponca Tribe of Oklahoma v.
Oklahoma, 89 F.3d 690, 691 n. 2 (10th Cir.1996).
Without compacts, there can be no legal Class III
gaming under IGRA.

The question for the tribes, then, is whether
there is any other viable route to the approval of
new gaming operations. One circuit court has
strongly suggested that, at least when the state fails
to bargain in good faith and asserts its Eleventh
Amendment immunity, IGRA's ban of Class III

gaming without a compact is not severable from the state-suit provision struck down in *Seminole*. United States v. Spokane Tribe, 139 F.3d 1297 (9th Cir.1998). It held that a tribe could not be preliminarily enjoined from Class III gaming if it had bargained in good faith for a compact. Another alternative, mentioned by the Supreme Court in *Seminole* without an expression of opinion as to its validity, is that which had been adopted by the Eleventh Circuit in the decision the Supreme Court reviewed in *Seminole*. The Eleventh Circuit relied on the Regulatory Act's severability clause, and held that the remaining procedures regarding compacts continued in force. Seminole Tribe of Florida v. Florida, 11 F.3d 1016, 1029 (11th Cir.1994). Under that alternative, a tribe may proceed as follows:

> One hundred and eighty days after the tribe first requests negotiations with the state, the tribe may file suit in district court. If the state pleads an Eleventh Amendment defense, the suit is dismissed, and the tribe, pursuant to 25 U.S.C. § 2710(d)(7)(B)(vii), then may notify the Secretary of the Interior of the tribe's failure to negotiate a compact with the state. The Secretary then may prescribe regulations governing class III gaming on the tribe's lands.

Id. at 1029.

This alternative would be the most efficient from the standpoint of the tribes, but there is some pulling and hauling between Congress and the Secretary of the Interior over the desirability of this solution. In the Department of the Interior Appropriations Act for fiscal 1998, Congress provided that the Secretary may not expend any funds during that fiscal year "to review or approve any initial Tribal–State compact for class III gaming entered into on or after the date of enactment of this Act. This provision shall not apply to any Tribal–State compact which has been approved by a State in accordance with State law and the Indian Gaming Regulatory Act." Pub. L. 105–83, 111 Stat. 1543, 1569 (1997). The Appropriations Act further provides that no compact shall become effective for failure of the Secretary to act upon it, subject to the same exception for compacts negotiated in accordance with state law and the Regulatory Act. Finally, the Appropriations Act includes an expression of the sense of the Senate that the Department of Justice should vigorously enforce provisions of the Regulatory Act requiring a compact for Class III gaming.

Although these provisions are curiously worded, they seem intended to impose a temporary moratorium on the Secretary's approval of Class III gaming in states that have not agreed upon a compact. The operative language, however, prohibits the use of funds to "approve a compact," while the Regulatory Act states that the Secretary shall "prescribe . . . procedures" for Class III gaming when the state has refused to enter a mediated compact. § 2710(d)(7)(B)(vii).

In any event, the Secretary has proposed regulations to effectuate the plan described by the Eleventh Circuit in *Seminole*. 63 Fed. Reg. 3289 (1998). The procedure takes effect after a state obtains a dismissal in federal court by claiming its Eleventh Amendment immunity. At that point, the tribe could submit a gaming plan to the Secretary, along with the tribe's position concerning whether the state failed to bargain in good faith. The state will then be invited to comment and submit a counter-proposal. If the Secretary determines that the state has not bargained in good faith, the Secretary will accept the tribe's plan if it complies with the Act and the state has not objected and offered counter-proposals. If the state has objected and offered counter-proposals, they will be accepted unless the tribe objects to them. If the tribe objects, the Secretary will send the matter to a mediator with the two "last best offers." The mediator then will select the one that best comports with the Regulatory Act and submit it to the Secretary, who may approve it or, if it is disapproved for failure to comport with the purposes of the Act, prescribe procedures that do so comport.

With regard to the scope of gaming, the Secretary takes the position that a state need not bargain over particular Class III games that the state completely prohibits for all purposes, but "games" apparently contemplates a category: "if a State prohibits an entire class of traditional games, it need not negotiate over the particular games within that category." 63 Fed. Reg. at 3293. The Secretary recognizes that problems are bound to arise concerning the proper breadth of a category, but specific rulings must await tribal requests. Id.

It is not clear whether the Supreme Court would agree that these substitute procedures are authorized by the Act. The Ninth Circuit expressed its doubts before *Seminole* in Spokane Tribe of Indians v. Washington, 28 F.3d 991, 997 (9th Cir.1994), vacated, 517 U.S. 1129 (1996), but now seems more favorably disposed. United States v. Spokane Tribe, ___ F.3d ___, 1998 WL 136213 (9th Cir.1998). If the Secretary's proposed rules are permitted by the Act, they doubtless provide the best refuge for the tribes if Congress does not prevent them from taking effect. Congress is also considering proposed amendments to the Regulatory Act that would give the Commission power to regulate Class III gaming, but it is uncertain whether and in what form these amendments may be enacted.

Another alternative that would be permissible under the Supreme Court's ruling in *Seminole* is for Congress expressly to authorize tribal suits against governors or other appropriate officials under the doctrine of *Ex Parte Young*. If that were done, the Regulatory Act could be enforced essentially as written. Again, however, there is no assurance that Congress is inclined to follow that path.

Yet another approach that is being attempted is for the tribes to induce the United States to sue recalcitrant states on their behalf, to enforce the duty to bargain in good faith. The Eleventh Amendment immunity of the states does not extend to actions brought by the United States on behalf of a tribe. See Arizona v. California, 460 U.S. 605, 614 (1983). One district court has entered summary judgment declaring the United States to have a duty to bring such a claim for several California tribes. Chemehuevi Indian Tribe v. Wilson, 987 F.Supp. 804 (N.D.Cal.1997). The court based its decision in part on 25 U.S.C.A. § 175, which directs the United States Attorney in districts where there are reservations to represent the tribes "in all suits at law and in equity." That provision, however, has been held not to eliminate the discretion of the United States concerning when to bring an action, although a majority of the court so holding indicated that the result might be different in more compelling circumstances. Shoshone–Bannock Tribes v. Reno, 56 F.3d 1476 (D.C.Cir.1995). Whether the United States will recognize the duty imposed by *Chemehuevi* remains to be seen.

The Eleventh Amendment does not prevent tribes from suing the states in state court, of course. IGRA grants jurisdiction to the federal courts to enforce the duty to bargain, but it does not state that federal jurisdiction is exclusive. The detailed scheme of the Act suggests that Congress had in mind only federal enforcement, however, and many of the provisions might not transfer easily to state court. The degree to which states have waived their sovereign immunity to suit in state court may also vary; it would be a different question from that addressed in *Seminole* whether IGRA overcame such immunity. The most important reason that the tribes will not quickly resort to the state courts, however, is that they do not view those courts as likely instruments for compelling state governments to comply with a federally-imposed duty to negotiate with the tribes.

One Arizona tribe may have succeeded in an innovative state-law approach to the problem posed by *Seminole*. The state governor refused to negotiate after having entered sixteen compacts with other tribes. The tribe proposed, and the voters adopted, an initiative requiring the governor to enter the "standard form" compact enjoyed by the other tribes if negotiations failed. The state supreme court held the initiative to be enforceable against the governor, and to be consistent with IGRA. Salt River Pima–Maricopa Indian Community v. Hull, 190 Ariz. 97, 945 P.2d 818 (1997).

While all of these battles are being fought, Class III gaming goes on, a great portion of it under more than 150 approved compacts and a not-insignificant further portion with no compacts at all and with a presently unrealized potential of federal prosecution. Additional tribes are seeking compacts but cannot precipitate bargaining. Eventually even the approved compacts will expire and the question of renegotiation will arise. Any of the states that resist renegotiation will place those gaming operations in doubt. The states for their part are uncertain of the degree to which they can insist on enforcement of their public policies. Whatever the ultimate outcome of the attempts to respond to the *Seminole* decision, no one argues that the present condition of uncertainty is satisfactory.

CHAPTER XI

INDIVIDUAL RIGHTS AND INDIAN LAW

A. RIGHTS OF INDIANS

1. INDIANS AND THE FEDERAL GOVERNMENT

In their relation to the federal government, Indians are entitled to the same constitutional rights as anyone else. The protections of the Bill of Rights extend to "persons," and nothing about their status removes Indians from that category. They are similarly entitled to invoke the protections of the various federal civil rights acts that have been passed to help effectuate constitutional guarantees.

There is, of course, one major constitutional distinction in the manner in which the federal government deals with Indians. Congress and the courts have created an entire body of law dealing with Indians as such. This treatment has led to challenges on the ground that legislation differentiating Indians from others violated the equal protection principles of the Fifth Amendment. These challenges have been uniformly rejected by the Supreme Court. In Morton v. Mancari, 417 U.S. 535 (1974), the Court upheld a statutory "Indian preference" in hiring by the Bureau of Indian Affairs. The Court relied upon the statute's purpose in aiding Indian self-government, and rejected the claim of unconstitutional discrimination in the following manner:

> Literally every piece of legislation dealing with Indian tribes and reservations, and certainly all legislation dealing with the BIA, single out for special treatment a constituency of tribal Indians living on or near reservations. If these laws, derived from historical relationships and explicitly designed to help only Indians, were deemed invidious racial discrimination, an entire Title of the United States Code [25 U.S.C.A.] would be effectively erased and the solemn commitment of the Government toward the Indians would be jeopardized. * * *

> * * *

> Contrary to the characterization made by appellees, this preference does not constitute "racial discrimination." Indeed, it is not even a "racial" preference. * * *

In a footnote, the Court added:

> The preference is not directed towards a "racial" group consisting of "Indians"; instead, it applies only to members of "federally recognized" tribes. This operates to exclude many individuals who are racially to be classified as "Indians." In this sense, the preference is political rather than racial in nature. * * *

417 U.S. at 552–53 & n. 24.

Equal protection claims have also arisen from the fact that the division of criminal and civil jurisdiction in Indian country often depends upon Indian status of the parties. These claims, too, have been unsuccessful. The most notable example is United States v. Antelope, 430 U.S. 641 (1977). In that case Indian defendants had killed a non-Indian while committing a felony in Indian country. They were prosecuted for first degree murder under federal law, which in those circumstances required no proof of premeditation. Had they been non-Indians, they would have been prosecuted under state law, which required proof of premeditation. The Supreme Court held that this disparity did not violate equal protection because the division of criminal jurisdiction by Indian status was an outgrowth of the entire legal structure dealing with Indians. Relying on *Mancari*, supra, the Court noted that "respondents were not subjected to federal criminal jurisdiction because they are of the Indian race but because they are enrolled members of the Coeur d'Alene Tribe." 430 U.S. at 646. The classification was therefore not racial. Moreover, the federal criminal law treated equally all those who were subject to it. See also Fisher v. District Court, 424 U.S. 382, 390–91 (1976).

As both *Mancari* and *Antelope* indicate, separate classification of Indians is permissible even when the classification is not tied to tribal self-government. The employment preference in *Mancari*, for example, was not limited to Indians who were members of the tribes being served by the BIA office in question. See also Johnson v. Shalala, 35 F.3d 402 (9th Cir.1994). Similarly, the federal government has been allowed to favor Indian and Alaska Native firms in awarding construction contracts, even though self-government was not involved and the preferences were not limited to members of the tribes for whom the projects were being constructed. Alaska Chapter, Associated General Contractors v. Pierce, 694 F.2d 1162 (9th Cir.1982). It was sufficient that the classification was rationally related to Congress' trust responsibility toward the Indians generally. Id. at 1166–1170. The same analysis would support the Indian preference exception to the employment discrimination provisions of the Civil Rights Act of 1964 (Title VII), 42 U.S.C.A. § 2000e–2(i). One court of appeals has suggested, however, that the *Mancari* principle shields from equal protection attack only those statutes that affect uniquely Indian interests. Williams v. Babbitt, 115 F.3d 657 (9th Cir.1997), cert. denied, 1998 WL 54253 (1998).

Enforcement of the right of free exercise of religion often takes a distinctive turn when Indians are involved. Many Indian religious beliefs and practices center on particular places or objects. The places may be on federal lands outside of any reservation. The objects may be eagle feathers or peyote. In these cases, federal management or regulation may interfere substantially with religious uses. In recognition of this problem, Congress in 1978 passed an unusual statute called the "American Indian Religious Freedom Act." It provides that it shall be the policy of the United States to protect and preserve for American Indians their inherent right of freedom to believe, express, and exercise the traditional religions of the American Indian, Eskimo, Aleut, and Native Hawaiians, including but not limited to access to sites, use and possession of sacred objects, and the freedom to worship through ceremonials and traditional rites.

42 U.S.C.A. § 1996. An Executive Order directs agencies administering federal lands to accommodate access to and ceremonial use of Indian religious sites to the extent practicable and not inconsistent with essential agency functions. Exec. Order No. 13007, 61 Fed. Reg. 26771 (1996). While the Act states the sense of Congress, it confers no judicially enforceable private right of action. Lyng v. Northwest Indian Cemetery Protective Ass'n, 485 U.S. 439, 455 (1988). Indians who seek to block federal (or state) action on religious grounds accordingly must usually prove a violation of the First Amendment Free Exercise Clause. Such controversies, when they come to court, are not truly Indian Law cases, even though they have a distinct Indian flavor. Their resolution depends upon general principles of First Amendment free exercise of religion, and not upon Indian status.

Several controversies have involved attempts by government to develop its public lands in a manner that adversely affects Indian religious practices. Initially, the lower courts resolved such controversies by balancing the governmental interest in developing the particular project against the burden it placed on Indian religion. The balancing nearly always came out in favor of the government. The courts rejected, for example, Indian attempts to prevent the government from inundating sacred places upstream from federal dams. Badoni v. Higginson, 638 F.2d 172 (10th Cir.1980), cert. denied, 452 U.S. 954 (1981); Sequoyah v. TVA, 620 F.2d 1159 (6th Cir.1980), cert. denied, 449 U.S. 953 (1980). They also rejected attempts to prevent expansion of a ski area on a sacred mountain in a national forest, Wilson v. Block, 708 F.2d 735 (D.C.Cir.1983), cert. denied, 464 U.S. 1056 (1984), and the establishment of a state park in sacred ground, Crow v. Gullet, 706 F.2d 856 (8th Cir. 1983), cert. denied, 464 U.S. 977 (1983).

In Lyng v. Northwest Indian Cemetery Protective Ass'n, 485 U.S. 439 (1988), the Supreme Court went even further. It held that, so long as the government did not coerce individuals into violating their religious beliefs or penalize their religious activity by denying them rights or benefits available to others, the government was free to develop its own property without regard to its interference with religious practices. Balancing was not appropriate. At issue was a proposal to improve a road and conduct logging operations in a region of national forest sacred to Yurok, Karok and Tolowa Indians. In rejecting the Indians' challenge, the Court stated:

> Even if we assume [that the road] will "virtually destroy the Indians' ability to practice their

religion" * * *, the Constitution simply does not provide a principle that could justify upholding respondents' legal claims. However much we might wish that it were otherwise, government simply could not operate if it were required to satisfy every citizen's religious needs and desires.

Id. at 1326–1327. This ruling presumably puts an end to free exercise challenges to governmental development projects. For example, *Lyng* was applied to defeat a free exercise challenge to the Forest Service's approval of a uranium mine near the Grand Canyon. See Havasupai Tribe v. United States, 752 F.Supp. 1471, 1484–86 (D.Ariz.1990), aff'd, 943 F.2d 32 (9th Cir.1991), cert. denied, 503 U.S. 959 (1992).

A somewhat different free exercise question is presented when an Indian claims that governmental action interferes with individual religious practices. Such claims are now greatly affected by the Supreme Court's decision in Employment Division v. Smith, 494 U.S. 872 (1990), discussed below. In the past, they led to a balancing of governmental and individual religious interests that produced mixed results. A right of Indian males to wear long hair for religious reasons was upheld against a prison regulation, Teterud v. Burns, 522 F.2d 357 (8th Cir.1975), but rejected in favor of a school dress code, New Rider v. Board of Education, 480 F.2d 693 (10th Cir.1973), cert. denied, 414 U.S. 1097 (1973). A free exercise claim of Indian prisoners of the right to wear headbands in a prison dining hall was defeated in Standing Deer v. Carlson, 831 F.2d

1525 (9th Cir.1987). The court held that, in the prison setting, it was sufficient that the regulation prohibiting headgear was logically connected to penological concerns of cleanliness, security and safety.

Some statutes and regulations incorporate exceptions to accommodate Indian religious interests in varying degrees. The federal Bald and Golden Eagle Protection Act, which prohibits the taking of eagles or the possession of eagle parts, authorizes exceptions "for the religious purposes of Indian tribes." 16 U.S.C.A. § 668a. Although a permit is required under the exception, that fact does not render the Act facially unconstitutional. United States v. Hugs, 109 F.3d 1375 (9th Cir.1997). Use of peyote by members of the Native American Church during church ceremonies has frequently been protected from the reach of criminal drug laws. E.g., 21 C.F.R. § 1307.31 (1987); People v. Woody, 61 Cal.2d 716, 40 Cal.Rptr. 69, 394 P.2d 813 (1964); State v. Whittingham, 19 Ariz.App. 27, 504 P.2d 950 (1973), cert. denied, 417 U.S. 946 (1974); see Peyote Way Church of God, Inc. v. Smith, 742 F.2d 193 (5th Cir.1984).

In Employment Division v. Smith, 494 U.S. 872 (1990), the Supreme Court was presented with the question whether such exceptions to peyote laws were required by the Free Exercise Clause. The case was brought by drug and alcohol abuse counselors who had been discharged for religious use of peyote and had been denied unemployment compensation. After ascertaining that the religious use of peyote was prohibited by Oregon's criminal laws, the Supreme Court held against the discharged workers. The Court ruled that, if the object of a generally applicable law is not to prohibit or burden religion, its incidental effect upon religion cannot give rise to a free exercise claim. The individual is not excused from compliance with such a law by reason of his or her religious beliefs. Id. at 878–79. Again, no balancing of interests was appropriate.

Congress reacted to *Smith* by enacting the Religious Freedom Restoration Act, 42 U.S.C.A. § 2000bb et seq. The Act prohibited government from substantially burdening a person's exercise of religion unless it can show that the burden furthers a compelling governmental interest and is the least restrictive means of furthering that interest. § 2000bb–1. The Supreme Court held the Restoration Act unconstitutional, however, ruling that Congress lacked the power to expand the constitutional right of free exercise by statute. City of Boerne v. Flores, 117 S.Ct. 2157 (1997). Although *Flores* involved application of the Act to a state's local subdivision, the Supreme Court's opinion left little doubt that the Act was generally invalid. *Smith* therefore remains controlling law.

For some years, Indian tribes have complained of the disturbance of Indian graves, and of the removal of remains and cultural artifacts from tribal control. Congress responded to these concerns by enacting the Native American Graves Protection and Repatriation Act of 1990, 25 U.S.C.A. § 3001–3013, 18 U.S.C.A. § 1170. The Act first establishes the ownership of cultural items excavated or discovered on federal or tribal land after November 16, 1990. Native American remains and associated funerary objects belong, first, to lineal descendants. If they cannot be identified, then those remains and objects, along with unassociated funerary objects, sacred objects, and objects of cultural patrimony, belong, in order of preference, to the tribe on whose land the remains or objects were found, or the tribe having the closest cultural relationship to them, or to the tribe that aboriginally occupied the area unless another tribe can show a stronger cultural relationship. § 3002. The act then requires each federal agency and every museum or institution receiving federal funds and holding such items to prepare an inventory of Indian remains and associated funerary objects, and a summary of unassociated funerary objects, sacred objects, and objects of cultural patrimony. §§ 3003, 3004. The Act then provides for repatriation of these items upon request of the appropriate descendant or tribe. § 3005. The repatriation provision, unlike the ownership provision, applies to remains or objects discovered at any time, even before the effective date of the Act, whether or not discovered on tribal or federal land. Pueblo of San Ildefonso v. Ridlon, 103 F.3d 936 (10th Cir.1996). The Act also establishes a Review Committee to oversee the inventory and repatriation process. § 3006.

A criminal provision of the Act prohibits trafficking in Native American human remains, or in Native American "cultural items." 18 U.S.C.A. § 1170.

Cultural items are defined elsewhere in the Act to include "cultural patrimony," which means "an object having ongoing historical, traditional, or cultural importance central to the Native American group or culture itself, rather than property owned by an individual Native American, and which, therefore, cannot be alienated * * * by any individual regardless of whether or not the individual is a member of the Indian tribe * * *." 25 U.S.C.A. § 3001(3)(D). This provision has been held not to be unconstitutionally vague as applied to trafficking in Navajo Yei B'Chei, imperfectly translated as ceremonial masks. United States v. Corrow, 119 F.3d 796 (10th Cir.), cert. denied, 118 S.Ct. 1089 (1998).

One rather celebrated case that has arisen under the Act concerns human a human skeleton over 9000 years old, found in the State of Washington. The remains were found on land in control of the Army Corps of Engineers, which gave notice of intention to deliver the remains to a group of Columbia River tribes for burial. A number of scientists and a pre-Christian European church brought an action to halt the transfer, contending that there was a dispute whether the remains were ethnologically related to current Indian tribes or, indeed, to any Indians at all. The scientists also claimed a first amendment right to study the remains. The district court remanded the matter to the Corps of Engineers, for further development of the record. Bonnichsen v. United States Dep't of Army, 969 F.Supp. 628 (D.Or.1997). The case presents an interesting clash between the spiritual interests of the tribes and the scientific interests of the non-Indian community.

2. INDIAN CITIZENSHIP

While most constitutional rights may not be denied to any "person," the right to vote and some other benefits may be restricted to citizens. Political participation in both federal and state government therefore depends substantially on citizenship.

Congress in 1924 conferred national citizenship on all Indians born in the United States. 8 U.S.C.A. § 1401(a)(2). Before that time, individual Indians could become citizens in a number of ways. The General Allotment Act, as well as some special allotment statutes, conferred citizenship upon Indians who received allotments. General Allotment Act, ch. 119, § 6, 24 Stat. 388, 390 (1887). That Act also provided citizenship for Indians who took up residence apart from their tribes and "adopted the habits of civilized life." Id.

While the 1924 statute makes all native-born Indians United States citizens, it is the Fourteenth Amendment that makes them citizens of the states where they reside as well. The status of Indians as citizens of the United States and of the individual states does not interfere with the Indians' relationship to their tribes or with the trust relationship between the tribes and the federal government. Winton v. Amos, 255 U.S. 373 (1921); United States v. Nice, 241 U.S. 591 (1916).

3. INDIANS AND THE STATE GOVERNMENTS

The Fourteenth Amendment is the most important guarantee against infringement of civil liberties by the states. Its due process and equal protection clauses protect all "persons" and its rarely used privileges and immunities clause protects "citizens." Indians clearly qualify on both counts, but historically states have often been reluctant to accord Indians those rights enjoyed under state law by non-Indians. These attitudes still linger, but the courts have made it clear that state discrimination against Indians because of their status is without support of law.

One area in which states have attempted to discriminate is in the furnishing of state services. The states attempt to justify the discrimination on the grounds that tribal Indians do not contribute substantially to the tax revenues of the state and that they are the special responsibility of the federal government. Both of these arguments have failed. States usually do not base services to their non-Indian citizens on proof of taxpaying status, and the federal government does not undertake to supply all needs for Indians. States have accordingly been forbidden to exclude Indians from public schools, e.g. Piper v. Big Pine Sch. Dist., 193 Cal. 664, 226 P. 926 (1924), from general relief services, Acosta v. County of San Diego, 126 Cal.App.2d 455, 272 P.2d 92 (1954), or from indigents' health services, County of Blaine v. Moore, 174 Mont. 114, 568 P.2d 1216

(1977); see McNabb v. Bowen, 829 F.2d 787, 794–95 (9th Cir.1987).

Voting by Indians was resisted by the states for many years on various grounds. One was non-payment of state taxes by Indians in Indian country, even though taxpayer status was not required of non-Indian voters. Another was that as wards of the federal government, Indians were under guardianship and not legally competent to vote—an argument that misconstrues the federal wardship of the tribes and runs counter to the federal Citizenship Act of 1924. A third ground was that residence in Indian country was not residence within the state for voting purposes—also an argument that had been rejected in other contexts (particularly those dealing with state power over non-Indians in Indian country). All of these state arguments have been discredited in court, and Indians are now entitled to vote in every state. See Harrison v. Laveen, 67 Ariz. 337, 196 P.2d 456 (1948); Montoya v. Bolack, 70 N.M. 196, 372 P.2d 387 (1962).

There has also been state resistance to Indians' holding state office. The fear has been expressed that Indians who were not subject to taxation in Indian country but who were eligible for state services might choose to inaugurate expensive service programs to be paid for entirely by non-Indian taxpayers. The same incentives, however, apply to any elected officeholder who is poor and therefore does not pay state taxes. In Shirley v. Superior Court, 109 Ariz. 510, 513 P.2d 939 (1973), cert. denied, 415 U.S. 917 (1974), the Supreme Court of

Arizona rejected the non-taxation argument and held that an Indian resident in Indian country was eligible for the office of county supervisor. The court also rejected arguments that no one should hold office who was immune from service of state process at his residence; the court pointed out that the Indian could always be recalled under state election law, and had to post a fidelity bond required of all officeholders. Immunity from state process was therefore of no consequence. In office-holding as in other areas, then, the Indian has the same rights in relation to the state as the non-Indian.

4.   INDIANS AND THE TRIBES

a.   The Constitution and the Tribes

Indians stand in an entirely different constitutional posture with regard to their tribes than they do with regard to the federal or state governments. The differences arise both from the structure of the federal Constitution and the nature of the tribes.

Nearly all of the civil liberties set forth in the Constitution are stated in terms of protection against governmental action. The Bill of Rights is a list of prohibitions against the federal government. The Fourteenth Amendment provides that no "State" shall deny due process or equal protection of the laws. The Indian tribes, however, are not the federal government nor are they states or subdivisions of either. It is therefore normally not possible for any person, Indian or non-Indian, to invoke the

Bill of Rights or the Fourteenth Amendment against a tribe. For example, in Talton v. Mayes, 163 U.S. 376 (1896), the Supreme Court held that the Cherokee Nation was not bound by the grand jury requirements imposed upon the federal government by the Fifth Amendment. After pointing out that the powers of the Cherokee Nation did not spring from the federal Constitution, the Court stated:

> [T]he fact has been fully recognized, that although possessed of these attributes of local self government, when exercising their tribal functions, all such rights are subject to the supreme legislative authority of the United States. * * * But the existence of the right in Congress to regulate the manner in which the local powers of the Cherokee nation shall be exercised does not render such local powers Federal powers arising from and created by the Constitution of the United States.

163 U.S. at 384. Similarly, in Native American Church v. Navajo Tribal Council, 272 F.2d 131 (10th Cir.1959), a court of appeals held that the First Amendment Free Exercise Clause does not apply to a tribe through the Fourteenth Amendment because "Indian tribes are not states. They have a status higher than that of states." Id. at 134.

The doctrine that constitutional guarantees against governmental action did not apply to the tribes underwent some erosion in the nineteen-sixties. In Colliflower v. Garland, 342 F.2d 369 (9th

Cir.1965), the court applied the Fifth Amendment Due Process Clause to the action of the tribal court of the Fort Belknap Indian Community. Because the tribal court was imposed on the tribe by the federal government and was still subject to some federal control, the court of appeals held that an action of the tribal court was part federal and part tribal. As such, it was subject to the Fifth Amendment. See also Settler v. Yakima Tribal Court, 419 F.2d 486 (9th Cir.1969), cert. denied, 398 U.S. 903 (1970). These cases depend, of course, on the establishment of links between the particular tribal activity involved and the federal government. They therefore did not result in full-scale application of the Bill of Rights to all tribal action. Their applicability even to tribal courts was largely or entirely repudiated years later by United States v. Wheeler, 435 U.S. 313 (1978), which held that the double jeopardy provision of the Fifth Amendment was not infringed when an Indian was convicted in federal court after having been convicted of a lesser included offense in tribal court. The Supreme Court reiterated that the tribe in punishing its members was exercising its own independent sovereignty that did not derive from the federal government. The second prosecution therefore did not offend the double jeopardy clause, as it would have if the tribal prosecution had been deemed wholly or partly federal.

The freedom of the tribes from constitutional restraints against governmental action therefore remains well supported. Not all constitutional guarantees are limited to governmental action; the Thirteenth Amendment prohibition of slavery applies to all persons and entities including Indians and Indian tribes. Today, however, the most important civil liberties are those set forth in the Bill of Rights and the Fourteenth Amendment and they are by their own terms unenforceable against the tribes. In 1968, Congress found this situation unacceptable and decided to intervene by statute. The result was the Indian Civil Rights Act.

b. The Indian Civil Rights Act of 1968

The Indian Civil Rights Act of 1968, 25 U.S.C.A. § 1301 et seq., was passed by Congress in order to impose most of the provisions of the Bill of Rights upon the tribes. The principal guarantees of the Act are found in 25 U.S.C.A. § 1302 which provides:

§ 1302   Constitutional rights

No Indian tribe in exercising powers of self-government shall—

(1) make or enforce any law prohibiting the free exercise of religion, or abridging the freedom of speech, or of the press, or the right of the people peaceably to assemble and to petition for a redress of grievances;

(2) violate the right of the people to be secure in their persons, houses, papers, and effects against unreasonable search and seizures, nor issue warrants, but upon probable cause, supported by oath or affirmation, and particularly describing the place to be searched and the person or thing to be seized;

(3) subject any person for the same offense to be twice put in jeopardy;

(4) compel any person in any criminal case to be a witness against himself;

(5) take any private property for a public use without just compensation;

(6) deny to any person in a criminal proceeding the right to a speedy and public trial, to be informed of the nature and cause of the accusation, to be confronted with the witnesses against him, to have compulsory process for obtaining witnesses in his favor, and at his own expense to have the assistance of counsel for his defense;

(7) require excessive bail, impose excessive fines, inflict cruel and unusual punishments, and in no event impose for conviction of any one offense any penalty or punishment greater than imprisonment for a term of one year and a fine of $5,000, or both;

(8) deny to any person within its jurisdiction the equal protection of its laws or deprive any person of liberty or property without due process of law;

(9) pass any bill of attainder or ex post facto law; or

(10) deny to any person accused of an offense punishable by imprisonment the right, upon request, to a trial by jury of not less than six persons.

The Act thus imposes on the tribes most of the Bill of Rights verbatim. There are notable exceptions, however. Clause (1) protects the free exercise of religion, but has no provision prohibiting the establishment of religion by a tribe. This omission was in conscious recognition of the fact that in some of the tribes, especially the Pueblos, government and religion and all the rest of life are inextricably interwoven. Divorcement of religion from government would have altered those tribes beyond recognition; Congress did not wish to go that far as long as the free exercise of religion by individuals was protected. Another point at which the protection of the Act falls short of that of the Constitution is Clause (6) which provides the right of an accused to have counsel "at his own expense." The Constitution requires state and federal government to supply counsel to indigents at government expense when the prosecution may result in imprisonment. Argersinger v. Hamlin, 407 U.S. 25 (1972). Fears of saddling the tribes with an excessive financial burden and the shortage of lawyers in Indian country apparently influenced Congress. See Tom v. Sutton, 533 F.2d 1101 (9th Cir.1976). The limited right to counsel under the Act has been held not to trigger the rule of Massiah v. United States, 377 U.S. 201 (1964), which renders inadmissible a confession taken in the absence of defense counsel from a defendant who has been charged. United States v. Doherty, 126 F.3d 769 (6th Cir.1997).

From its passage the Indian Civil Rights Act has engendered controversy. Tribal governments tended to see the Act as an undue federal intrusion into tribal affairs. Some individual Indians and many non-Indians saw the Act as a valuable protection against arbitrary tribal action. The extent to which the Act intrudes upon tribal government is partially dependent upon the manner in which it is interpreted. Several courts have stated that guarantees of due process and equal protection should be applied flexibly and adapted to the tribal context. E.g., Wounded Head v. Tribal Council of Oglala Sioux Tribe, 507 F.2d 1079, 1082–83 (8th Cir.1975); Randall v. Yakima Nation Tribal Court, 841 F.2d 897, 900 (9th Cir.1988). It is accordingly not safe to assume that, in the limited circumstances in which federal courts now apply the Act, the guarantees of the Indian Civil Rights Act will be enforced in exactly the same way as their counterparts in the Constitution. On the other hand, federal courts are most familiar with due process and equal protection law generated in a non-Indian context, and there is likely to be some tendency to apply that law to the tribes without modification. One court of appeals, for example, held that the equal protection clause of the Civil Rights Act required application of the one person, one vote rule in tribal elections. White Eagle v. One Feather, 478 F.2d 1311 (8th Cir.1973). Another held that the search and seizure provisions of the Act are identical to those of the Fourth Amendment. United States v. Strong, 778 F.2d 1393, 1395 (9th Cir.1985). A third, while acknowledging that due process concepts generally must be applied with sensitivity to their tribal context, held that when tribal court procedures parallel those of Anglo–Saxon law, there was no need to weigh tribal interests. Randall v. Yakima Nation Tribal Court, 841 F.2d 897 (9th Cir.1988). Thus due process was violated when a tribal appellate court dismissed an appeal on the ground that the trial court had failed promptly to address a request for in forma pauperis status. Id.

Three additional developments have limited the degree to which the Indian Civil Rights Act acts as a federal intrusion upon tribal autonomy. The first is the widespread adoption of the rule that a party aggrieved by tribal action must first exhaust tribal remedies before invoking the aid of the federal courts (even though exhaustion is not normally required under other federal civil rights statutes). E.g., O'Neal v. Cheyenne River Sioux Tribe, 482 F.2d 1140 (8th Cir.1973); McCurdy v. Steele, 506 F.2d 653 (10th Cir.1974). The rule doubtless derives added force from the Supreme Court's strong endorsement of tribal court exhaustion in National Farmers Union Ins. Cos. v. Crow Tribe, 471 U.S. 845 (1985), even though *Crow Tribe* did not arise under the Indian Civil Rights Act. Thus one court of appeals upheld the dismissal of a confrontation clause claim in a habeas petition, because it had not been raised before the tribal court of appeals. Selam v. Warm Springs Tribal Correctional Facility, 134 F.3d 948 (9th Cir.1998). Such a result is also supported by a strong tradition of exhaustion in the federal law of habeas corpus, now the only means of federal review of tribal court action.

A second limitation upon federal intrusion into tribal autonomy arises from the reluctance of some federal courts to delve into "internal tribal matters" even though federal law might arguably permit intervention. See, e.g., Prairie Band of Pottawatomie Tribe v. Udall, 355 F.2d 364 (10th Cir.), cert. denied, 385 U.S. 831 (1966); Tewa Tesuque v. Morton, 498 F.2d 240 (10th Cir.1974), cert. denied, 420 U.S. 962 (1975). The doctrine has perhaps been most often invoked in regard to questions of eligibility for tribal membership or office. See Groundhog v. Keeler, 442 F.2d 674 (10th Cir.1971).

The third and by far the most important limitation upon federal authority under the Indian Civil Rights Act arises from the decision of the Supreme Court in Santa Clara Pueblo v. Martinez, 436 U.S. 49 (1978). That case involved a rule of the Pueblo making ineligible for membership the children born to female members married to a person outside the tribe. In contrast, children of marriages of male members to spouses outside the tribe were eligible. A female member of the Pueblo whose children were excluded by the rule brought suit against the tribe and its Governor, alleging a violation of the equal protection clause of the Indian Civil Rights Act. The Supreme Court did not reach the merits of her claim, but dismissed the suit on procedural grounds of great significance.

First, the Court held that the tribe was immune from suit as a sovereign. This ruling was counter to numerous lower court decisions that had held the Indian Civil Rights Act to be a congressional waiver of tribal sovereign immunity to the extent necessary to enforce the provisions of the Act. The fact that the tribe was held immune in *Santa Clara* did not end that particular case, because injunctive relief was being sought and the tribal Governor was still a defendant. In some instances, however, the tribe may be an indispensable party, and tribal immunity will be a complete bar to suit. In addition, the existence of tribal immunity severely restricts (and in a practical sense eliminates) the availability of damages as a remedy.

The Supreme Court in *Santa Clara* then went on to make an even more important procedural ruling. In § 1303 of the Civil Rights Act, Congress had provided:

25 U.S.C.A. § 1303. Habeas corpus

The privilege of the writ of habeas corpus shall be available to any person, in a court of the United States, to test the legality of his detention by order of an Indian tribe.

The Supreme Court in *Santa Clara* held that this section furnished the exclusive federal remedy under the Act. This ruling, too, was contrary to numerous lower federal court decisions in which remedies had been liberally implied in order to effectuate the substantive provisions of the Act. In support of its decision, the Supreme Court emphasized the desire of Congress not to intrude unnecessarily upon tribal self-government. The Court pointed out that remedies other than habeas corpus (especially in civil cases) were likely to lead to federal court interference with tribal affairs.

The effect of this ruling in *Santa Clara* was to eliminate the jurisdictional base upon which most decisional law under the Indian Civil Rights Act had rested. Because the remedy of habeas corpus is available only to test the legality of detention by a tribe, its use will necessarily be confined almost entirely to reviewing actions of the tribal courts or police in criminal cases. Violations of equal protection or takings of property without compensation, for example, are unlikely to result in detention and consequently may not be remedied in federal courts. See Crowe v. Eastern Band of Cherokee Indians, Inc., 584 F.2d 45 (4th Cir.1978). One circuit has carved out an exception to the *Santa Clara* rule and has permitted a non-Indian corporation that was denied a tribal forum to bring an Indian Civil Rights Act claim in federal court. Dry Creek Lodge, Inc. v. Arapahoe and Shoshone Tribes, 623 F.2d 682 (10th Cir.1980), cert. denied, 449 U.S. 1118 (1981). The tribal remedy must actually have been sought and refused. White v. Pueblo of San Juan, 728 F.2d 1307, 1312 (10th Cir.1984). At least one other circuit, however, has held that *Santa Clara* simply forecloses any relief other than habeas corpus in federal court under the Indian Civil Rights Act. R. J. Williams Co. v. Fort Belknap Housing Authority, 719 F.2d 979, 981 (9th Cir.1983), cert. denied, 472 U.S. 1016 (1985).

Perhaps the most interesting case to arise under the federal habeas corpus jurisdiction of the Indian

Civil Rights Act was Poodry v. Tonawanda Band of
Seneca Indians, 85 F.3d 874 (1st Cir.1996). There
certain tribal members had been informed by tribal
officials that they were guilty of attempting to over-
throw the tribal government and were therefore
banished forever from the reservation and stripped
of all rights of membership. The First Circuit held
that banishment was a severe punishment, involving a sufficient restraint on liberty to qualify as
"detention" and permit federal review by habeas
corpus under the Act, § 1303.

More commonly, however, *Santa Clara* results in
a narrow federal review confined to the typical
criminal sentence of imprisonment. The *Santa
Clara* decision has been highly controversial. It
unquestionably reduces the degree of federal interference in tribal self-government, but it also leaves
many potential violations of federal law without a
federal remedy. Enforcement of much of the Indian
Civil Rights Act is therefore left entirely to the
tribal courts. Some tribal court systems are reasonably well equipped for the task; others are not. In
either case, the effectuation of the non-criminal
portions of the Indian Civil Rights Act lies entirely
with them.

B. RIGHTS OF NON–INDIANS

Non–Indians, like Indians, cannot invoke the Bill
of Rights or the Fourteenth Amendment against
tribal action, because the tribes are neither the
federal government nor states. It is perhaps not

surprising, therefore, that the first case arising under the Indian Civil Rights Act involved an attempt by a non-Indian to invoke the protections of the Act against tribal action. Dodge v. Nakai, 298 F.Supp. 26 (D.Ariz.1969). The court there held that non-Indians were entitled to the protection of the Act, which extends most of its guarantees to "persons" affected by tribal action. 25 U.S.C.A. § 1302.

Two recent Supreme Court decisions combine, however, to reduce severely the number of occasions upon which non-Indians will be in a position to seek the protection of the Indian Civil Rights Act in federal court. The first decision is Oliphant v. Suquamish Indian Tribe, 435 U.S. 191 (1978). In that case, the Supreme Court held that under the statutory framework established by Congress, tribal courts had no criminal jurisdiction over non-Indians. See Chapter VII, Section D(2), supra. The second decision is Santa Clara Pueblo v. Martinez, 436 U.S. 49 (1978), discussed in the previous section. There the Court held that habeas corpus was the sole remedy by which enforcement of the Indian Civil Rights Act could be obtained in federal court. The result of that ruling is that federal court enforcement of the Act is confined almost entirely to review of tribal criminal matters. Since *Oliphant* prevents the tribes from exercising criminal jurisdiction over non-Indians, there will be little opportunity for non-Indians to bring Indian Civil Rights Act cases in federal court. Non–Indians seeking to enforce their rights under the non-criminal portions of the Act will have to rely, as the Indians must, upon tribal courts. If the tribe refuses to provide a forum, one circuit will permit the claim to be raised in federal court. Dry Creek Lodge, Inc. v. Arapahoe and Shoshone Tribes, 623 F.2d 682 (10th Cir.1980), cert. denied, 449 U.S. 1118 (1981); but see R. J. Williams Co. v. Fort Belknap Housing Authority, 719 F.2d 979, 981 (9th Cir.1983), both discussed in the preceding section.

Of course, when federal or state rather than tribal action is challenged by non-Indians, the Constitution and the federal courts are available to supply relief when it is due. Non–Indians have attacked federal and state governmental action on equal protection grounds when Indians were singled out for special treatment, but those attacks have not generally been successful. In Morton v. Mancari, 417 U.S. 535 (1974), the Supreme Court upheld an employment preference for Indians in the Bureau of Indian Affairs. Similar preferences had existed in federal statutes since 1834. The Court held that the preference was not invidious race discrimination, but instead was a political classification designed to encourage Indian tribal self-government and to fulfill the special federal responsibility to Indians. The statutory preference consequently did not offend the equal protection principles of the Fifth Amendment.

In Livingston v. Ewing, 601 F.2d 1110 (10th Cir.), cert. denied, 444 U.S. 870 (1979), a court of appeals upheld policies of the Museum and City of Santa Fe permitting only Indians to sell artifacts under the portal of the museum on the town square. The discrimination against non-Indians was held not to be stigmatizing, and the classification was held justified by the state interest in preserving historical and ethnological interest in fine arts. The court therefore held that the Fourteenth Amendment was not violated.

Other notable statutory provisions affect the status of non-Indians in the context of individual rights. One is Title VII of the Civil Rights Act of 1964, which outlaws employment discrimination based on race, color, religion, sex or national origin, but which has an express exception for employers who publicly discriminate in favor of Indians "living on or near a reservation." 42 U.S.C.A. § 2000e–2(i). Another is 25 U.S.C.A. § 194, which provides that in trials involving title to property where an Indian is on one side and a "white person" on the other, "the burden of proof shall rest upon the white person, whenever the Indian shall make out a presumption of title in himself from the fact of previous possession or ownership." That statute was applied by the Supreme Court in Wilson v. Omaha Indian Tribe, 442 U.S. 653 (1979), but no equal protection challenge was before the Court. The circuit court had rejected such a challenge on the strength of *Morton v. Mancari*. Omaha Indian Tribe v. Wilson, 575 F.2d 620, 631 n. 18 (8th Cir.1978). A different court of appeals has suggested, however, that *Mancari* shields from equal protection attack only those statutes affecting uniquely Indian interests; it stated that a serious equal protection problem would be presented by a governmentally-mandated monopoly of the reindeer industry by Alaska Natives. Williams v. Babbitt, 115 F.3d 657 (9th Cir.1997), cert. denied, 1998 WL 54253 (1998).

CHAPTER XII

INDIAN LANDS

A. INTRODUCTION

Indian lands may be held in a variety of ways, each of which presents its own problems and advantages. Two points must be made at the outset of any review of the subject. The first is that the term "Indian lands" refers to those lands that are held by Indians or tribes under some restriction or with some attribute peculiar to the Indian status of its legal or beneficial owners. Today any Indian can purchase real property (such as a residence in Phoenix or Chicago) in the public market and thereby acquire a fee title that is freely disposable. That real property is not "Indian land."

The second point is that the ownership pattern of Indian lands, which is the subject of this chapter, is a matter separate from the questions of what constitutes a reservation and what is meant by Indian country. The latter concepts, which are particularly important for jurisdictional purposes, are discussed in Chapter VII, Section B, under the heading "Indian Country."

The unique statutory system under which Alaska Natives hold their land is discussed, along with other Alaska Native matters, in Chapter XIII.

B. ABORIGINAL TITLE

In the first Trade and Intercourse Act, 1 Stat. 137 (1790), Congress provided that non-Indians could not acquire lands from Indians except by treaty entered pursuant to the federal Constitution. While providing a measure of protection for existing Indian landholdings, that legislation made no attempt to characterize the nature of the Indian interest in those lands. It remained for Chief Justice Marshall and the Supreme Court to define the title by which Indian tribes held land, and to determine the incidents of that title.

The Supreme Court's definition came in the case of Johnson v. McIntosh, 21 U.S. (8 Wheat.) 543 (1823). There the Court held that Indian tribes were incapable of conveying their land directly to individuals even before passage of the Trade and Intercourse Acts. In reaching its decision, the Court explored at length the legal relation between the European colonizers of America, the Indian tribes, and the land. Chief Justice Marshall concluded that discovery conferred upon the European sovereign a title good against all other European governments. The United States succeeded to that title to the extent that it was held by the British. As for the Indians:

They were admitted to be the rightful occupants of the soil, with a legal as well as just claim to retain possession of it, and to use it according to their own discretion; but their rights to complete sovereignty, as independent nations, were neces-

> sarily diminished, and their power to dispose of
> the soil at their own will, to whomsoever they
> pleased, was denied by the original fundamental
> principle, that discovery gave exclusive title to
> those who made it.

21 U.S. (8 Wheat.) at 574. The United States was
accordingly free to grant to others land held by
Indian tribes, but the grantee took title subject to
the Indian "right of occupancy." Most important
from the standpoint of the Indians, however, was
Marshall's point that the United States, and *only*
the United States, could extinguish the Indian right
of occupancy, "either by purchase or conquest." Id.
at 587.

Although Marshall softened his language somewhat in the later *Cherokee Cases*, supra Chapter II,
Section C, and shifted his emphasis from conquest
to purchase as the preferred method of extinguishment, his formulation of Indian land title in Johnson v. McIntosh has remained essentially intact.
Indian tribes that occupied and used land to the
exclusion of others (except for mere temporary in-
cursions) had an interest denoted as a "right of
occupancy." This right later came to be known as
"original Indian title" or, more frequently today, as
"aboriginal title." That title cannot be compromised
by any other party except the federal government.
Oneida Indian Nation v. County of Oneida, 414 U.S.
661 (1974). The federal government can extinguish
aboriginal title by purchase, which is the usual
method, or simply by taking it. Such a taking will
not be "lightly implied." United States v. Santa Fe

Pacific R. Co., 314 U.S. 339, 354 (1941); see County of Oneida v. Oneida Indian Nation, 470 U.S. 226, 247–48 (1985). If aboriginal title is not extinguished, a conveyance of fee to a purchaser transfers no more than a reversion that matures only when aboriginal title ends. Catawba Indian Tribe v. South Carolina, 865 F.2d 1444, 1448 (4th Cir.1989). A taking by the federal government of lands held by aboriginal title (usually referred to as an "extinguishment" of aboriginal title) does not give rise to any right of compensation under the Fifth Amendment. Tee–Hit–Ton Indians v. United States, 348 U.S. 272 (1955). In this respect aboriginal title is to be distinguished from "recognized title," discussed in Section D, below. A taking by the federal government of land held by aboriginal title may, however, provide the basis for a claim under the Indian Claims Commission Act of 1946. See Section E, below.

There have been many disputes over whether aboriginally held land has been taken. The federal intent to extinguish title must be clear, but can take various forms. Treatment of the land in a manner wholly inconsistent with continued tribal occupancy suffices. Thus, military action removing the Indians from the land, followed by inclusion of the land in a National Forest and active federal management of the land for forest purposes, was sufficient to establish a taking in United States v. Gemmill, 535 F.2d 1145 (9th Cir.1976). Ambiguous acts such as inclusion of the land in a federal grazing district may be insufficient to establish a taking, however. See

United States v. Dann, 706 F.2d 919 (9th Cir.1983), rev'd on other grounds, 470 U.S. 39 (1985). Payment by the United States of a tribe's claim for taking of land establishes that the aboriginal title has been extinguished. Western Shoshone Nat'l Council v. Molini, 951 F.2d 200 (9th Cir.1991).

Virtually all of the cases dealing with aboriginal title, from Johnson v. McIntosh onward, have viewed such title as being that of the tribe, rather than its individual members. Similarly, the Trade and Intercourse Acts have been held to protect tribal title, so that those Acts cannot be invoked by individual Indians suing on their own behalf. James v. Watt, 716 F.2d 71 (1st Cir.1983). It can easily be argued that the very concept of aboriginal title requires that the title be tribal.

In Cramer v. United States, 261 U.S. 219 (1923), however, the Supreme Court held that individual Indians may also claim a right of occupancy that predates competing claims of record title acquired by non-Indians.

Unquestionably it has been the policy of the Federal Government from the beginning to respect the Indian right of occupancy, which could only be interfered with or determined by the United States. * * * It is true that this policy has had in view the original nomadic tribal occupancy, but it is likewise true that in its essential spirit it applies to individual Indian occupancy as well. * * *

Id. at 227. The Court later characterized this right of occupancy as "individual aboriginal title," United States v. Dann, 470 U.S. 39, 50 (1985). The Ninth Circuit subsequently held that individual Indians (or their lineal ancestors) could acquire aboriginal title to land by settling on it before it was withdrawn from settlement, and could acquire aboriginal grazing rights by grazing cattle prior to withdrawal of the land from open grazing by enactment of the Taylor Grazing Act of 1934. The individual aboriginal grazing rights were limited to the numbers and type of livestock being grazed at the time of the withdrawal, however. United States v. Dann, 873 F.2d 1189 (9th Cir.), cert. denied, 493 U.S. 890 (1989). Individual aboriginal title does not arise as part of tribal aboriginal title; it must arise separately on its own. Id. Individual aboriginal title must be maintained, directly or by lineal ancestors, continuously from a time before the land was withdrawn. United States v. Kent, 945 F.2d 1441 (9th Cir.1991).

C. THE EASTERN LAND CLAIMS

In recent times, several eastern tribes have asserted land claims based on aboriginal title. In Oneida Indian Nation v. County of Oneida, 414 U.S. 661 (1974), the Oneidas brought a claim for lands ceded to the State of New York by the tribe without the consent of the federal government, in violation of the Trade and Intercourse Act of 1790, 1 Stat. 137. The lower courts held that the tribe did not assert a federal claim and dismissed for lack of jurisdiction. The Supreme Court reversed. Although the Oneidas had entered treaties with the federal government before ceding the disputed lands to the state, the Supreme Court did not rely on those treaties as having created "recognized title" in the Oneidas. Instead, the Court discussed at length the nature of aboriginal (original Indian) title and held that a tribe relying upon it clearly asserted a federal claim. Later, the Court held that the Oneidas retained a federal common law right to sue on their claim, and that the right was not barred by limitations or laches. County of Oneida v. Oneida Indian Nation, 470 U.S. 226 (1985).

Other eastern tribes brought claims based on aboriginal title that was not the subject of any federal treaty. See, e. g. Narragansett Tribe v. Southern Rhode Island Land Development Corp., 418 F.Supp. 798 (D.R.I.1976); Mashpee Tribe v. New Seabury Corp., 592 F.2d 575 (1st Cir.), cert. denied, 444 U.S. 866 (1979); Schaghticoke Tribe v. Kent Sch. Corp., 423 F.Supp. 780 (D.Conn.1976); Mohegan Tribe v. Connecticut, 483 F.Supp. 597 (D.Conn.1980), aff'd, 638 F.2d 612 (2d Cir.), cert. denied, 452 U.S. 968 (1981). The most notable example was the Passamaquoddy Tribe, which claimed large areas of Maine that had been deeded to the state (then Massachusetts) by a treaty in which the federal government did not participate and which it did not ratify. See Joint Tribal Council of Passamaquoddy Tribe v. Morton, 528 F.2d 370 (1st Cir.1975). Despite a long history of dealing with the state rather than the federal government, the tribe was held entitled to federal trust services in pursuing its claims based on aboriginal title. Id. The controversy culminated in passage of the Maine Indian Claims Settlement Act, 25 U.S.C.A. § 1721 et seq., which extinguished the Indians' aboriginal title and provided federal funds for purchase of lands for three Maine tribes. Other such claims have been similarly resolved. E.g., Rhode Island Indian Claims Settlement Act, 25 U.S.C.A. § 1701 et seq.; Florida Indian Land Claims Settlement Act, 25 U.S.C.A. § 1741 et seq.; Connecticut Indian Land Claims Settlement Act, 25 U.S.C.A. § 1751 et seq.

All of these claims are based on one of the fundamental principles of aboriginal title: tribal rights to the land may be conveyed or extinguished only by the federal government. A prima facie case for an aboriginal land claim has been held to consist of the following elements: (1) that the claimant is an Indian tribe, (2) that the land is tribal land, (3) that the United States never consented to its alienation, (4) that the trust relationship between the tribe and the United States has not been terminated or abandoned. Golden Hill Paugussett Tribe v. Weicker, 39 F.3d 51, 56 (2d Cir.1994). The last element must be regarded with caution, however. Recognition for purposes of an aboriginal claim does not invariably equate to recognition for all other purposes. Thus a tribe whose constitution had been revoked by federal action still retained the tribal existence necessary to pursue an aboriginal title claim. See Catawba Indian Tribe v. South Carolina, 718 F.2d 1291 (4th

Cir.1983), rev'd on other grounds, 476 U.S. 498 (1986). The requirement of federal approval for transfer of Indian land has been held by the Second Circuit to have arisen with the establishment of federal power under the Constitution; during the period of the Articles of Confederation states could purchase Indian land within their borders and thereby extinguish aboriginal title without the consent of the Confederal Congress. Oneida Indian Nation v. State of New York, 860 F.2d 1145 (2d Cir.1988), cert. denied, 493 U.S. 871 (1989).

Recent eastern aboriginal title claims often have involved huge tracts of land. The very size of the claims makes them tactically difficult to pursue, because the option is always open to the federal government, at least in theory, to extinguish without compensation the aboriginal title upon which the claims are based. While any such action would be a drastic method of defeating tribal claims, fear of the possibility has provided a substantial incentive for tribes to settle their claims rather than pursuing them to final judgment.

In the western states, Indian lands were customarily ceded by treaty with the United States. Land claims based on aboriginal title accordingly are rarely found there outside of the framework of the Indian Claims Commission Act. One exception was a claim asserted by a band of Western Shoshone in Nevada; the Supreme Court held that the tribal claim was defeated by the payment of funds into trust for the Tribe, in satisfaction of an award of the Claims Commission. United States v. Dann, 470 U.S. 39 (1985).

D. RECOGNIZED TITLE

Recognized title is title to Indian lands that has been recognized by federal treaty or statute. A treaty may, for example, recognize tribal title by describing a particular land area as being reserved to the tribe. That parcel may or may not have been part of the aboriginal territory of the tribe. Whether or not a treaty recognized title to particular land is a question of intent, and is sometimes the subject of great controversy. See Northwestern Bands of Shoshone Indians v. United States, 324 U.S. 335 (1945). Where a reservation is expressly set out by treaty or statute, however, there is little question that the tribe has recognized title.

The primary advantage of recognized title is its relative permanence. Recognized title is "property" within the meaning of the Fifth Amendment, so that its taking by the federal government gives rise to a right of compensation. United States v. Creek Nation, 295 U.S. 103 (1935). Moreover, legal interest may be charged against the federal government for a Fifth Amendment taking, a fact of great importance when the taking may have occurred a century before judgment. See United States v. Sioux Nation, 448 U.S. 371 (1980). Where the tribe's land title is recognized, a taking of timber or mineral rights is also compensable under the Fifth Amendment, because the tribe's interest in the land is presumed to include timber and minerals in the absence of an expression to the contrary in the governing treaty or statute. United States v. Shoshone Tribe, 304 U.S. 111 (1938).

Although most reservations in existence today were either established or confirmed by treaty or statute, there are some reservations that were created in whole or part by presidential executive orders. It has been argued by commentators that the effect of such orders is to recognize the tribe's title, so that subsequent federal taking of the land is compensable under the Fifth Amendment. Judicial authority, however, supports the contrary view that mere executive orders confer no such right, and that lands set aside by that method may be taken by the federal government without compensation. Sioux Tribe v. United States, 316 U.S. 317 (1942); Hynes v. Grimes Packing Co., 337 U.S. 86, 103 (1949). Of course, territory originally reserved by executive order may subsequently be recognized by statute so as to create a compensable property right in the occupying tribe. Since 1919 (1918 in the case of Arizona and New Mexico), reservations have been required to be created by statute and not executive order. 43 U.S.C.A. § 150; 25 U.S.C.A. § 211.

E. INDIAN CLAIMS

The fact that aboriginal title was not viewed as a compensable property right was only one of the obstacles standing in the way of tribes that sought redress for injuries suffered at the hands of the federal government. The United States could not be sued without its consent. The Court of Claims had been established to permit litigation of certain types of suits against the government but claims based on violation of Indian treaties were excluded from its jurisdiction in 1863. Act of March 3, 1863, ch. 92, § 9, 12 Stat. 765, 767. Special congressional acts were therefore commonly required before tribes could bring suit. On various occasions, Congress did pass statutes permitting suits by particular tribes, but these acts were often narrowly construed by the courts in a manner that defeated recovery. See Northwestern Bands of Shoshone Indians v. United States, 324 U.S. 335 (1945).

Dissatisfaction with the existing method of handling claims led to passage of the Indian Claims Commission Act of 1946, 25 U.S.C.A. §§ 70–70v. The Act established the Indian Claims Commission to hear suits brought by tribes, bands or other identifiable groups of Indians. Appeal was permitted to the Court of Claims and by certiorari to the Supreme Court. The Act was liberal in defining the scope of permissible claims. In addition to regular claims in law or equity (including those in tort), the Act authorized recovery for the following:

25 U.S.C.A. § 70a:

* * *

(3) claims which would result if the treaties, contracts, and agreements between the claimant and the United States were revised on the ground

of fraud, duress, unconscionable consideration, mutual or unilateral mistake, whether of law or fact, or any other ground cognizable by a court of equity;

(4) claims arising from the taking by the United States, whether as the result of a treaty of cession or otherwise, of lands owned or occupied by the claimant without the payment for such lands of compensation agreed to by the claimant; and

(5) claims based upon fair and honorable dealings that are not recognized by any existing rule of law or equity.

The Act solved a number of problems. Takings of land held by aboriginal title became compensable, as did any number of other unfair actions of the federal government, whether or not arising from a treaty. The sovereign immunity of the United States was waived. The defense of laches, which had sometimes presented an insuperable barrier to recovery, was also waived. 25 U.S.C.A. § 70a.

The intent of Congress in passing the Act had been to settle once and for all the claims arising from the government's historical dealings with the Indians. As a result, payment of an award under the Act defeats any further tribal claim of an aboriginal right to occupy the lands for which compensation was paid. United States v. Dann, 470 U.S. 39 (1985); see Navajo Tribe v. New Mexico, 809 F.2d 1455 (10th Cir.1987); Western Shoshone Nat'l Council v. Molini, 951 F.2d 200 (9th Cir.1991), cert.

denied, 506 U.S. 822 (1992). The Act empowered the Commission to hear claims accruing prior to August 13, 1946; those accruing later must be brought to the Court of Federal Claims and their permissible scope is much narrower (claims arising under federal law or executive order or otherwise cognizable if brought by non-Indians, 28 U.S.C.A. § 1505; see United States v. Mitchell, 445 U.S. 535, 538–40 (1980)). Although the ambitious purpose of Congress in passing the Indian Claims Commission Act was not entirely accomplished, large numbers of claims were adjudicated by the Commission during its life, which ended in 1978, and substantial relief was granted to many tribes and Indian groups. Nearly all of this relief was compensation for land taken or unfairly purchased from the tribes.

It should not be assumed, however, that compensation under the Act was total. One of the most serious limitations was that the usual rule was applied forbidding the award of interest against the United States except for Fifth Amendment takings. See United States v. Sioux Nation, 448 U.S. 371, 387 & n. 16 (1980). An award for land measured by nineteenth century values without interest falls many times short of restoring a tribe to the position it would have occupied had it retained the lost land. The Act also permitted the government to offset certain payments made to the claimant tribe in the past, but these deductions were sharply limited in comparison with prior practice and could only be allowed if the Commission found that the entire course of dealings between the government and the tribe warranted it. 25 U.S.C.A. § 70a.

F. INDIAN LANDHOLDING TODAY

Lands presently set aside for Indians, whether by treaty, statute or executive order, may be held in various patterns of tenure. Nearly all of the land is in trust, with the United States holding naked legal title and the Indians enjoying the beneficial interest. The beneficial ownership of the Indians usually does not include ownership of beds of navigable waters, unless Congress made very clear its intent to convey such an interest. United States v. Pend Oreille Pub. Util. Dist. No. 1, 926 F.2d 1502 (9th Cir.), cert. denied, 502 U.S. 956 (1991); Yankton Sioux Tribe v. South Dakota, 796 F.2d 241 (8th Cir.1986), cert. denied, 483 U.S. 1005 (1987). Within the typical trust arrangement of land tenure, differences exist in the nature of the beneficial holdings. In a few cases where land is held for tribes with a restraint on alienation, even the usual trust title is absent.

When a tribe purchases fee land, there is no restraint on alienability. Lummi Indian Tribe v. Whatcom County, Washington, 5 F.3d 1355 (9th Cir.1993), cert. denied, 512 U.S. 1228 (1994). The Secretary of the Interior is authorized, however, to acquire lands in trust for the benefit of Indians. 25 U.S.C. § 465; 25 C.F.R. §§ 151.10–151.12. Although this power has been exercised in many instances, the Eighth Circuit held § 465 to be an unconstitutional delegation of legislative power to the Secretary. South Dakota v. United States Dep't of Interior, 69 F.3d 878 (8th Cir.1995). That decision was vacated, 117 S.Ct. 286 (1996), and the mandate recalled, 106 F.3d 247 (8th Cir.1996), when the government retreated from its position that a decision to acquire lands in trust was unreviewable. It seems likely, therefore, that an acquisition under § 465 that is reviewable under the Administrative Procedure Act would be viewed by a majority of the Supreme Court as constitutional. The procedure was assumed to be constitutional during such judicial review in McAlpine v. United States, 112 F.3d 1429 (10th Cir.), cert. denied, 118 S.Ct. 447 (1997), but the parties there did not challenge the constitutionality of § 465.

1. COMMUNALLY HELD LAND

One method by which large tracts of reservation land is held, particularly in the Southwest, is communal tribal ownership. The United States holds the legal title, and the undivided beneficial interest is held by the tribe as a single entity. There are two major advantages to this type of ownership. The first is that the land base of the tribe is given maximum protection because of the continuity of beneficial ownership. The second is that management of the land is relatively easy when decisions over leasing and development can be made by a single owner, even though that owner must go through its own form of institutional decision-making. Changes in the use or in the distribution of benefits from use of the land do not infringe any legally protectible rights of individual tribal members. United States v. Jim, 409 U.S. 80 (1972). Although communal ownership is relatively trouble-free when it is exercised by a single tribe, joint exercise has occasionally led to large difficulties. Land communally but jointly held by both the Hopi and Navajo tribes has been the subject of dispute for decades, leading to an equally disputed partition. See, e.g., Masayesva for and on Behalf of Hopi Tribe v. Hale, 118 F.3d 1371 (9th Cir.1997), cert. denied, 118 S.Ct. 1048 (1998).

2. ASSIGNMENTS

When land is communally held by the tribe, individual members may simply share in the enjoyment of the entire property without having any claim at all to an identifiable piece of land. In practice, however, tribal members usually require some method of knowing that it is permissible for them to erect a residence on a given spot, to graze stock in a particular area, or to engage in other activities requiring a relatively fixed location. This need is customarily met by the tribe's conferring a license upon the individual to use particular land. That license may go by many names, but it is commonly referred to as an "assignment." The terms of assignments may vary greatly in duration and scope. They often expire after a term of years without any guaranteed right of renewal, and they usually are

personal to the assignee. In practice, however, there
is a pronounced tendency to renew an assignment
once given and to permit descendants to acquire the
assignment of a deceased assignee.

3. ALLOTMENTS

The allotment system of landholding is in total
contrast to communal ownership by the tribe. Under various statutes, particularly the General Allotment (Dawes) Act of 1887, 25 U.S.C.A. § 331 et
seq., Congress provided for Indian lands to be allotted to individual Indians. Tribally held lands were
consequently divided into small farm-sized tracts to
be held by individuals. The land was to remain in
trust for a certain period, usually 25 years, and then
was to become a totally alienable and taxable fee
interest in the hands of the Indian. Many allotments did pass out of trust status under this or
similar provisions, and most of that land is no
longer in Indian hands. See, e.g., Cross v. State of
Washington, 911 F.2d 341 (9th Cir.1990), cert. denied, 499 U.S. 922 (1991). In many cases, however,
trust periods were extended by statute and in 1934
the Indian Reorganization Act indefinitely extended
the trust period of all allotments still in trust. 25
U.S.C.A. § 462. The Act also provided that no further lands were to be allotted. 25 U.S.C.A. § 461.
There was, however, a great amount of Indian land
allotted and still in trust at the time of the Reorganization Act, and large numbers of allotments consequently remain today.

The legal title to existing allotments is held by the United States, with the entire beneficial interest being in the individual allottees. Decisions concerning the use or disposition of the land accordingly must be made by the allottees, with the concurrence of the United States. Indeed, the tribe has been held not to have a right of action to enforce restrictions in an Allotment Act against non-Indian purchase in excess of a certain acreage. Crow Tribe of Indians v. Campbell Farming Co., 31 F.3d 768 (9th Cir.1994), cert. denied, 514 U.S. 1018 (1995). The bare trust title of the United States does not create a duty on its part to manage the land's resources. United States v. Mitchell, 445 U.S. 535 (1980) (*Mitchell I*). Comprehensive statutes and regulations do, however, establish duties of the federal government to manage timber resources of allotted lands, and violations of those duties are compensable. United States v. Mitchell, 463 U.S. 206 (1983) (*Mitchell II*). Statutes restricting the sale of trust land without prior approval of the Secretary were held to apply to invalidate the sale of a prime skeleton of a Tyrannosaurus Rex (named "Sue") that was excavated from an individual trust allotment; the fossil in place qualified as land. Black Hills Inst. of Geologic Research v. South Dakota School of Mines and Tech., 12 F.3d 737 (8th Cir.1993), cert. denied, 513 U.S. 810 (1994). Allotments may not be condemned by local governments or utilities without the consent of the United States. United

States v. Pend Oreille County Pub. Util. Dist. No. 1, 135 F.3d 602 (9th Cir.1998).

The allotment system has led to immense practical problems. The fact that allotted tracts were usually 40 or 80 acres would in itself create problems of land management for large-scale leasing and development projects. The small size of the tracts is only a minor part of the problem, however. Allotted lands may be disposed of by a will approved by the Secretary of Interior, 25 U.S.C.A. § 373, but in most cases wills are not executed. In the absence of a will, the interest of a deceased allottee descends according to the law of intestate succession of the state where the allotment is located. 25 U.S.C.A. § 348. The result of this system of descent operating on trust land is that over a period of generations the beneficial interest of many allotments has come to be shared by as many as a hundred allottees. Productive use of the lands is then a near impossibility because the consent of all allottees is necessary for leasing. Intestacy also sometimes results in allotted land passing to non-Indians, which removes it from trust status altogether and creates "checkerboard" patterns of Indian and non-Indian land that further complicate proper land use.

To combat the problems caused by fractionated allotments, Congress passed the Indian Land Consolidation Act, 96 Stat. 2517 (1983). It provided, among other things, that an undivided interest representing less than 2% of an allotted tract and yielding less than $100 annual income, could not pass by intestacy or devise, but escheated to the tribe. The Supreme Court, however, held the provision to be an unconstitutional taking of property in violation of the Fifth Amendment. Hodel v. Irving, 481 U.S. 704 (1987). While *Irving* was pending, Congress amended the Act in 1984 to require the income of less than $100 annually to persist over five years, to permit devise and descent of fractional interests to other holders of fractional interests in the same land, and to permit the tribe to adopt alternative remedies with the approval of the Secretary. Once again, however, the Supreme Court held the Act unconstitutional. Babbitt v. Youpee, 117 S.Ct. 727 (1997). The narrow 1984 amendments did not prevent the Act from effecting a taking of property of some value without just compensation. A remedy therefore remains elusive. Other statutes that provide for forced purchase of fractional interests by or for the tribe may represent a more viable approach to the problem. See 25 U.S.C.A. §§ 607, 608; Hunger v. Andrus, 476 F.Supp. 357 (D.S.D. 1979). In the meantime, allotments continue to cause grave problems for those reservations that are partly or entirely subject to them.

4. NEW MEXICO PUEBLOS

While the New Mexico Pueblos hold their lands communally, their title is virtually unique. Most of the Pueblo lands were acquired in fee under Spanish rule. When New Mexico Territory was acquired by the United States as a result of the Mexican War, the Treaty of Guadalupe Hidalgo, 9 Stat. 922

(1848), guaranteed property rights acquired under the Spanish and Mexican governments. See Mountain States Tel. & Tel. Co. v. Pueblo of Santa Ana, 472 U.S. 237 (1985). The Pueblos accordingly own most of their lands in fee, rather than having the United States hold the legal title for them.

The practical effects of the Pueblos' distinctive form of ownership are now minimal. The Pueblos are in a trust relationship with the federal government, United States v. Sandoval, 231 U.S. 28 (1913), and their lands cannot be alienated without the consent of the United States, United States v. Candelaria, 271 U.S. 432 (1926). Water rights are reserved for Pueblo lands in the same manner as they are for other Indian lands. New Mexico v. Aamodt, 537 F.2d 1102 (10th Cir.1976), cert. denied, 429 U.S. 1121 (1977).

G.　LEASING OF INDIAN LANDS

Indian lands, whether tribally held or allotted, may be leased with the approval of the Secretary of the Interior. 25 U.S.C.A. § 415. Permissible duration varies with the nature of the lease and the location of the land, but the most common limit is 25 years. On some reservations, 99 year leases are permitted. Id. Particular leases may be affected by various statutes and regulations too numerous to set forth here. Notable among them are the Omnibus Indian Mineral Leasing Act, 25 U.S.C.A. § 396a–g; the National Environmental Policy Act (NEPA), 42 U.S.C.A. § 4321 et seq.; and portions of the Surface Mining Control and Reclamation Act of 1977, 30 U.S.C.A. § 1300(c).

Supervision of leasing is one of the most extensive reservation activities of the Bureau of Indian Affairs, and it has sometimes been a controversial one. Leases may be granted for such purposes as farming, grazing, housing and industrial developments, timber cutting, mining, and oil and gas exploration and production. Some of these uses are almost certain to cause major intrusions into the social structure of the landholding tribe. Under the Secretary's regulations and tribal leases approved by the Secretary, the lessee's interest is subject to foreclosure. See Red Mountain Machinery Co. v. Grace Investment Co., 29 F.3d 1408 (9th Cir.), cert. denied, 513 U.S. 1044 (1994). In addition, numbers of leases in the past seem to have provided abnormally low financial returns to the tribes. Allegations of such mismanagement were held to state a compensable claim for violation of the federal trust responsibility in United States v. Mitchell, 463 U.S. 206 (1983) (*Mitchell II*). On the other hand, when the Secretary denied approval of a subsidiary agreement in order to cause mineral leases to terminate, solely for the purpose of permitting Indian lessors to negotiate more favorable lease terms, the Tenth Circuit held the Secretary's action to be an abuse of discretion. Woods Petroleum Corp. v. Department of Interior, 47 F.3d 1032 (10th Cir.), cert. denied, 516 U.S. 808 (1995). In view of the conflicting interests represented in leasing of Indian lands, leasing decisions are almost certain to be a continuing subject of dispute.

CHAPTER XIII

ALASKA NATIVES

A. INTRODUCTION

Federal policy toward Alaska Natives (Indians, Eskimos and Aleuts), evolved under very different conditions from those prevailing in what are now the lower forty-eight states, with distinctive legal consequences. The Treaty of Cession by which the United States purchased Alaska from Russia in 1867 provided that the inhabitants who chose to remain, "with the exception of uncivilized native tribes," would be entitled to the rights of citizens. "The uncivilized tribes will be subject to such laws and regulations as the United States may, from time to time, adopt in regard to aboriginal tribes of that country." 15 Stat. 539, 542. Despite this opening, there was very little federal attention paid to the Alaska Natives for many decades thereafter. The Alaska Organic Act of 1884 similarly looked to future legislation: "[T]he Indians or other persons in said district shall not be disturbed in the possession of any lands actually in their use or occupation or now claimed by them but the terms under which such persons may acquire title to such lands is reserved for future legislation by Congress." 23 Stat. 24, 26. That future legislation, too, was slow

367

in coming, although some statutes were enacted
that contained similar provisos protecting Native
possession.

Totally absent from Alaska were many of the
events that shaped Indian law to the south during
the eighteenth century. There was no federal policing of jurisdictional lines between the federal government, the tribes, and the local governments.
There was consequently little judicial attention paid
to that subject. There was no substantial pressure
from non-Indian settlers desiring land occupied by
the Natives. There were accordingly no military
encounters and no removal. Perhaps most important, there were no treaties describing land claimed
under aboriginal title, ceding parts of it, and securing recognized title to remaining portions. With no
contest over most land, there was no need to define
either the nature or the extent of Alaska Native
land claims. The territorial court, after some uncertainty, did hold, however, that Alaska Natives were
wards of the federal government, and that the lands
they occupied were not subject to purchase by third
parties. United States v. Berrigan, 2 Alaska 442
(1905).

For the reasons just stated, most Alaska Natives
did not become occupants of reservations. The only
statutory reservation was that of the Annette Islands, established in 1891 for Metlakatla Indians
who had recently migrated from British Columbia.
25 U.S.C.A. § 495. That reservation was held to
include by implication adjacent waters. Alaska Pacific Fisheries v. United States, 248 U.S. 78 (1918).

Although other "reserves" were established in varying sizes (often quite small) by executive order during the first decades of the twentieth century, the legality and status of those reserves was never clearly established. In 1934, Congress enacted the Indian Reorganization Act ("IRA"), which authorized the Secretary of the Interior to establish new reservations. 25 U.S.C.A. § 467. Two years later, most of the Reorganization Act was made expressly applicable to Alaska, and Native groups not yet recognized were authorized to organize to adopt constitutions and by-laws. 25 U.S.C.A. § 473a. Pursuant to the authority conferred by the Act, the Secretary ultimately succeeded in establishing six IRA reservations: Venetie, Karluk, Akutan, Diomede, Unalakleet, and Wales. The Supreme Court held, however, that a reservation so established was temporary in nature, and could be revoked by Congress without payment of compensation. Hynes v. Grimes Packing Co., 337 U.S. 86 (1949). In any event, the great majority of Alaska Natives continued to live outside of reservations on land they long had occupied. The boundaries of their occupancy and the nature of their tenure remained uncertain.

Alaska Natives other than Aleuts were authorized to acquire homestead allotments by the Alaska Native Allotment Act of 1906. 34 Stat. 197. The Act was amended to make Aleuts eligible in 1956. The Act was repealed by the Alaska Native Claims Settlement Act in 1971, but pending applications were protected. Allotment claims therefore continue to be litigated. See Alaska v. Babbitt, 75 F.3d 449 (9th

Cir.), cert. denied, 117 S.Ct. 70 (1996). Many of the protected pending claims were later granted legislatively by the Alaska National Interest Lands Conservation Act. See 43 U.S.C.A. § 1634(a); cf. Alaska v. Babbitt, 38 F.3d 1068 (9th Cir.1994). Alaska Natives could also acquire townsite plots under the Alaska Native Townsite Act of 1926, 44 Stat. 629, repealed in 1976. That statute provided for Native communities to place township lands into trusteeship, from which individual townsite plots could be conveyed to individual Natives. Both types of individual title were subject to restraints on alienation. A Native community did not have to be incorporated to be eligible. Aleknagik Natives Ltd. v. United States, 886 F.2d 237 (9th Cir.1989).

With Natives living in scattered locations and attracting little federal attention, it is not surprising that state courts more or less regularly exercised jurisdiction over them. Perhaps in recognition of this fact, Alaska was added in 1958 to the list of mandatory states covered by Public Law 280. See Chapter VIII, supra. Alaska was thereby given criminal and civil adjudicatory jurisdiction over "All Indian country within the Territory." 72 Stat. 545. The criminal provision was subsequently amended in 1970 to provide that the Metlakatla Indian Community of the Annette Islands could exercise jurisdiction over offenses in Indian country in the same manner as tribes not covered by Public Law 280. See 18 U.S.C.A. § 1162(a). The result of the amendment was that both the tribe and the state exercised concurrent criminal jurisdiction. Booth v. State, 903 P.2d 1079 (Alaska App.1995).

None of these land tenure or jurisdictional provisions, however, purported to address the question of the nature and extent of Native Alaskan aboriginal land claims. Their nature was finally illuminated in Tee–Hit–Ton Indians v. United States, 348 U.S. 272 (1955). That case dealt with a claim by the Tee–Hit–Ton group of Tlingit Indians for the taking of timber by the United States from land to which the Tee–Hit–Tons claimed aboriginal title. The Supreme Court held that the Alaska Indians' title was of the same nature as the aboriginal title, or right of occupancy, once held by the Indians to the south. Such title was good against third parties, but was subject to extinguishment by the federal government without compensation. Thus the nature, but by no means the extent, of the Alaska aboriginal holdings was made clear.

The Alaska Statehood Act provided that Alaska disclaimed all right and title "to any lands or other property (including fishing rights), the right or title to which may be held by any Indians, Eskimos, or Aleuts* * *or is held by the United States in trust for said natives." 72 Stat. 339 (1958). The Act also authorized the State to select huge tracts from the vacant public lands within the former Territory. It soon became clear that the question of competing aboriginal land claims would have to be addressed. Impending development of oil production and pipeline facilities added greatly to the impetus. The result was the Alaska Native Claims Settlement Act.

B. ALASKA NATIVE CLAIMS SETTLEMENT ACT ("ANCSA")

In the Alaska Native Claims Settlement Act of 1971, 43 U.S.C.A. §§ 1601–1628, Congress not only provided for the extinguishment of Alaskan aboriginal title; it also created a unique system of landholding that has ramifications well beyond the field of land tenure. The Act and its numerous amendments are many-faceted and very detailed; only the major provisions will be dealt with here.

First, the Act extinguished "[a]ll aboriginal titles, if any, and claims of aboriginal title in Alaska based on use and occupancy, including submerged land underneath all water areas, both inland and offshore, and including any aboriginal hunting or fishing rights that may exist." 43 U.S.C.A. § 1603. It is noteworthy that the Act did not acknowledge whether or not such aboriginal title existed; it simply extinguished such title "if any." It also extinguished all claims based on aboriginal title, including pre-Act claims of trespass. § 1603(c); United States v. Atlantic Richfield Co., 612 F.2d 1132 (9th Cir.), cert. denied, 449 U.S. 888 (1980). The Act did not proceed on the theory of the Indian Claims Commission Act, which provided a means for tribes to prove the existence of their particular aboriginal title and to be compensated for its taking, measured by the value of the right. ANCSA did not attempt to determine what claims of which groups were extinguished, and to pay value to each group accordingly. It extinguished and, as discussed below, compensated without regard to the value of particular claims.

The extinguishment of aboriginal claims "in Alaska" is almost certainly confined to claims within the geographical boundaries of the State, extending three miles into the sea from its coastline. See Amoco Production Co. v. Village of Gambell, 480 U.S. 531, 552 (1987). Thus a question remains open whether Alaska Native groups could still successfully claim aboriginal hunting and fishing rights in the outer continental shelf. See Village of Gambell v. Hodel, 869 F.2d 1273 (9th Cir.1989), dismissed as moot, 999 F.2d 403 (9th Cir.1993).

In part payment for the extinguishment of aboriginal title, the Act establishes an Alaska Native Fund of more than $962,500,000, of which $462,500,000 was to be appropriated and $500,000,000 was to come from mineral lease payments. For the rest of the compensation, Native groups were authorized to select approximately 40 million acres of federal public land, to be held under the unique system established by the Act. Selections were to be made from lands withdrawn in or near Native villages; the withdrawal included lands so described that had been "selected by" but not "patented to, the State under the Alaska Statehood Act." This withdrawal was held to cover lands selected but not patented to the State under the Alaska Mental Health Enabling Act, which predated but was reconfirmed in the

Statehood Act. Tyonek Native Corp. v. Secretary of Interior, 836 F.2d 1237 (9th Cir.1988). Two million acres were authorized to be withdrawn by the Secretary to convey cemetery sites to regional corporations, and lands to Native groups not qualifying as villages, to Natives in specified towns who formed urban corporations, and to individual Natives occupying homesites of up to 160 acres. § 1613(h); see Haynes v. United States, 891 F.2d 235 (9th Cir. 1989). "Native groups" are communities composed of less than 25 Natives who are in a majority in their locality. § 1602(d). Thus establishment of the boundaries of a "locality" often determines whether members of the Native group are in a majority. Relative proximity of residents, compared to less densely populated surroundings, and sharing of common interests in services or facilities are factors in determining that an area constitutes a locality. Minchumina Natives, Inc. v. U.S. Dep't of Interior, 60 F.3d 1363 (9th cir.1995). Members enrolled in another village do not qualify as members of the group, but do qualify as residents of the locality for purposes of determining a majority. Chugach Alaska Corp. v. Lujan, 915 F.2d 454 (9th Cir.1990).

The Act provided for the establishment under state law of regional and village corporations in which enrolled Natives would receive corporate stock. Alaska was to be divided into twelve regions, "composed as far as practicable of Natives having a common heritage and sharing common interests," each region to have its own regional corporation. The Act proposed the regions, composed of existing

Native associations, with modification permitted for good cause. A thirteenth regional corporation was also authorized, and later established, for nonresident Natives. 43 U.S.C.A. § 1606. The Act also provided for each Native village entitled to receive lands to incorporate, with its articles of incorporation subject to approval of the Regional corporation for its region. § 1607. The village corporations were permitted to select 22 million acres from land where they were located and adjoining areas in proportion to the population of the village; regional corporations were entitled to select lands from an additional 16 million acres, which they then were to reallocate to villages within their regions. § 1611. After these selections, patents to the surface estates were to be issued to the village corporations. Upon receipt of patents, the village corporations are required to convey to certain occupants and governments tracts actually occupied as residences, businesses or municipalities (with allowance for expansion), and certain federal operations. § 1613. That process would still leave the village corporations with large tracts of surface estate. The regional corporations are then given the subsurface rights in all of those lands (with certain exceptions when subsurface rights were already reserved). Most of the revenues received by the regional corporations from the subsurface estates are shared with all twelve of the geographic regional corporations according to their populations. § 1606(i).

The Native corporations receive title to their estates in fee. The Act imposed no restraint on alienation of those lands by their corporate owners, but it did restrain alienation of Natives' corporate stock for twenty years. In the absence of such controlling provisions of ANCSA, the corporations were subject to state corporation law, such as the requirement that distributions to shareholders be equal. See Hanson v. Kake Tribal Corp., 939 P.2d 1320 (Alaska 1997). The ANCSA Amendments of 1987 (actually enacted in 1988) permitted the corporations to extend the restraints on alienation of their stock beyond that term. Pub. L. 100–241, 101 Stat. 1788. In addition, Native corporations were authorized to transfer their assets to state-chartered trusts, which had no power to transfer lands and which were not subject to the rule against perpetuities. The trusts are "to promote the health, education, and welfare of its beneficiaries." 43 U.S.C.A. § 1629e(b)(1). The provision of ANCSA authorizing the trusts partially preempts state corporation law and permits unequal distributions, such as an old-age benefit payments, by the trust. Broad v. Sealaska Corp., 85 F.3d 422 (9th Cir.1996), cert. denied, 117 S.Ct. 768 (1997). The 1987 ANSCA amendments also modified the Alaska National Interest Lands Conservation Act to protect undeveloped Native fee lands from property taxation and from certain types of foreclosure and involuntary transfer. 43 U.S.C.A. § 1636. The power to transfer lands voluntarily remains, however. This ability to alienate, as well as the corporate ownership, distinguishes Alaska Native landholding from all other Indian land tenure.

ANCSA also revoked all reserves previously established in Alaska, except for the Annette Islands Reserve. Enrolled members of the Metlakatla Indian community of the Annette Islands Reserve were excluded from benefits under ANCSA. § 1618(a). Corporations of villages occupying reserves revoked by the Act were given the option of taking fee title to the surface and subsurface estates of the prior reserves. If the corporation chose that option, however, it and its members became ineligible for other benefits under ANCSA, including land selections and distribution of funds or stock in regional corporations. § 1618(b).

One goal of ANCSA that clearly has not been realized is that of accomplishing the settlement "without litigation." § 1601(b). The Act's complicated land selection and ownership system, divided between regional and village corporations, raised many questions requiring judicial resolution. The land surrounding villages that was withdrawn by ANCSA for Native selection was withdrawn "subject to valid existing rights." § 1610(a)(1). This clause has been interpreted to protect expectancies, such as a municipality's segregation of land for future subdivision, and a state lessee's option to purchase the land in the future upon certain conditions. Aleknagik Natives, Ltd. v. United States, 806 F.2d 924 (9th Cir.1986); Seldovia Native Ass'n, Inc. v. Lujan, 904 F.2d 1335 (9th Cir.1990).

Some disputes have arisen from the reconveyance provision, which among other things requires village corporations receiving surface estates to reconvey without consideration to Natives or non-Natives occupying the tracts "as a primary place of residence, or as a primary place of business, or as a subsistence campsite, or as headquarters for reindeer husbandry." § 1613(c)(1). The village corporation, in determining whether to reconvey to a particular occupant, acts as a federal delegee and is subject to due process requirements of notice to the prospective claimant. Ogle v. Salamatof Native Ass'n, Inc. 906 F.Supp. 1321 (D.Alaska 1995). The reconveyance clause creates a statutory duty, but does not create a fiduciary or trust relationship between the village and the occupant entitled to reconveyance. Id. Predictable issues have arisen over qualified uses. The City of Ketchikan was unsuccessful in claiming that the largest of its four power plants was the city utility's "primary place of business." Nor could the city's utility qualify under another clause providing for reconveyance to non-profit organizations. City of Ketchikan v. Cape Fox Corp., 85 F.3d 1381 (9th Cir.1996). A cabin site used by hunting guides qualified, however, as a primary place of that business. Hakala v. Atxam Corp., 753 P.2d 1144 (Alaska 1988). Occupancy of a cabin as a primary residence qualified even if the occupancy was under a use permit from the Forest Service. Buettner v. Kavilco, Inc., 860 F.2d 341 (9th Cir.1988).

Another source of dispute is the division between surface and subsurface estates. The issue first arose with regard to sand and gravel on land entirely owned by a regional corporation. If sand and gravel were part of the surface estate, then revenues from their extraction belonged entirely to the regional corporation owning the land. If sand and gravel were part of the subsurface estate, then 70% of the revenues had to be shared with other regional corporations. § 1606(i). The sand and gravel were held to be part of the subsurface estate. Chugach Natives, Inc. v. Doyon, Ltd., 588 F.2d 723 (9th Cir. 1978). The same result was reached when the surface estate belonged to a village corporation and the subsurface to a regional corporation. Tyonek Native Corp. v. Cook Inlet Region, Inc., 853 F.2d 727 (9th Cir.1988). Later cases, however, recognize that the surface estate sometimes cannot be developed at all without exploitation of sand and gravel on the spot. Consequently, when there is no other practical source for those materials, an equitable servitude is imposed on the subsurface estate owner. The subsurface owner cannot unreasonably deny the surface owner access to sand and gravel necessary for surface development. The surface owner must, however, pay a reasonable price for the sand and gravel; the purchaser has the burden of demonstrating that the price demanded by the subsurface owner is unreasonable. Koniag, Inc. v. Koncor Forest Resource, 39 F.3d 991 (9th Cir.1994); Shee Atika v. Sealaska Corp., 39 F.3d 247 (9th Cir.1994).

C. GOVERNMENTAL STATUS OF NATIVE ORGANIZATIONS

The unique legal organization of Alaska Native organizations has raised questions whether they enjoy all of the governmental prerogatives of tribes in the lower forty-eight states. The issues concern their relationship to the federal government and the degree of their sovereignty for purposes of self-government, governmental control over their lands, and sovereign immunity. On these questions, the federal courts and the Supreme Court of Alaska have frequently reached different results. The Supreme Court of the United States, however, recently has made clear that Alaska Native groups cannot govern ANCSA corporately-held land as "Indian country." Alaska v. Native Village of Venetie, 118 S.Ct. 948 (1998).

1.   FEDERAL TRUST RELATIONSHIP

In 1918, the Supreme Court had no difficulty accepting the proposition that establishing a reserve for Alaska Natives served "a recognized public purpose-that of safe-guarding and advancing a dependent Indian People dwelling within the United States." Alaska Pacific Fisheries v. United States, 248 U.S. 78, 88 (1918). Those are terms of trust relationship. Although ANCSA declares that settlement should occur without "*creating* a* * *lengthy wardship or trusteeship,*" § 1601(b)(emphasis added), it did not state that it was terminating any such relationship. It probably did not expressly preserve the relationship either. ANCSA states that it shall not diminish "any obligation of the United States* * *to protect and promote the rights or welfare of Natives *as citizens of the United States or*

Alaska," § 1601(c)(emphasis added), but the final clause can be read to limit the statement to little more than a guarantee of equal protection. One circuit observed that ANCSA "arguably precludes the existence of a general trust responsibility to the Eskimoes." North Slope Borough v. Andrus, 642 F.2d 589, 612 n. 151 (D.C.Cir.1980). The Ninth Circuit, in which Alaska lies, appeared to recognize a federal trust responsibility comparable to that toward other Indians, even after passage of the Alaska Native Claims Settlement Act. Alaska Chapter, Associated General Contractors v. Pierce, 694 F.2d 1162, 1168–69 n. 10 (9th Cir.1982). That court later clearly embraced this position in State ex rel. Yukon Flats School Dist. v. Native Village of Venetie Tribal Gov't, 101 F.3d 1286 (9th Cir.1996), rev'd on other grounds, 118 S.Ct. 948 (1998).

Congress has included Alaska Natives in post-ANCSA legislation implementing the trust responsibility in various ways. The Indian Self–Determination and Education Assistance Act of 1975, which permits tribes to contract to administer federal Indian programs, defines "Indian tribe" to include "any Alaska Native village or regional or village corporation as defined in or established pursuant to [ANCSA] which is recognized as eligible for the special programs and services provided by the United States to Indians because of their status as Indians." 25 U.S.C.A. § 450b(e)(as amended); see Cook Inlet Native Ass'n v. Bowen, 810 F.2d 1471 (9th Cir.1987). A similar definition appears in the Tribally Controlled Community College Assistance

Act, 25 U.S.C.A. § 1801(2), and the Indian Health Care Improvement Act, 25 U.S.C.A. § 1603(d), although the significance of the latter inclusion is tempered by the fact that the same section extends coverage of the Act to terminated Indians, with whom there is no trust relationship. § 1603(c). The Indian Child Welfare Act, however, begins with a recitation of the "special relationship between the United States and the Indian tribes and their members and the Federal responsibility to Indian people" and then includes as tribes Alaska Native villages as defined in ANCSA. 25 U.S.C.A. § 1903(8).

Congress made clear that recognition of Indian tribes was a prerogative of the Secretary of the Interior when it required the Secretary to publish "a list of all Indian tribes which the Secretary recognizes to be eligible for the special programs and services provided by the United States to Indians because of their status as Indians." 25 U.S.C.A. § 479a–1. The Secretary now includes more than 200 Alaska Native organizations in his list of tribes recognized as having the immunities and privileges of "acknowledged Indian tribes by virtue of their government-to-government relationship with the United States* * *." 62 Fed. Reg. 55270 (1997). In the face of this recognition by the Executive Branch, as well as the congressional statutes referred to above, it seems clear today that there exists a trust relationship between the recognized Alaska Native organizations and the federal government.

2. INDIAN COUNTRY

One of the major uncertainties overhanging Alaska Native governmental power has been the question whether Native lands held pursuant to ANCSA were "Indian country." See Chapter VII, Section B, supra. The issue is one of great jurisdictional importance. If Native villages occupied their lands as Indian country, they presumably would be able to exercise all of the powers of reservation tribes in the lower forty-eight states. See Chapter VII, supra. They would have power to exercise criminal jurisdiction over Alaska Natives and other Indians within their territory. 25 U.S.C. § 1301(2). They would also have civil and regulatory jurisdiction over much member and nonmember activity (except nonmember activities on any nonmember-owned fee lands) within their Indian country. See Chapter VII, Section F(2); Chapter IX, Sections D & G, supra. Moreover, the State of Alaska would be precluded from exercising general regulatory jurisdiction within that same territory. See Chapter VIII, Section D, supra.

"Indian country" is defined by 18 U.S.C. § 1151 to encompass (a) land within Indian reservations, (b) "dependent Indian communities," and (c) allotments under Indian title. The only reservation left in Alaska after the enactment of ANCSA is the Annette Islands Reserve of the Metlakatla Indians; that reserve is indisputably Indian country. There are also Native allotments in Alaska, but they usually have not been a source of jurisdictional controversy. One exception is Jones v. State, 936 P.2d 1263 (Alaska App.1997), in which the court expressed doubt that Alaska Native allotments could qualify as Indian country. The prime jurisdictional question, however, has been whether lands held by Native entities under ANCSA comprise "dependent Indian communities."

The Supreme Court answered that question in the negative in Alaska v. Native Village of Venetie Tribal Government, 118 S.Ct. 948 (1998). The issue arose when the Village attempted to impose a tax on a contractor building a state school on fee land held by the Village pursuant to ANCSA. The land had been a reserve until that status was revoked by ANCSA; the two Native corporations connected with the former reserve elected to take title to the former reserve lands, and to forego any other benefits under ANCSA. See 25 U.S.C.A. § 1618(b). They then transferred the land to the Village. The Village held the land without restrictions on alienation.

The Supreme Court held that, for land to be a dependent Indian community, it had to have been set aside by the federal government for the use of Indians, and had to be under the superintendence of the federal government. Lands held by the Village pursuant to ANCSA failed to meet both requirements. ANCSA's transfer of lands to state-chartered corporations, without restraints on alienation, did not set the land aside for use of the Natives; the corporations or the Village could transfer the land out of Native ownership at any time. Transfer of the land to corporations chartered and regulated by the state was inconsistent with supervision by the federal government. Active supervision of the lands, not of the tribe, was the requirement, and the federal government must supervise the land essentially as a guardian. Thus lands held by the Alaska Native groups pursuant to ANCSA did not qualify as Indian country. The Village's attempt to tax the contractor accordingly failed. As a consequence of this *Venetie* decision, Alaska Native villages are left without any jurisdiction based on territorial power, and the State of Alaska is left with adjudicatory, regulatory, and legislative jurisdiction over ANCSA-held lands.

3.   TRIBAL SELF–GOVERNMENT

Questions then arise concerning the degree to which Alaska Native entities may exercise governmental power without a territorial basis. Even without Indian country, over 200 Native entities remain federally recognized governmental bodies. Indeed, in 1994, the requirements for federal acknowledgment were modified to make clear that occupation of a particular territory was not a prerequisite. See 59 Fed.Reg. 9280, 9286–87; 25 C.F.R. § 83.7. What powers do these governments have after *Venetie*? The answers are not entirely clear, but some insight may be gained from events preceding the Supreme Court's decision. In 1988, the Alaska Supreme Court took the position that most villages and Native groups in Alaska were "not self-governing or in any meaningful sense sovereign." Native Village of

Stevens v. Alaska Management & Planning, 757 P.2d 32, 34 (Alaska 1988). The exception was the Metlakatla Indian Community of the Annette Islands Reserve. Id.; see Atkinson v. Haldane, 569 P.2d 151 (Alaska 1977). *Stevens* relied upon a history of state jurisdiction over Alaska Natives. It concluded that organization of the tribe under section 16 of the IRA, 25 U.S.C. § 476, was not sufficient to make the entity sovereign for purposes of immunity. See also Hydaburg Cooperative Ass'n v. Hydaburg Fisheries, 826 P.2d 751 (Alaska 1992). After reviewing the Alaska Indian Reorganization Act and ANCSA, the Court in *Stevens* concluded that "Congress has demonstrated its intent that Alaska Native communities not be accorded sovereign tribal status." 757 P.2d at 41. It accordingly rejected a defense of tribal sovereign immunity.

At about the same time, the Ninth Circuit took a more individualized and fact-bound approach to the sovereign power of any particular village. Although it agreed that organization under section 16 of the Indian Reorganization Act, 25 U.S.C.A. § 476, did not automatically establish sovereignty, it held that sovereignty could be established by a showing of federal recognition or, failing that, by other historical factors. Alaska v. Native Village of Venetie, 856 F.2d 1384, 1387 (9th Cir.1988); Native Village of Tyonek v. Puckett, 957 F.2d 631, 635 (9th Cir. 1992). The Ninth Circuit further defined its position in Native Village of Venetie I.R.A. Council v. Alaska, 944 F.2d 548 (9th Cir.1991). It rejected early views that Alaska Native groups simply did not qualify as independent sovereigns, see In re Sah Quah, 31 Fed. 327 (D.Alaska 1886), and held that "[i]f the native villages of Venetie and Fort Yukon are the modern-day successors to sovereign historical bands of natives, the villages are to be afforded the same rights and responsibilities as are sovereign bands of native Americans in the continental United States." *Venetie*, 944 F.2d at 559. The Alaska Supreme Court, however, refused to accept the reasoning of *Venetie I.R.A.*, and adhered to its view in *Stevens* that "Congress intended that most Alaska Native groups not be treated as sovereigns." Matter of F.P., 843 P.2d 1214, 1215 (Alaska 1992), cert. denied, 508 U.S. 950 (1993). The Alaska Supreme Court earlier, however, had recognized a Native group organized under section 16 of the IRA, 25 U.S.C. § 476, as a "tribe" for the limited purpose of protecting its land under that provision from foreclosure by a city for nonpayment of taxes. Matter of City of Nome, 780 P.2d 363 (Alaska 1989); see also Hydaburg Cooperative Ass'n v. Hydaburg Fisheries, 925 P.2d 246 (Alaska 1996).

All of these cases, however, were decided before the Department of the Interior revised its list of entities entitled to receive federal benefits. Prior to 1988, the intent of the Department in including an Alaskan entity on its list had not been made clear, see Harrison v. State, 791 P.2d 359, 364 n. 8 (Alaska App.1990). In 1988 the list was expanded to include all Alaskan entities entitled to receive federal funds or services even if they were not regarded as "tribes" by the Department. In 1993, however, the Department recognized the ambiguity caused by its actions and published a narrower list of "villages and regional tribes [that] have functioned as political entities exercising governmental authority and are, therefore acknowledged to have 'the immunities and privileges available to other federally acknowledged Indian tribes by virtue of their status as Indian tribes * * *.' " 58 Fed.Reg. 54364, 54365 (1993). The Department stated its intent to clarify that the listed tribes "have the same governmental status as other federally acknowledged Indian tribes * * * with a government-to-government relationship with the United States * * *." Id. at 54366. Because recognition of a tribe by the Executive Branch is generally a nonjusticiable political question, judicial acceptance of the sovereign status of the listed villages should follow. See Atkinson v. Haldane, 569 P.2d at 163.

What governmental power may such a recognized tribal government exercise without territory, simply because it is a sovereign body? Under normal circumstances, the inherent power of tribal self-government at the least includes the minimal attributes of sovereignty set forth in United States v. Wheeler, 435 U.S. 313, 322 & n. 18 (1978)-the power to enforce criminal laws against tribal members, to determine tribal membership, to regulate domestic relations among tribal members, and to prescribe rules of inheritance. Thus the Ninth Circuit held that, if a Native Village was a sovereign entity, it had inherent authority to make child-custody determinations for its members. Native Village of Venetie I.R.A. Council v. Alaska, 944 F.2d 548 (9th Cir.1991).

Prior to this decision of the Ninth Circuit, the Supreme Court of Alaska had held that tribal courts had no jurisdiction to adjudicate child custody because exclusive custody over such matters was granted to the state courts by Public Law 280. Native Village of Nenana v. Department of Health & Social Services, 722 P.2d 219 (Alaska), cert. denied, 479 U.S. 1008 (1986). The Alaska Court relied upon the Indian Child Welfare Act, 25 U.S.C.A. § 1918(a), which provides that "[a]ny Indian tribe which became subject to State jurisdiction [pursuant to Public Law 280] or pursuant to any other federal law may reassume jurisdiction over Indian child custody proceedings" upon approval of the Secretary after a petition that includes "a suitable plan to exercise such jurisdiction." In rejecting this same argument, the Ninth Circuit in *Venetie I.R.A.* endorsed the view that Public Law 280 did not deprive tribes of concurrent civil jurisdiction. See Chapter VIII, Section C, supra. The reassumption provision of the Indian Child Welfare Act was not thereby rendered superfluous, because reassumption under § 1918(a) could lead to exclusive or primary, rather than merely concurrent, tribal jurisdiction. *Venetie I.R.A.*, 944 F.2d at 561. The Supreme Court of Alaska has since refused to accept the Ninth Circuit's view, see Matter of F.P., 843 P.2d 1214 (Alaska 1992), cert. denied, 508 U.S. 950 (1993), so the federal and state courts remain in conflict on this question.

This debate takes on an interesting color after the United States Supreme Court's decision in *Venetie*. Public Law 280 extended state criminal and civil jurisdiction into "Indian country." 18 U.S.C.A. § 1162(a); 28 U.S.C.A. § 1360(a). Under *Venetie*, however, there was no Indian country (other than the Annette Islands Reserve) upon which Public Law 280 could operate. It may be, however, that ANCSA itself subjected the Native villages to state jurisdiction, and thus is an "other federal law" subjecting the villages to state jurisdiction within the meaning of the Indian Child Welfare Act. The State of Alaska might say that ANCSA subjected to state jurisdiction only those villages that had reserves revoked by ANCSA, and that other villages had always been under state jurisdiction. In any event, the larger point is that the inherent jurisdiction of the Village over child custody upheld by the Ninth Circuit in *Venetie I.R.A.* did *not* depend on territory at all; Public Law 280 was held to be irrelevant to that inherent (and concurrent) jurisdiction.

There is little reason to doubt that several other inherent powers of tribal self-government set forth in *Wheeler* may be exercised by Native governments without a territorial base. The basis of jurisdiction emphasized in *Wheeler* is tribal membership, and it supports such matters of internal self-governance as determination of membership, regulation of domestic relations among members, and regulation of inheritance. Wheeler, 435 U.S. at 322 n.18. It may also support jurisdiction to enforce civil ordinances

regarding members' transfer of tribal artifacts. See
Chilkat Indian Village v. Johnson, 870 F.2d 1469
(9th Cir.1989). Membership might even support the
other attribute of inherent sovereignty set forth in
Wheeler-the power to exercise criminal jurisdiction
over tribal members. See Duro v. Reina, 495 U.S.
676, 693 (1990). The point is problematical, however, because criminal jurisdiction normally has a
territorial element. A tribe has been permitted to
exercise criminal jurisdiction over tribal members
exercising treaty fishing rights off-reservation, Settler v. Lameer, 507 F.2d 231 (9th Cir.1974), but that
ruling retained a geographical (but not Indian country) element of "usual and accustomed" treaty fishing locations. Finally, Native villages ought to be
able to exercise whatever governmental powers
might be necessary to administer programs made
available or delegated to them by the federal government in recognition or implementation of the
federal-tribal government-to-government relationship.

With regard to nonmembers, it is possible that
certain kinds of consensual activity might subject
them to the exercise of civil governmental power by
Native villages. See Duro, 495 U.S. at 688; Montana
v. United States, 450 U.S. 544, 565 (1981). It is
clear, however, that without Indian country jurisdiction, Native villages may not exercise governmental authority, such as taxation, over nonconsen-
sual activities of nonmembers on ANCSA-held
lands. Venetie, supra; Alyeska Pipeline Service Co.
v. Kluti Kaah Native Village, 101 F.3d 610 (9th

392 U.S. 78 (1918). 1962

Cir.1996). The villages or their corporations do enjoy the usual rights of landowners, of course, but those prerogatives do not derive from governmental status.

D. HUNTING AND FISHING

Hunting and fishing has always been of extreme importance to Alaska Natives. The subject early attracted the attention of the Supreme Court in Alaska Pacific Fisheries v. United States, 248 U.S. 78 (1918). The Court there held that Congress, in setting aside a reserve for the Metlakatla Indians "the body of lands known as the Annette Islands" included by implication the adjacent waters, because the fishery was the Indians' primary means of subsistence. The Court returned to the subject in Metlakatla Indian Community v. Egan, 369 U.S. 45 (1962), which upheld the power of the Secretary of the Interior to authorize the use of fish traps by Indians in those waters in contravention of state law.

In the companion case of Organized Village of Kake v. Egan, 369 U.S. 60 (1962), the Court reached a different result when the Secretary attempted to authorize the use of fish traps by Village fishermen in waters not part of any reserve. The Court held that the Secretary was not authorized to issue any such permits. One point in issue was the effect of the clause in the Alaska Statehood Act providing that the State "forever disclaim[ed] all right and title * * * to any lands or other property

(including fishing rights), the right or title to which
may be held by any Indians, Eskimos, or Aleuts"
and that such lands or property "shall be and
remain under the absolute jurisdiction and control
of the United States * * *." 72 Stat. 339 (1958).
The Court held that the reference to fishing rights
was intended neither to recognize nor to extinguish
any aboriginal or possessory rights held by the
Natives; it was intended merely to maintain the
status quo. The provision for "absolute jurisdiction
and control" by the United States "was a disclaimer
of proprietary rather than governmental interest."
369 U.S. at 69. Moreover, "absolute jurisdiction"
did not necessarily mean "exclusive jurisdiction."
Id. at 68. Consequently, the State could exercise
jurisdiction and control over the Native fishing, and
thus could ban the fish traps.

Alaska Native hunting and fishing thus generally
proceeded under state regulation. There were, of
course, no treaties and therefore no treaty hunting
or fishing rights to be asserted. Any uncertainty
concerning the nature and extent of aboriginal
rights to hunt and fish ended in 1971 with the
passage of the Alaska Native Claims Settlement
Act. It extinguished "any aboriginal hunting or
fishing rights that may exist." 43 U.S.C.A.
§ 1603(b). Because the extinguishment was of aboriginal title "in Alaska," it left a possibility that
Natives could claim aboriginal rights beyond the
three-mile limit from shore. See Village of Gambell
v. Hodel, 869 F.2d 1273 (9th Cir.1989), dismissed as
moot, 999 F.2d 403 (9th Cir.1993). Within the

State, however, no pre-existing rights remained and any distinctive treatment of Native hunting and fishing out of Indian country therefore had to be a creature of statute or regulation.

One federal statute that has a substantial impact on Native hunting and fishing is the Alaska National Interest Lands Conservation Act ("ANILCA"), 16 U.S.C.A. § 3101 et seq., enacted in 1980. ANILCA provides, among other things, a system for managing huge amounts of land withdrawn by the federal government for various public purposes. One of the stated purposes of the Act is "to provide the opportunity for rural residents engaged in a subsistence way of life to continue to do so." § 3101(c). The Act was clearly intended to protect subsistence uses of Alaska Natives, but its coverage was broadened to rural residents because of objections that the state constitution might prohibit subsistence preferences based exclusively on Native status.

ANILCA declares "nonwasteful subsistence uses of fish and wildlife" to be the priority consumptive uses of those resources on the public lands of Alaska. § 3112(2). When there are insufficient populations of fish or game to meet subsistence requirements, priority among subsistence users is based on three criteria: whether the subsistence use is a "mainstay of livelihood," local residency, and availability of alternative resources. § 3114. "Subsistence use" means the "customary and traditional uses by rural Alaska residents * * * for direct personal or family consumption as food, shelter, fuel, clothing, tools, or transportation; for the making

and selling of handicraft articles out of nonedible
byproducts * * *; for barter, or sharing for personal
of family consumption; and for customary trade."
§ 3113. Customary trade may include cash sales,
and a ban on such sales has been held to violate
ANILCA. United States v. Alexander, 938 F.2d 942
(9th Cir.1991). "Public lands" include not only federal lands, but lands selected by Alaska under the
Statehood Act and by Native corporations under
ANCSA. § 3102(3). "Public lands" consequently includes a huge proportion of Alaska. It does not,
however, include the continental shelf beyond the
three mile limit of the State boundary. Amoco Production Co. v. Village of Gambell, 480 U.S. 531
(1987). Public lands also do not include navigable
waters over which the federal government reserves
only a navigational servitude. Alaska v. Babbitt, 72
F.3d 698, 702–03 (9th Cir.1995), cert. denied, 116
S.Ct. 1672 (1996). There is a conflict of authority
over the status of waters (including navigable waters) reserved as appurtenant to federally reserved
lands. The Ninth Circuit has held that such waters
are public lands within the meaning of ANILCA. Id.
at 703–04. The Supreme Court of Alaska has held
that they are not. Totemoff v. State, 905 P.2d 954,
964 (Alaska 1995), cert. denied, 517 U.S. 1244
(1996).

ANILCA provides for the Secretary of the Interior
to divide public lands into regions, to create local
advisory committees, and to make rules to preserve
the priority of subsistence uses of fish and wildlife.
§ 3115(a), (b), (c). These provisions are rendered

inoperative, however, if the State "enacts and implements laws of general applicability that are consistent with the subsistence preference. § 3115(d). In other words, if the State wishes to avoid federal regulation of hunting and fishing on public lands, it must enact a general system of fish and game regulations that protect and give priority to subsistence uses of rural residents. "Given the choice between federal regulation or self-regulation with federal oversight, Alaska chose the latter." Kenaitze Indian Tribe v. Alaska, 860 F.2d 312, 314 (9th Cir.1988), cert. denied, 491 U.S. 905 (1989). Alaska thus enacted laws providing a subsistence use priority for rural residents, but its narrow definition of "rural" was held to be inconsistent with ANILCA. Id. More substantial difficulties followed when the Supreme Court of Alaska held that confining the priority to rural residents violated the state constitution. McDowell v. State, 785 P.2d 1 (Alaska 1989). The State's laws were then declared to be out of compliance with ANILCA and the federal government consequently began regulating fish and game on public lands. See Native Village of Quinhagak v. United States, 35 F.3d 388, 390 (9th Cir.1994). Although a good argument can be made that the scheme of ANILCA renders such federal regulation exclusive, the Supreme Court of Alaska subsequently held that the State had concurrent jurisdiction to regulate subsistence hunting on public lands, so long as its regulation was not inconsistent with federal regulations. Totemoff v. State, 905 P.2d 954 (Alaska 1995), cert. denied, 517 U.S. 1244 (1996).

In addition to the provisions discussed above, ANILCA contains measures for monitoring and enforcing the Act's subsistence preference, along with a judicial remedy for persons aggrieved by state or federal failure to provide priority for subsistence uses. §§ 3116, 3117. It requires federal agency heads to evaluate the effect of land use decisions on subsistence uses, and to provide notice and hearing if an action would substantially restrict subsistence uses. § 3120. The Act includes many other provisions of general and specific application that are too numerous to describe here.

Alaska's own hunting and fishing laws continue to provide a preference for subsistence uses. When the stocks of fish and game are insufficient for subsistence and competing uses, competing uses must yield. There is also a system for determining preference among subsistence users, although residence may not be used in such a determination. State v. Kenaitze Indian Tribe, 894 P.2d 632 (Alaska 1995); see Alaska Stat. § 16.05.258. The State may declare areas where the subsistence preference does not apply. Kenaitze, 894 P.2d at 639–42. The Supreme Court of Alaska has disapproved intervention by a lower court to secure a preference for a particular subsistence hunt; the effects of such a move on competing subsistence users and the entire game population must be taken into account. State v. Kluti Kaah Native Village, 831 P.2d 1270 (Alaska 1992). An intermediate court has held that Alaska's hunting laws are not merely regulatory, but are "criminal/prohibitory" for purposes of Public Law

280, see Chapter VIII, Section D, supra, and therefore may be applied on an Indian allotment even if it is Indian country. Jones v. State, 936 P.2d 1263 (Alaska App.1997).

Several federal statutes of general applicability contain exceptions for Alaska Native subsistence hunting and fishing. The Endangered Species Act provides that endangered or threatened species may be taken for subsistence purposes by "any Indian, Aleut, or Eskimo who is an Alaskan Native who resides in Alaska" or by "any non-native permanent resident of an Alaskan Native village." 16 U.S.C.A. § 1539(e). The exemption has been upheld against an equal protection attack by Native Hawaiians; the classification is rationally based "upon food supply and culture." United States v. Nuesca, 945 F.2d 254, 257 (9th Cir.1991). The Marine Mammal Protection Act imposes a moratorium on the taking of marine mammals, but contains an exception for "any Indian, Aleut, or Eskimo who resides in Alaska and who dwells on the coast of the North Pacific Ocean or the Arctic Ocean." 16 U.S.C.A. § 1371(b). The taking must be for purposes of subsistence or creation of Native artifacts, and must not be conducted "in a wasteful manner." Id. Several treaties regarding migratory birds include protections for Native subsistence, and the Secretary of the Interior is authorized by statute to issue regulations "to assure that the taking of migratory birds and the collection of their eggs, by the indigenous inhabitants of the State of Alaska, shall be permitted for their own nutritional and other essential needs * * *." 16 U.S.C.A. § 712(a). Finally, more distant from the subject of wild game, the Reindeer Act and its administration have secured a virtual monopoly of the reindeer business for Alaska Natives. See 25 U.S.C.A. § 500 et seq. In order to avoid serious constitutional questions, however, the Act has been interpreted not to prohibit non-Natives from entering the business. See Williams v. Babbitt, 115 F.3d 657 (9th Cir.1997), cert. denied, 1998 WL 54253 (1998). The number and substance of these various statutory provisions reflect the undeniable importance of hunting and fishing to the Alaska Native culture and economy.

CHAPTER XIV

INDIAN WATER RIGHTS

A. THE APPROPRIATIVE SYSTEM
OF WATER RIGHTS

Disputes over Indian water rights are necessarily concentrated in the water-scarce states of the West. To understand these disputes and the evolving legal principles applicable to them, it is necessary to examine briefly the two major systems of water rights in the United States—the "riparian" system of the water-abundant states of the East and the "appropriative" system of the arid West.

Under the riparian system, the owner of land that borders a lake or stream has the right to the reasonable use of the water. That right runs with the land and cannot be separated from it. It continues to exist whether or not it is exercised. The reasonableness of any use of any given amount of water depends entirely on the circumstances of that use, with the primary limitation being that it must not interfere unduly with any other riparian owner's reasonable use of the water. All riparian owners are entitled to a continuation of the flow. If the source of the water is affected by drought, then the right of each riparian owner is diminished proportionally.

The appropriative system operates on entirely different premises. It evolved at a time when nearly all of the land in the West was federally owned, and the primary demands for water were for mining. Mines were often located at considerable distance from the source of the water, and substantial investment was required to construct systems for transporting it. In later years, agriculture became a primary use, and it also required substantial investment in irrigation systems. Miners and farmers both needed assurances of continued supplies of water before they undertook these investments.

The result of these circumstances was the growth of the appropriative system. Under that regime, water rights are not appurtenant to the land. The right to water belongs to the first user who appropriates it and puts it to beneficial use. That appropriator is guaranteed the right to continue to take the same amount of water from the source without interference by any later appropriator. The appropriator retains that right only so long as he or she continues to put the water to beneficial use. "Use it or lose it" is consequently one of the slogans describing the appropriative system.

In case of drought, the entire share of the latest appropriator is lost before the share of the next latest begins to diminish. Appropriation dates are therefore of immense importance, and the older the better. When a stream is almost fully appropriated, new appropriators are at great risk of losing future supplies in short years, but the older appropriators enjoy a high degree of security.

Although the appropriative system evolved on federal land, it is a creature of local custom rather than federal law. Congress by various statutes recognized these customs, and in the Desert Land Entries Act of 1877, 43 U.S.C.A. §§ 321–25, declared all non-navigable water available to appropriation in the present states of California, Oregon, Washington, Idaho, Montana, Wyoming, Utah, Colorado, Nevada, Arizona, New Mexico, and North and South Dakota. These appropriations are governed by state law. California Oregon Power Co. v. Beaver Portland Cement Co., 295 U.S. 142 (1935). State law varies greatly from the relatively pure appropriative system of Colorado to the mixture of appropriative and riparian systems in California and Oregon. Details of state law also differ in regard to requirements for registration of appropriations, the period of non-use that causes forfeiture, priorities of use, and method of resolving disputes. The organizing principles of appropriation remain the same, however: water may be appropriated separately from land; the first appropriator in time is first in right; and water not put to beneficial use is lost to the appropriator.

B. INDIAN WATER RIGHTS: THE *WINTERS* DOCTRINE

Indian water rights do not fall entirely into either the appropriative or the riparian category. Their foundation lies in the Supreme Court decision of Winters v. United States, 207 U.S. 564 (1908). That case involved the Fort Belknap Reservation in Montana, which had been created by an 1888 agreement out of a much larger area previously set aside for the concerned tribes. The agreement described one boundary of the reservation as being the middle of the Milk River, but it made no mention of rights to the use of water. Thereafter, non-Indian settlers off the reservation built dams that diverted the flow of the river and interfered with agricultural uses by the Indians. The settlers claimed that they had appropriated the water after the reservation was established but prior to any use of water by the Indians. The Supreme Court found it unnecessary to determine the truth of the settlers' claims of prior use, because it held that when the Fort Belknap lands were reserved by the 1888 agreement, water rights for the Indians were also reserved by necessary implication. The Court thought it unreasonable to assume that Indians would reserve lands for farming and pastoral purposes without also reserving the water to make those uses possible. The Court also held that this implied reservation of water was unaffected by the subsequent admission of Montana into the Union "upon an equal footing with the original States."

Despite the clear ruling of *Winters*, Indian water rights were largely ignored for many decades thereafter. The United States was far more interested in encouraging non-Indian settlement than it was in developing and protecting Indian water resources. Indeed, during those years the United States represented the tribes in several water rights adjudications that severely compromised the tribes' *Winters* rights, and those decrees in several instances still control the tribes' access to water. See, e.g., United States v. Gila Valley Irr. Dist., 920 F.Supp. 1444 (D.Ariz.1996), aff'd, 117 F.3d 425 (9th Cir.1997). The Supreme Court was not called upon further to define Indian water rights until 1963, in the case of Arizona v. California, 373 U.S. 546 (1963). In that major litigation over the lower Colorado River, the Court had to determine the water rights accruing to tribes along the river whose reservations had been established by both statute and executive order. The Court viewed the question as one of the intention of Congress or the President, and held that neither one could have meant to establish reservations without reserving for the use of the Indians the water necessary to make the land habitable and productive. The Court held that the water rights were effectively reserved as of the time of creation of the reservation.

The other major issue presented by Arizona v. California concerned the quantity of water reserved. Competing users contended that the water rights should be limited to amounts likely to be needed by the relatively sparse Indian population in the foreseeable future. The Supreme Court rejected that measure and instead ruled that the tribes were entitled to enough water to irrigate all the *practicably irrigable acreage* on the reservations—a much more generous measure. Once that quantity is e tablished in litigation, however, res judicata applies, the decree may not be reopened on the ground that some reservation lands were omitted. Arizona v. California, 460 U.S. 605 (1983).

From the *Winters* and *Arizona v. California* cases, it is possible to summarize some of the characteristics of reserved Indian water rights, commonly referred to as "*Winters* rights":

1. *Winters* rights are creatures of federal law, which defines their extent.

2. Establishment of a reservation by treaty, statute or executive order includes an implied reservation of water rights in sources within or bordering the reservation.

3. The water rights are reserved as of the date of creation of the applicable portion of the reservation. Competing users with prior appropriation dates under state law take precedence over the Indian rights, but those with later dates are subordinate.

4. The quantity of water reserved for Indian use is that amount sufficient to irrigate all the practicably irrigable acreage of the reservation.

5. *Winters* rights to water are not lost by nonuse.

It may be seen from this summary that Indian water rights have some of the characteristics of appropriative rights, such as a date of appropriation and the total priority of a prior appropriator over a later one in times of short supply. On the other hand, they also have some of the characteristics of riparian rights; they apply most clearly to Indian land bordering or surrounding the water, and they are not lost by non-use.

While maximum irrigable acreage provides the measure of Indian water rights under *Arizona v. California*, the special master to whom that case was referred stated that this measure did not necessarily mean that the water had to be used for agricultural purposes. S. Rifkind, Report of the Special Master—Arizona v. California 265 (1962), quoted in D. Getches, D. Rosenfelt & C. Wilkinson, Federal Indian Law 598 (1979). If a tribe decides to use its quantified share of agricultural water for industrial or other purposes, it therefore may do so. See Colville Confederated Tribes v. Walton, 647 F.2d 42, 48 (9th Cir.), cert. denied, 454 U.S. 1092 (1981); United States v. Anderson, 736 F.2d 1358, 1365 (9th Cir.1984); but see In re Big Horn River System, 835 P.2d 273, 278 (Wyo.1992). Courts have generally been inclined to recognize the need for flexibility in the manner in which reservations meet the needs of their inhabitants. United States v. Finch, 548 F.2d 822, 832 (9th Cir.1976), vacated on other grounds, 433 U.S. 676 (1977); Conrad Investment Co. v. United States, 161 Fed. 829, 831 (9th Cir.1908).

Where a reservation is established with express or implicit purposes beyond agriculture, such as fishing, then water is also reserved in quantities sufficient to sustain that use. United States v. Adair, 723 F.2d 1394, 1408–11 (9th Cir.1983), cert. denied, 467 U.S. 1252 (1984); Colville Confederated Tribes v. Walton, 647 F.2d at 48.

Although the purpose for which the federal government reserves other types of lands may be strictly construed, United States v. New Mexico, 438 U.S. 696 (1978) (national forest), the purposes of Indian reservations are necessarily entitled to broader interpretation if the goal of Indian self-sufficiency is to be attained. United States v. Finch, 548 F.2d at 827–32.

Although *Winters* and nearly all subsequent decisions dealt with surface water, there seems little doubt that Indian reserved rights also exist in "ground water" (perhaps better termed "underground water") beneath the reservation. The United States was held to have reserved ground water rights to Death Valley National Monument in Cappaert v. United States, 426 U.S. 128 (1976).

An expansive interpretation of *Winters* rights would also reserve for Indian use water from off-reservation sources if determined to be necessary to meet reservation needs. One such award appears to have been made without discussion in the Arizona v. California decree, 376 U.S. 340, 344 (1964); see Note, *Indian Reserved Rights: The Winters of Our Discontent*, 88 Yale L.J. 1689, 1697 n. 54 (1979). Extension of *Winters* rights beyond the reservation is sufficiently disruptive of the entire appropriative system, however, that it is likely to occur only in cases of dire need or where congressional intent is express or clear from a pattern of historical usage. The Department of Justice refused to undertake litigation on behalf of a tribe to pursue a claim to off-reservation water rights based on a treaty right to hunt (and implicitly to fish) on ceded lands. Shoshone–Bannock Tribes v. Reno, 56 F.3d 1476 (D.C.Cir.1995).

Many Indian tribes are just beginning to assert their unexercised water rights, and each assertion is almost certain to engender bitter controversy. Non–Indians contend that recognition of long-dormant Indian rights defeats the entire purpose of the appropriative system, which was to create certainty that would stimulate beneficial use. They argue that appropriators who saw unused water and spent large sums in creating transportation and irrigation systems ought not to be shut out today by the Indians. The tribes contend, however, that the reason for their non-use of the water was the failure of the United States to fulfill its responsibility as trustee in developing and protecting water resources, and that it would only compound injury to deprive the tribes of their water forever. *Winters* and its progeny have decided this argument in favor of the Indians, but that fact has by no means ended the controversy.

The greatest uncertainty resulting from Indian water rights arises from the fact that in many cases the rights have not been quantified. Competing users and the Indians themselves know that a reservation is entitled to enough water to irrigate its practicably irrigable acreage, but no one knows exactly how much water that is. One solution to that problem is adjudication, as in Arizona v. California. Adjudications have not come easily, however. The United States historically has not been vigorous in litigating to establish or preserve Indian water rights. The tribes themselves can bring suit, but the cost of such litigation is frequently prohibitive. All water users of a given source must be joined, with the result that mere service of process in a major river adjudication can run into tens of thousands of dollars. Surveys to determine irrigability may cost hundreds of thousands. The expenses of trial itself are even greater. For these reasons, alternative suggestions have been made for quantification of Indian water rights by negotiation, administrative action or legislation, but little progress has yet been made in that direction. An exception was the legislative settlement of the groundwater claims of the Ak–Chin Reservation in Arizona. Pub. L. 95–328, 92 Stat. 409 (1978).

C. *WINTERS* RIGHTS IN ALLOTTED LAND

When tribal land is converted into allotments, the Indian allottees succeed to the tribe's *Winters* rights for that land. United States v. Powers, 305 U.S. 527 (1939). Whether and to what extent those rights transfer to a non-Indian who subsequently acquires the allotment has been a matter of some dispute. Non–Indian transferees' rights were protected by the decision in *Powers*, but the nature and extent of those rights was not considered. Id. at 533. They were considered to be equal to Indian rights in United States v. Ahtanum Irrigation Dist., 236 F.2d 321, 342 (9th Cir.1956), cert. denied, 352 U.S. 988

(1957). That view has been elaborated to embrace the following propositions: (1) an Indian allottee is entitled to that share of the reservation's irrigation water rights that his allotment's irrigable acreage bears to the total irrigable acreage of the reservation; (2) when the Indian allottee sells to a non-Indian, the purchaser acquires the allotment's reserved water rights; (3) the priority date of those rights remains the date when the reservation was created; (4) the non-Indian allottee, unlike his Indian predecessor, loses his reserved right if he does not use it; he is therefore limited to the quantity of water from his reserved right that he appropriates with reasonable diligence after the transfer of title. Colville Confederated Tribes v. Walton, 647 F.2d 42 (9th Cir.1981), cert. denied, 454 U.S. 1092 (1981), appeal after remand 752 F.2d 397 (9th Cir.1985), cert. denied, 475 U.S. 1010 (1986). This formulation is a compromise. If no reserved rights at all were transferable, the Indian seller of an allotment would be prevented from realizing most of its value upon sale. On the other hand, if the sale price were maximized by permitting transfer of a right that could not be lost by non-use, the non-Indian transferee might assert dormant claims years later, in competition with reserved rights of the tribe or remaining Indian allottees. The *Walton* rule applies only when a non-Indian acquires an allotment from an Indian allottee; it does not apply to once-tribal land that was ceded back to the United States and subsequently homesteaded. The homesteader must acquire water under state rules. In re Big Horn

River System, 899 P.2d 848 (Wyo.1995); United
States v. Anderson, 736 F.2d 1358, 1363 (9th Cir.
1984).

D. LEASE OR SALE OF
WINTERS RIGHTS

It is well established that Indian water rights
may be leased to non-Indians along with a lease of
Indian lands. Skeem v. United States, 273 Fed. 93
(9th Cir.1921). The practice is quite common. It is
less clear whether *Winters* rights may be leased
separately to non-Indians for use on other land.
Because tribes are not confined to any particular
use of their agricultural water, see Section B, supra,
there would seem to be no reason to prohibit them
from leasing it as an alternative means of making
the reservation self-sufficient. Use of such water by
non-Indian lessees would not be inconsistent with
the trust nature of *Winters* rights so long as the
tribe retained the reversionary interest.

Outright sale of Indian water rights might be
inconsistent with the trust responsibility, because it
would quite possibly threaten the continued existence of the tribal land base. The issue is likely to
arise rarely in the future because of extreme resistance by the tribes to the permanent alienation of
tribal property.

E. *WINTERS* RIGHTS AS PROPERTY

The question has sometimes been raised whether
Winters rights are property to which tribes hold

recognized title, so that any taking of those rights by the federal government would be subject to compensation under the Fifth Amendment. See Chapter XII, Section D, supra. Although the question has not been settled, it seems almost certain that the status of *Winters* rights is the same as that of the land they serve. As a result, *Winters* rights arising by implication from a treaty or statute establishing a reservation are property to which title is recognized, as are the reservation lands themselves.

When Indian lands are set aside solely by executive order, the tribal title apparently remains unrecognized for Fifth Amendment purposes. See Chapter XII, Section D, supra. It follows that *Winters* rights pertaining to those lands would also be unrecognized and subject to taking without compensation by the federal government.

Winters rights arising from the establishment of a reservation take the date of that establishment as their appropriation date. In some cases, however, a tribe may claim aboriginal occupation of the land long prior to that time. The nature and extent of water rights attending such occupation has only recently come under examination. Initially, these rights would be held under original Indian title and would accordingly be subject to taking without compensation by the federal government (but not subject to taking in any manner by others). The rights become recognized, however, when a reservation is established by treaty or statute on the lands in question. United States v. Adair, 723 F.2d 1394, 1412–15 (9th Cir.1983), cert. denied, 467 U.S. 1252

(1984). Thus the Klamath Tribe's aboriginal hunting and fishing became the foundation for a reserved water right for those purposes when their reservation was established. The amount of water reserved was that quantity sufficient to provide the Indians with a moderate livelihood from hunting and fishing, not the amount enjoyed in aboriginal times, or at the time the reservation was established. The priority date, however, was time immemorial. Id.

F. JURISDICTION TO ADJUDICATE WATER RIGHTS

The United States holds the legal title to *Winters* rights as trustee for the tribes. It consequently is an indispensable party to any adjudication of those rights. It may not, however, be sued without its consent. Traditionally, the United States has not consented to be sued in state court. When it has brought suit itself, it has done so in federal court under the jurisdiction conferred by 28 U.S.C.A. § 1345. As a result, federal court has been the customary forum for the adjudication of Indian water rights.

In 1952, however, Congress consented to suit in state court by the McCarran Amendment, which includes the following provision:

43 U.S.C.A. § 666

(a) Consent is hereby given to join the United States as a defendant in any suit (1) for the adjudication of rights to the use of water of a river system or other source, or (2) for the administration of such rights, where it appears that the United States is the owner of or is in the process of acquiring water rights by appropriation under State law, by purchase, by exchange, or otherwise, and the United States is a necessary party to such suit. The United States, when a party to any such suit, shall (1) be deemed to have waived any right to plead that the State laws are inapplicable or that the United States is not amenable thereto by reason of its sovereignty, and (2) shall be subject to the judgments, orders, and decrees of the court having jurisdiction * * *.

Although at one time it was uncertain whether this provision applied to suits involving reserved Indian water rights, that point was settled in Colorado River Water Conservation Dist. v. United States, 424 U.S. 800 (1976). In that case the United States had actually initiated a suit in federal court when a subsequent litigation was begun under the state adjudication system. The Supreme Court held that the McCarran Amendment rendered the United States as trustee for Indian water rights subject to suit in state court. It also ruled that the federal court should have abstained in favor of the state litigation, even though the federal court had concurrent jurisdiction. The Court relied on the fact that no proceedings had taken place in federal court except for the filing of the complaint.

The Court also made it clear in *Colorado River* that the nature and extent of reserved Indian water rights remain matters of federal law, even though they are subject to adjudication in state court. Federal question review is therefore available in the Supreme Court. Despite these assurances, the prospect of state adjudication of their water rights causes great apprehension on the part of Indian tribes. They believe that the state forum is likely to be unsympathetic to Indian rights, and that the applicability of federal law does not provide great protection against bias. Indeed, one state supreme court has held that state and not federal law governs the question whether a tribe may change the use of its reserved *Winters* water from agriculture to instream fisheries! In re Big Horn River System, 835 P.2d 273 (Wyo.1992). Even when federal law is acknowledged to govern, water rights cases often depend upon detailed fact determinations, such as the extent of practicably irrigable acreage of a reservation, that are very difficult to upset upon review. For this reason, many tribes have hastened to initiate water rights litigation in federal court, and have attempted to undertake sufficient discovery and other proceedings there to forestall abstention in favor of later-initiated state court proceedings. In general, these tactics have failed, and the federal courts have yielded to the states for general watershed adjudications involving Indian rights.

Legal challenges to state court adjudication have also been unsuccessful. In Arizona v. San Carlos Apache Tribe, 463 U.S. 545 (1983), the United States and several tribes argued: (1) that state enabling acts requiring the states to disclaim jurisdiction over Indian lands precluded the states from adjudicating Indian water rights; (2) that federal Indian policy similarly precluded the states from acting; and (3) that abstention by the federal courts was improper when the suit was brought by a tribe itself, and sought only an adjudication of tribal water rights. The Supreme Court rejected all of these arguments. It held that any barriers to state court adjudication erected by enabling acts or federal policy were dismantled by the McCarran Amendment. It also strongly endorsed abstention, stating that parallel federal and state proceedings were wasteful and inconsistent with the thrust of the McCarran Amendment.

The United States and the Klamath Tribe challenged Oregon's attempt to adjudicate their water rights on the ground that Oregon's procedure was not a "suit" within the meaning of the McCarran Amendment's waiver of sovereign immunity. United States v. Oregon, 44 F.3d 758 (9th Cir.1994), cert. denied, 516 U.S. 943 (1995). Oregon's procedure was administrative, subject to judicial review when parties filed objections to the administrative report. The court of appeals held that this procedure qualified as a "suit" for purposes of the McCarran Amendment. 44 F.3d at 765–77. The court also held that the failure of Oregon's adjudication to include groundwater did not deprive it of the comprehensiveness deemed necessary to qualify as an adjudication of a "river system" within the meaning of the Amendment. The United States and the Tribe were therefore required to submit to Oregon's procedure.

More extreme legal challenges to state court adjudication have also failed. One tribe attempted, unsuccessfully, to enjoin federal officers from taking necessary steps to submit the tribe's water claim to state court for adjudication. United States v. White Mountain Apache Tribe, 784 F.2d 917 (9th Cir. 1986).

There is no question, therefore, that the focus of Indian water rights litigation has shifted to the state courts. Several general water rights adjudications involving entire watersheds are under way in the states, and will remain so for several years. The federal courts have correspondingly withdrawn from the field.

On occasion, nevertheless, a federal court is called upon to make a ruling concerning the existence or extent of Indian water rights in order to settle a collateral controversy. The existence of a pending general adjudication in state court, expected to last for years, does not prevent the federal court from acting in such cases. Thus federal courts have been permitted or required to adjudicate tribal reserved rights, at least for purposes of decision, when necessary to protect tribal fisheries. United States v. Adair, 723 F.2d 1394 (9th Cir.1983), cert. denied, 467 U.S. 1252 (1984); Joint Board of Control of the Flathead, Mission and Jocko Irrigation Districts v. United States, 832 F.2d 1127 (9th Cir.1987); see Kittitas Reclamation District v. Sunnyside Valley Irrigation District, 763 F.2d 1032 (9th Cir.1985), cert. denied, 474 U.S. 1032 (1985).

One other area of collateral jurisdictional contention concerns state power to regulate water use by non-Indians on fee lands they own within reservations. In one instance, where the stream lay wholly within the reservation, the state was held to be preempted from regulating allotted water use. Colville Confederated Tribes v. Walton, 647 F.2d 42, 51–53 (9th Cir.1981). In another, where the stream lay largely outside the reservation and only formed a boundary of the reservation for part of its course, the state was allowed to regulate water use by non-Indians on their fee lands within the reservation. United States v. Anderson, 736 F.2d 1358 (9th Cir.1984). Conversely, a tribe has been held without power under Montana v. United States, 450 U.S. 544 (1981), to regulate non-Indian use of "surplus" water (water in excess of that needed to satisfy *Winters* rights) on fee lands within the reservation or off-reservation. Holly v. Confederated Tribes and Bands of Yakima Indian Nation, 655 F.Supp. 557 (E.D.Wash.1985), aff'd, 812 F.2d 714 (9th Cir.), cert. denied, 484 U.S. 823 (1987).

CHAPTER XV

INDIAN HUNTING AND FISHING RIGHTS

A. INTRODUCTION

The most intense controversies in current Indian affairs are probably those concerning hunting and fishing. The right to take game and fish has always been of immense economic importance to many tribes, and it has equally great cultural significance for most Indians. Attempts to exercise hunting and fishing rights have brought Indians into conflict with non-Indians who have very strong economic and sporting motivations of their own. One result has been a great deal of litigation.

Legal problems of Indian hunting and fishing are exceptionally complicated. Not only is the right to hunt and fish a form of tribal property, but it also involves an activity that calls for regulation and policing. All of the problems of conflicting jurisdiction that exist in the general criminal law field, see Chapter VII, supra, consequently appear here. Jurisdiction may thus depend on whether the hunting and fishing is done by an Indian or non-Indian, whether it takes place in or out of Indian country, and whether a treaty modifies the usual jurisdictional rules. In addition to these complexi-

419

ties, migratory fish and game present problems of regulation and conservation that are almost overwhelming.

The subject is perhaps best attacked by first examining the basic nature of Indian hunting and fishing rights without the complications that are introduced when the state strongly asserts a competing conservation interest. Those complications can then be explored in the context of recent confrontations between tribes and states over fishing rights, particularly in the State of Washington. Finally, problems of jurisdiction over non-Indian hunting and fishing in Indian country can be addressed. Issues peculiar to Alaska are treated separately in Chapter XIII, Section D.

B. BASIC INDIAN HUNTING AND FISHING RIGHTS

It is well settled that the establishment of a reservation by treaty, statute or agreement includes an implied right of Indians to hunt and fish on that reservation free of regulation by the state. Menominee Tribe v. United States, 391 U.S. 404 (1968). That right is shared by tribes placed together on a reservation by the United States, even when one of them was placed there in violation of a treaty with the other. Northern Arapahoe Tribe v. Hodel, 808 F.2d 741 (10th Cir.1987). States have rarely contested the right because of their general lack of power to regulate Indians in Indian country. See McClanahan v. Arizona State Tax Com'n, 411 U.S.

164 (1973). The Indians' immunity from state law
applies on the reservation even in states that have
been granted criminal jurisdiction over Indian country by Public Law 280, for that statute provides
that it shall not "deprive any Indian or any Indian
tribe, band, or community of any right, privilege, or
immunity afforded under Federal treaty, agreement, or statute with respect to hunting, trapping,
or fishing or the control, licensing, or regulation
thereof." 18 U.S.C.A. § 1162(b). Nor may state law
be applied to Indian hunting and fishing in Indian
country by way of the Assimilative Crimes Act, 18
U.S.C.A. § 13. Cheyenne–Arapaho Tribes v. Oklahoma, 618 F.2d 665 (10th Cir.1980). The state may
also be preempted from prohibiting the possession
or sale off-reservation of fish or game by Indians
who had taken them on their reservations. People v.
McCovey, 36 Cal.3d 517, 205 Cal.Rptr. 643, 685
P.2d 687 (1984), cert. denied, 469 U.S. 1062 (1984);
Mattz v. Superior Court, 46 Cal.3d 355, 758 P.2d
606, 250 Cal.Rptr. 278 (1988), cert. denied, 489 U.S.
1078 (1989); contra Bailey v. State, 409 N.W.2d 33
(Minn.App.1987).

Indeed, the implied treaty right to hunt and fish
free from state law has been held to survive a
congressional termination of the trust relationship
between the tribe and the federal government; the
hunting and fishing rights are not extinguished in
the absence of a clear indication of congressional
intent to that effect. Menominee Tribe v. United
States, 391 U.S. 404 (1968); United States v. Felter,
752 F.2d 1505 (10th Cir.1985). Such rights have

been upheld even for Indians who withdrew from the tribe upon termination of its trust relationship. Kimball v. Callahan, 493 F.2d 564 (9th Cir.), cert. denied, 419 U.S. 1019 (1974), and Kimball v. Callahan, 590 F.2d 768 (9th Cir.), cert. denied, 444 U.S. 826 (1979); but see United States v. Von Murdock, 132 F.3d 534 (10th Cir.1997). Failure of the federal government to recognize a group of Indians as a tribe does not prevent the group from exercising treaty rights if it descended from a treaty signatory and has maintained an organized tribal structure. United States v. Washington, 520 F.2d 676, 692–93 (9th Cir.1975), cert. denied, 423 U.S. 1086 (1976). A group that fails to maintain cohesion with the treaty tribe, however, does not retain the treaty right. United States v. Oregon, 29 F.3d 481 (9th Cir. 1994), amended, 43 F.3d 1284, cert. denied, 515 U.S. 1102 (1995).

A tribe may also reserve by treaty the right to hunt or fish off-reservation. United States v. Winans, 198 U.S. 371 (1905). Where a treaty reserves the right to fish at "all usual and accustomed places," the state may not preclude access to those places, id., nor may it require a license fee of Indians to fish there. Tulee v. Washington, 315 U.S. 681 (1942). The treaty right also encompasses the ability to erect structures at those sites, although their permissible nature and degree of permanence are subject to dispute. See Sohappy v. Hodel, 911 F.2d 1312 (9th Cir.1990). The "usual and accustomed places" are those of the tribes that signed the treaty. A non-treaty tribe that later affiliates with one of the treaty tribes may share the treaty tribe's right to fish its accustomed places, but the affiliating tribe acquires no treaty right to fish *its* own accustomed places. Wahkiakum Band of Chinook Indians v. Bateman, 655 F.2d 176 (9th Cir. 1981); State v. Goodell, 84 Or.App. 398, 734 P.2d 10, rev. denied, 303 Or. 455, 737 P.2d 1248 (1987). If two treaty tribes merge, the resulting merged tribe may exercise the treaty rights of both predecessors. See United States v. Suquamish Indian Tribe, 901 F.2d 772 (9th Cir.1990).

A tribal member exercising the treaty right to hunt on "open and unclaimed lands" within his tribe's aboriginal territory but outside of its reservation cannot be subjected to state season limitations. State v. Stasso, 172 Mont. 242, 563 P.2d 562 (1977). An unrestricted right to hunt on "open and unclaimed lands" even may include public lands outside of the tribe's original territory. State v. Buchanan, 87 Wash.App. 189, 941 P.2d 683 (1997). An agreement ratified by Congress guaranteeing the right to hunt on ceded lands "in common with all other persons" grants the same immunity. Antoine v. Washington, 420 U.S. 194 (1975). The state may, however, impose certain regulations essential to conservation; see Section C, infra. A treaty reserving the "right of hunting" on ceded lands also reserves the right to continue fishing commercially in adjacent waters without a state license. People v. LeBlanc, 399 Mich. 31, 248 N.W.2d 199 (1976).

The status of *temporary* rights reserved by treaty is somewhat more precarious. Reserved treaty rights to hunt, fish and gather on ceded lands "during the pleasure of the President of the United States" were protected from implied abrogation by later orders or treaties in Lac Courte Oreilles Band v. Voigt, 700 F.2d 341 (7th Cir.), cert. denied, 464 U.S. 805 (1983), and Lac Courte Oreilles Band v. Wisconsin, 760 F.2d 177 (7th Cir.1985). The court held that even temporary rights guaranteed by treaty are protected to a greater degree than aboriginal rights, and cannot be extinguished by implication. 700 F.2d at 356. The Tenth Circuit has held, however, that a treaty "right to hunt on the unoccupied lands of the United States so long as game may be found thereon" was understood to be temporary and was abrogated by the admission of Wyoming into the Union "on an equal footing with the original States." Crow Tribe of Indians v. Repsis, 73 F.3d 982 (10th Cir.1995), cert. denied, 517 U.S. 1221 (1996). The Tenth Circuit relied on a similar "equal footing" ruling applied to identical treaty language in Ward v. Race Horse, 163 U.S. 504 (1896). Many observers had thought this rationale of *Race Horse* to have been undermined by United States v. Winans, 198 U.S. 371, 382–83 (1905). In *Crow Tribe*, however, the Tenth Circuit emphasized the temporary nature of the treaty right and insisted that, for such rights, *"Race Horse* is alive and well." *Crow Tribe*, 73 F.3d at 994.

A somewhat different approach was taken by the Eighth Circuit in dealing with claims of several Chippewa bands to hunt, fish, and gather under an 1837 treaty guaranteeing those rights "during the

pleasure of the President of the United States." See
Mille Lacs Band of Chippewa Indians v. Minnesota,
124 F.3d 904 (8th Cir.1997), pet. for cert. filed, 66
U.S.L.W. 3607 (1998). The Eighth Circuit held that
this right was not understood by the Indians to be
temporary. Unlike the right involved in *Race Horse*
and *Crow Tribe*, it applied to all land, not simply
unoccupied land of the United States which is necessarily a temporary category. Such treaty rights
had often been exercised consistently with a state's
right of sovereignty. The Chippewas' right therefore
was not abrogated by admission of Minnesota into
the Union on an equal footing with the original
states. Id. at 926–29. It was also not abrogated by
an 1850 executive order of President Taylor pur-
porting to revoke the "temporary" privileges granted to the Chippewas in 1837 and requiring their
removal to their reservations. The executive order,
the court held, was unauthorized because the President had no statutory power unilaterally to order
removal and the removal provision was not severable from the extinguishment provision. Id. at 914–
18. The treaty rights were held exercisable on all
public and private land in the ceded territory open
to hunting generally, but not to private land open
only with permission of the owner. Id. at 933–34.

When a tribe cedes title to lands without any
indication of intent to retain hunting or fishing
rights, the state is free to regulate Indians there.
Oregon Dept. of Fish & Wildlife v. Klamath Indian
Tribe, 473 U.S. 753 (1985). In the absence of treaty

rights, of course, Indians outside of Indian country are subject to the same state laws as anyone else.

Wholly apart from treaty, a tribe may possess aboriginal rights to hunting and fishing, but like other aboriginal title, it can be extinguished by the federal government. Extinguishment of aboriginal land title also extinguishes aboriginal hunting and fishing rights, unless they are reserved in a treaty, statute or executive order. Confederated Tribes of Chehalis Indian Reservation v. Washington, 96 F.3d 334 (9th Cir.1996), cert. denied, 117 S.Ct. 1432 (1997). Payment of a claim for taking of aboriginal land title therefore forecloses further enjoyment of an aboriginal right to hunt and fish the lands taken. Western Shoshone Nat'l Council v. Molini, 951 F.2d 200 (9th Cir.1991), cert. denied, 506 U.S. 822 (1992).

The tribe itself has power to regulate Indian hunting and fishing on the reservation, whether or not it chooses to exercise it. United States v. Jackson, 600 F.2d 1283 (9th Cir.1979). That power extends to the regulation of hunting and fishing by Indians on non-Indian fee lands. Lower Brule Sioux Tribe v. South Dakota, 711 F.2d 809, 827 (8th Cir.1983), cert. denied, 464 U.S. 1042 (1984). The tribe also has the power to regulate Indian hunting or fishing conducted off-reservation pursuant to treaty. Settler v. Lameer, 507 F.2d 231 (9th Cir. 1974).

The federal government's plenary power over Indian affairs extends to the regulation of Indian hunting and fishing. Indeed, Congress can wholly abrogate a treaty hunting right, as it did in the Eagle Protection Act, 16 U.S.C.A. § 668(a). United States v. Dion, 476 U.S. 734 (1986). The Secretary of Interior has issued regulations governing Indian fishing on a few reservations, see 25 C.F.R.Pts. 241 and 242, and has provided for identification of treaty Indians fishing off-reservation, 25 C.F.R.Pt. 249. The Secretary has been held to be authorized under the trust power to ban commercial fishing by Indians on their reservation, and he need not show the kind of imminent threat to conservation required for state regulation of treaty fishing. United States v. Eberhardt, 789 F.2d 1354 (9th Cir.1986). The Secretary similarly may regulate Indian hunting. Northern Arapahoe Tribe v. Hodel, 808 F.2d 741 (10th Cir.1987). In general, however, the federal government has been very sparing in the exercise of its power to regulate Indian hunting and fishing. But see Section D, infra. The matter has accordingly been left largely for tribal regulation. In one instance where the tribe failed to act, federal authorities prosecuted a tribal member under a federal trespass statute that forbids unauthorized entry upon Indian lands for the purpose of hunting, trapping or fishing, 18 U.S.C.A. § 1165. The statute was held inapplicable to Indians. United States v. Jackson, 600 F.2d 1283 (9th Cir.1979). In 1981, however, Congress amended the Lacey Act to prohibit transport of or traffic in fish or wildlife taken, possessed or sold in violation of any federal, state or tribal law. 16 U.S.C.A. § 3372(a). That prohibition was held applicable to Indians in United States v. Sohappy, 770 F.2d 816 (9th Cir.1985), cert. denied, 477 U.S. 906 (1986). If an Indian is charged under the Lacey Act with violating a state law applicable to Indian treaty fishing, the prosecution must prove that the state law was necessary for conservation of the fish. Id. If an Indian claiming a treaty right is charged under the Lacey Act for a violation of state law that would also constitute a violation of tribal law, no such showing is required. United States v. Williams, 898 F.2d 727 (9th Cir.1990); cf. State v. McCormack, 117 Wash.2d 141, 812 P.2d 483 (1991), cert. denied, 502 U.S. 1111 (1992). Of course, federal statutes of general applicability such as the Airborne Hunting Act, 16 U.S.C.A. § 742j–1, apply to Indians in Indian country just as they apply to everyone else everywhere. United States v. Stone, 112 F.3d 971 (8th Cir.1997).

C. INDIAN RIGHTS AND STATE CON-SERVATION; THE WASHINGTON FISHING CASES

The most severe conflict between Indian fishing rights and competing non-Indian interests arose over the right to fish for salmon and steelhead trout in the Pacific Northwest. Those fish are anadromous, which means that they hatch in rivers, then journey far out to sea and ultimately return to their original rivers to spawn. They are sought after not only by Indians, but by non-Indian sport and commercial fishermen both in the rivers and at sea. If too many fish from a particular river's run are caught, then fishing in that river is destroyed and may not be restored for decades, if ever. Wholly unrestricted fishing by all parties would probably lead to that result in some rivers. Consequently, Washington and other states attempted to regulate not only non-Indian fishing, but the entire salmon and steelhead fishery. The result was a number of Supreme Court cases wrestling with the conflicting interests and the issues that they presented.

The first major case was Puyallup Tribe v. Department of Game, 391 U.S. 392 (1968) (*Puyallup I*). The tribes involved in that case had entered a treaty in 1854 which contained the following clause:

> The right of taking fish, at all usual and accustomed grounds and stations, is further secured to said Indians, in common with all citizens of the Territory * * *.

Treaty with the Nisqually and Other Indians, art. III, 10 Stat. 1132, 1133 (1854). That clause, or one virtually identical to it, appeared in a number of treaties entered by northwestern tribes in the 1850's. It confers off-reservation fishing rights, which the tribes in *Puyallup I* were exercising by the use of set nets in the streams. The Indians were fishing both for their own needs and for commercial purposes. The State of Washington banned the use of nets in the streams and sought to apply this prohibition to the Indians. The Supreme Court assumed that Indians fished with nets and for commercial purposes at the time of the treaty, but noted that the treaty said nothing to guarantee a particular manner of fishing. The Court then held:

> The right to fish "at all usual and accustomed" places may, of course, not be qualified by the State, even though all Indians born in the United States are now citizens of the United States. * * * But the manner of fishing, the size of the take, the restriction of commercial fishing, and the like may be regulated by the State in the interests of conservation, provided the regulation meets appropriate standards and does not discriminate against the Indians.

391 U.S. at 398. The Court noted that the Washington courts had made no finding on whether the particular regulation was a "reasonable and necessary" conservation measure, and therefore remanded the case, with the additional enigmatic comment that the state court's findings "must also cover the issue of equal protection implicit in the phrase 'in common with'." Id. at 403.

Puyallup I was an important departure from prior law because it permitted some state regulation of the exercise of Indian treaty rights. To be sure, that regulation had to meet "appropriate standards." The Supreme Court later explained that "[t]he 'appropriate standards' requirement means that the State must demonstrate that its regulation is a reasonable and necessary conservation measure, * * * *and* that its application to the Indians is necessary in the interests of conservation." Antoine v. Washington, 420 U.S. 194, 207 (1975). Even with that subsequently-developed limitation, however, *Puyallup I* still meant that states for the first time could legally exercise control over federal Indian rights.

After the remand in *Puyallup I*, Washington authorities decided to permit Indian net fishing of salmon, but they banned net fishing of steelhead altogether. The matter returned to the Supreme Court, which pointed out that limiting steelhead fishing to hook-and-line had the effect of granting the entire run to non-Indian sports fishermen. The Court held that this result discriminated against the Indians and consequently did not meet the standard set in the previous *Puyallup* decision. Department of Game v. Puyallup Tribe, 414 U.S. 44 (1973) (*Puyallup II*). Some accommodation between non-Indian and Indian rights had to be found, said the Court, but if a total ban was essential to save the steelhead from extinction, that ban could be applied to Indians.

After the second remand, Washington authorities permitted Indians to net steelhead, but limited their take to 45% of the natural run. At about the same time, an unexpected collateral development took place. A federal court of appeals held that the Puyallup Reservation, which many had thought abandoned, still existed. United States v. Washington, 496 F.2d 620 (9th Cir.), cert. denied, 419 U.S. 1032 (1974). As a consequence, many of the "accustomed grounds and stations" dealt with in *Puyallup I* and *II* suddenly were found to be on-reservation sites (although the land was no longer Indian-held).

In the third appeal, the tribe therefore argued that the state could not regulate its fishing in those locations at all. The Supreme Court rejected that contention, stating that its prior decisions established that the Indians' right to fish at the accustomed places was not exclusive, and that a fair apportionment of fish could not be made between non-Indians and Indians if the Indians could take an unlimited number of fish within the reservation. Puyallup Tribe, Inc. v. Department of Game, 433 U.S. 165 (1977) (*Puyallup III*). The Court also upheld the standards of conservation necessity applied by the state courts.

In the course of the three *Puyallup* cases, then, the law moved from an original (and perhaps not severely tested) position that the state could not regulate treaty fishing rights at all, to a radically different one permitting it to regulate Indian fishing both on and off-reservation when necessary for purposes of conservation. It was not clear, however, to what degree the state's power over on-reservation fishing was a product of the peculiar history of the *Puyallup* litigation, which began as an off-reservation case and ended as an on-reservation one. It seems clear enough that, where the fishery is shared, the state is entitled to limit the total on-reservation catch so that it does not destroy the non-Indian population's share of the runs. Washington v. Washington State Commercial Passenger Fishing Vessel Ass'n, 443 U.S. 658, 681–82 (1979). The state may also be able to limit Indian fishing methods where essential to preserve the run from extinction. Any regulation beyond that point would appear to run counter to the usual exclusion of state regulatory power over Indians in Indian country. The Supreme Court has cited *Puyallup III* to support the proposition that "in exceptional circumstances a State may assert jurisdiction over the on-reservation activities of tribal members," New Mexico v. Mescalero Apache Tribe, 462 U.S. 324, 331–32 & n. 15 (1983), but instances of such regulation have proved to be rare indeed. See Chapter IX, Section F, supra. The unusual history of the *Puyallup* cases is almost certainly the sole explanation for the unique ruling of *Puyallup III* that the tribe's right to on-reservation stations was nonexclusive; the Court reached a contrary conclusion in *Washington State Commercial Passenger Fishing Vessel Association*, 443 U.S. at 683–84.

Meanwhile, during the pendency of the *Puyallup* litigation, the United States had brought suit in United States District Court on behalf of seven tribes asserting rights under similar treaty clauses. The district court found the Indians entitled to 50% of the harvestable run of fish, minus a few percentage points representing fish that were not needed by the tribes. United States v. Washington, 384 F.Supp. 312 (W.D.Wash.1974), aff'd, 520 F.2d 676 (9th Cir.1975), cert. denied, 423 U.S. 1086 (1976). The decision was bitterly and in some cases violently resisted. Litigation was begun in state court which culminated in decisions by the Washington Supreme Court holding that the state could not comply with the federal ruling, that the treaty conferred upon the Indians no greater right than that enjoyed by other citizens, and that any other interpretation more favorable to the Indians would violate the Equal Protection Clause. Puget Sound Gillnetters Ass'n v. Moos, 88 Wash.2d 677, 565 P.2d 1151 (1977); Washington State Commercial Passenger Fishing Vessel Ass'n v. Tollefson, 89 Wash.2d 276, 571 P.2d 1373 (1977). The federal district court thereupon issued orders enabling it to supervise the state fishery in order to preserve treaty rights. United States v. Washington, 459 F.Supp. 1020 (W.D.Wash.), aff'd, 573 F.2d 1123 (9th Cir.1978).

These state and federal decisions were all reviewed by the U.S. Supreme Court in Washington v. Washington State Commercial Passenger Fishing Vessel Ass'n, 443 U.S. 658 (1979). The Supreme Court rejected the Washington court's holdings entirely. It ruled that the equal protection issue was foreclosed by the *Puyallup* cases. It also disagreed with the state court's treaty interpretation. While "in common with all citizens of the Territory" might normally be read to confer only an equal opportunity to fish on the same terms as others, the Supreme Court believed that the right of "taking fish" would have been understood by the Indians to guarantee the tribes an actual share of the fish. The federal district court's percentage allocation was therefore approved. The Supreme court in the course of its opinion also set forth the following propositions, which undoubtedly set the future pattern for enforcement of treaty rights in migratory fish:

1.   It is logical to establish a 50% share of the harvestable run as the "ceiling" for the Indian fishery. Reductions may then be made for fish not needed, as when a tribe has dwindled to very small numbers.

2.   The state may set the figure of the harvestable run (the total number of fish that may be caught without endangering the future of the run) for each stream.

3.   All fish from those runs caught by treaty Indians count against the Indian share, whether caught on or off reservation.

4.   All fish from those runs caught by non-Indian citizens of the state count against their share, whether or not caught in state waters.

5.   Indians may reserve for their exclusive use all fishing stations within the reservation.

The Court's resolution of this entire controversy probably makes up in pragmatism whatever it lacks in theoretical symmetry. The state continues to be able to regulate treaty fishing rights, but only in the imposition of aggregate catch limits necessary for conservation. Similar limits may be imposed by federal courts adjudicating fishing cases. United States v. Oregon, 657 F.2d 1009, 1016 (9th Cir. 1981). The Indians are guaranteed a substantial portion of the run. The decision is a response to the practical problems attending a shared fishery, and certainly should not be understood as permitting state limitation of Indian rights to take game and fish that never leave the reservation. See United

States v. Washington, 694 F.2d 188 (9th Cir.1982), cert. denied, 463 U.S. 1207 (1983).

The Supreme Court's standards have been applied or elaborated upon in continuing litigation of treaty fishing in Washington and Oregon. The Indian share of 50% includes state-produced hatchery fish. United States v. Washington, 759 F.2d 1353 (9th Cir.1985) (en banc). The 50% applies to the whole harvestable run, not simply the total fish actually caught. United States v. Washington, 774 F.2d 1470 (9th Cir.1985). Either party may exceed its share when the other takes less than its share, so long as the total catch does not exceed the harvestable limit. United States v. Washington, 761 F.2d 1404 (9th Cir.1985). The 50% figure has also been employed in other treaty cases. See, e.g., Lac Courte Oreilles Band of Lake Superior Chippewa Indians v. Wisconsin, 775 F.Supp. 321 (W.D.Wis. 1991).

Allocation of anadromous fish among the competing treaty and nontreaty fishing interests has been a continuous process, accomplished largely by agreement of parties under the continuing supervision of the federal courts. See, e.g., United States v. Oregon, 913 F.2d 576 (9th Cir.1990), cert. denied, 501 U.S. 1250 (1991). Controversy continues over the degree of necessity the state must show to support conservation regulations restricting treaty fishing. The state may even close accustomed stations if conservation interests justify. United States v. Oregon, 718 F.2d 299 (9th Cir.1983); see Shoshone–Bannock Tribes v. Fish and Game Comm'n, 42 F.3d 1278 (9th Cir.1994). The state must show more than mere benefit to the fish run, but it need not show that the fish species is actually endangered. Id. Generally, state regulation of treaty fishing must be the least restrictive consistent with the necessary escapement of fish to preserve future runs; it must treat the treaty rights as co-equal to other uses; and it must accord the tribes a fair opportunity to take, by reasonable means, a fair portion of the fish from each run. United States v. Oregon, 769 F.2d 1410 (9th Cir.1985). Federal regulation of ocean fishing, by enforcing conservation closures run-by-run, also helps to guarantee that treaty fishermen will have an opportunity to take their share from each separate run. See Washington State Charterboat Ass'n v. Baldrige, 702 F.2d 820 (9th Cir.1983), cert. denied, 464 U.S. 1053 (1984).

The most recent application of the Washington treaties concerned shellfish gathering. The treaties providing for a right of the Indians to take fish "at all usual and accustomed grounds and stations" included a proviso: "That they shall not take shell fish from any beds staked or cultivated by citizens." The Ninth Circuit held that the treaty clearly guaranteed a right to take shellfish, and that the proviso excluded treaty Indians only from artificial beds created by private owners; it did not prevent access to natural beds claimed or improved by those owners, nor to artificial beds created by the state. United States v. Washington, 135 F.3d 618 (9th

Cir.1998). In implementing the treaty, the court followed the formula of the salmon cases, awarding the Indians one half of the harvestable shellfish within their accustomed fishing grounds, with an adjustment for harvest from privately-owned beds. With regard to beds owned by private growers, the court awarded the Indians the right to harvest one half of the shellfish that would be produced by such beds without the efforts of the owners to enhance production. The court also imposed restrictions on exercise of the treaty right arising from the nature of the resource, consisting as it does largely of fixed beds, frequently in privately owned tidelands. Harvest from most beds was confined to five days per year, and owners were given considerable control over the manner of harvest. The Indians were not given a right of crossing private lands to get to the beds unless they showed that there was no other practical means of access. On the other hand, the tribes' rights were not confined to customary shellfish stations, but included all of their accustomed fishing stations for all species. The treaty right was held not to be inconsistent with the admission of Washington into the Union on an equal footing with the original states. The court's implementation of the treaty right represents an understandable compromise. As in the case of anadromous fish, exercise of the treaty right to gather shellfish will require continuous administration, ideally with a high degree of agreement among the competing parties.

D. THE ALTERNATIVE OF FEDERAL REGULATION; THE GREAT LAKES

Another conflict over Indian off-reservation rights arose in regard to fishing in the Great Lakes. In People v. LeBlanc, 399 Mich. 31, 248 N.W.2d 199 (1976), state authorities charged a Chippewa tribal member with fishing in Lake Superior without a commercial license and with using a prohibited device—a gill net. The Michigan Supreme Court held that the fishing was guaranteed by treaty and that the state could not require a license. It held that the state could, however, impose its gill net regulations, but only if: (1) the prohibition was necessary for the preservation of the fish; (2) the application of the prohibition to the treaty Indians was also necessary for the preservation of the fish; and (3) the regulation did not discriminate against the Chippewas. In so ruling, the court was adhering to the standards set by the Supreme Court in *Puyallup I* and *II* as elaborated by Antoine v. Washington, supra, Section C.

Subsequently, a federal district court held that the state was utterly without power to regulate the manner of exercise of Indian treaty rights to Great Lakes fishing. United States v. Michigan, 471 F.Supp. 192 (W.D.Mich.1979). Shortly thereafter, the Secretary of Interior issued fairly detailed regulations governing Indian treaty fishing in the Great Lakes. The regulations closed certain areas, restricted others, prohibited netting of some species, and regulated the mesh size of gill nets. As a result, the federal court of appeals remanded the preceding district court decision for a determination whether the federal regulations were intended to and did preempt the state law. The preemption issue disappeared, however, when the Secretary permitted the federal regulations to expire; the alternative of federal regulation was accordingly never truly tested. See United States v. Michigan, 653 F.2d 277 (6th Cir.), cert. denied, 454 U.S. 1124 (1981), 712 F.2d 242 (6th Cir.1983).

There is no question, however, that federal regulations authorized by Congress can supersede conflicting state laws regarding Indian hunting and fishing. Metlakatla Indian Community v. Egan, 369 U.S. 45 (1962). The only questions likely to arise are whether a given regulation is intended to preempt state law and, if so, whether it is authorized by Congress. In People v. McCovey, 36 Cal.3d 517, 205 Cal.Rptr. 643, 685 P.2d 687, cert. denied, 469 U.S. 1062 (1984), and Mattz v. Superior Court, 46 Cal.3d 355, 758 P.2d 606, 250 Cal.Rptr. 278 (1988), cert. denied, 489 U.S. 1078 (1989), federal regulation of Indian fishing was held to preempt state laws. In Organized Village of Kake v. Egan, 369 U.S. 60 (1962), the Supreme Court held that the general powers conferred upon the executive by 25 U.S.C.A. §§ 2 and 9 to manage Indian affairs and effectuate any act relating to them were insufficient to support regulation of fish traps in conflict with state law. That case, however, arose under the distinctive historical and legislative conditions of Alaska and no treaty or reservation was involved. It seems likely that the Secretary's powers would be more generously interpreted where a treaty or statute guaranteed the fishing in question.

Valid federal regulation offers a method of meeting conservation goals without permitting state regulation of a federal treaty right. It is most likely to be acceptable where the need is simply for a limitation of the method of fishing, which appears to have been the case in the Great Lakes. Where conservation demands an actual apportionment of the fish, federal regulation could also be the instrument, although it would doubtless meet the same opposition faced by the federal courts, possibly with less success. In any event, apportionment would take the federal executive authorities farther into problems of state fish management than they as yet have been willing to go.

E. NON–INDIAN HUNTING AND FISHING IN INDIAN COUNTRY

Non–Indian hunting and fishing in Indian country has also given rise to jurisdictional problems. The federal government, the tribe, and the state are all potential regulators.

The federal government unquestionably has power to control hunting and fishing by non-Indians in Indian country, but for the most part it has not chosen to exercise that power. There are two statutory exceptions. One is 18 U.S.C.A. § 1165, which makes it a federal crime to enter Indian lands without permission "for the purpose of hunting, trapping or fishing." The tribes may give permission to enter by means of a licensing system for non-Indians, and hunting or fishing without a tribal permit is then subject to federal prosecution under § 1165. See United States v. Pollmann, 364 F.Supp. 995 (D.Mont.1973).

The other exception is the Lacey Act, which was amended in 1981 to prohibit transport of or traffic in fish, wildlife or plants taken or possessed in violation of federal, state or tribal law. Mere possession of such fish, wildlife or plants in territory within the exclusive jurisdiction of the United States (which includes Indian country, 18 U.S.C.A. § 1152) is also prohibited. 16 U.S.C.A. § 3372(a). Like the trespass statute, the Lacey Act amendments place the force of federal law behind any state or tribal law regulating non-Indian hunting and fishing on reservations. Federal enforcement of both statutes is sufficiently sporadic, however, that they clearly do not substitute for comprehensive regulation of non-Indian hunting and fishing.

The tribe has power to exclude non-Indians from hunting or fishing on Indian lands. Washington v. Washington State Commercial Passenger Fishing Vessel Ass'n, 443 U.S. 658, 683–84 (1979). In Montana v. United States, 450 U.S. 544 (1981), however, the Supreme Court held that a tribe had no power to regulate non-Indian hunting and fishing on fee lands owned by non-Indians within the reservation. The Court pointed out that there were no allegations that the non-Indian activities on fee lands threatened the tribe's welfare, that the state had abdicated its responsibility of conservation, or that its regulations interfered with tribal hunting and fishing rights. Id. at 566 & n. 16. Although this language suggested that tribes in the future might be able to make the necessary showing and regulate non-Indian hunting or fishing on fee lands, such efforts thus far have met with failure. See Lower Brule Sioux Tribe v. South Dakota, 104 F.3d 1017 (8th Cir.), cert. denied, 118 S.Ct. 64 (1997); South Dakota v. Bourland, 39 F.3d 868 (8th Cir.1994). Tribal success is even less likely after the Supreme Court's decision in Strate v. A–1 Contractors, 117 S.Ct. 1404 (1997), which construed narrowly *Montana*'s exception for threats to tribal welfare.

The federal trespass statute, 18 U.S.C.A. § 1165, does not apply to fee lands within reservations. The Lacey Act Amendments do apply on such lands, 16 U.S.C.A. § 3372(a)(3), but do not enlarge or diminish "the authority of any State or Indian tribe to regulate the activities of persons within Indian reservations." Id. at § 3378(c)(3). The Lacey Act, therefore, can add nothing to the determination of whether the tribe or the state governs the actions of non-Indians on the reservation.

The tribe has power to license hunting and fishing by non-Indians on reservation lands held in trust for the tribe or individual Indians. Montana v. United States, supra; New Mexico v. Mescalero Apache Tribe, 462 U.S. 324 (1983). Tribal regulation of non-Indians has been greatly complicated, however, by Oliphant v. Suquamish Indian Tribe,

435 U.S. 191 (1978), which held that tribes have no criminal jurisdiction over non-Indians. Enforcement of tribal game and fish regulations against non-Indians must therefore be accomplished by the use of civil sanctions. See Montana v. United States, supra. Tribal imposition of a forfeiture of arms or other property of non-Indians has been held an impermissible criminal penalty. Quechan Tribe v. Rowe, 531 F.2d 408 (9th Cir.1976). The remedy of expulsion from Indian lands remains available to the tribe, however, and the aid of federal authorities may be enlisted to prosecute violators of tribal game and fish laws under the trespass provision of 18 U.S.C.A. § 1165 or under the Lacey Act amendments, 16 U.S.C.A. § 3372(a).

In the absence of preemption by federal or tribal authority, the state has the power to regulate hunting and fishing by non-Indians in Indian country. Confederated Tribes of the Colville Indian Reservation v. Washington, 591 F.2d 89 (9th Cir.1979); Quechan Tribe v. Rowe, supra. Some tribes cooperate with the state by requiring both tribal and state licenses of non-Indians, or by agreeing to some other division of regulatory jurisdiction. See United States v. Big Eagle, 881 F.2d 539 (8th Cir.1989), cert. denied, 493 U.S. 1084 (1990). The state does not, of course, have the power to authorize non-Indians to enter Indian lands when the tribe chooses to exclude them. Montana v. United States, supra.

The greatest jurisdictional problems arise when the tribe purports to enact a comprehensive system of regulation that permits hunting and fishing by non-Indians in a manner prohibited by the state. The tribe's purpose is normally to develop non-Indian hunting and fishing as a source of tribal income, and that purpose is aided if limits or seasons are more generous than the state's. It is positively hindered if non-Indians must pay license fees to both the tribe and the state. The tribes have therefore contended that a comprehensive tribal system preempts state law.

This contention met with mixed results in the lower federal courts, but ultimately succeeded in New Mexico v. Mescalero Apache Tribe, 462 U.S. 324 (1983). In that case the tribe and the federal government had undertaken a joint and extensive program of developing reservation game and fish resources. Resort facilities had been built, in part to attract nonmember hunters and fishermen. The state, on the other hand, did not contribute to reservation game and fish resources, and there was no substantial off-reservation effect of on-reservation hunting and fishing. In light of these facts and the strong federal policy favoring tribal self-development, the Supreme Court held that the state was preempted by federal law from regulating nonmember hunting and fishing on the reservation. Because the Court's preemption analysis involves a fact-specific weighing and balancing of the interests at stake, id. at 334, the possibility exists that other, somewhat less comprehensive tribal programs would be unsuccessful in preventing the state from concurrent regulation of nonmember hunting and fishing. Much of the language of the Supreme Court in *Mescalero* suggests, however, that preemption is to be the rule.

Concurrent jurisdiction would empower New Mexico wholly to supplant tribal regulations. The State would be able to dictate the terms on which nonmembers are permitted to utilize the reservation's resources. The Tribe would thus exercise its authority over the reservation only at the sufferance of the State. The tribal authority to regulate hunting and fishing by nonmembers, which has been repeatedly confirmed by federal treaties and laws * * * would have a rather hollow ring if tribal authority amounted to no more than this.

Id. at 338. The same can surely be said in any other case in which the issue arises. True, the state interest still must be considered, and it would be much stronger in a case where the game or fish migrated on and off the reservation, and where the state had contributed to creation and maintenance of the resources. Absent migration, however, the result of *Mescalero* will almost certainly follow. That outcome should surprise no one, in light of the historical, cultural, economic and proprietary interests of the tribes in their own fish and game.

INDEX

References are to Pages

HUNTING AND FISHING—Cont'd
Federal regulation, 426–428, 437, 439–441
   Great Lakes, 439–440
   Non–Indians, 441–446
   Preemption of state, 274–275, 421, 440–441, 444–446
Fishing methods, 429–431, 432–433
Fishing water rights, 406
Migratory fish, 428–437
Off-reservation, 422–425
On-reservation, 420
   Non–Indians, 74, 441–446
Public Law 280, p. 421
State regulation, 423, 430–433, 444–446
Termination, 108–110, 421–422
Treaty rights generally, 101–102, 233–234, 421–425, 429–438, 439
Tribal regulation, 426, 443–446

INDIAN
Blood quantum, 7–9
Defined, 7–9, 112
"Terminated" tribe, 7

INDIAN CHILD WELFARE ACT
See Civil Jurisdiction, State; Civil Jurisdiction, Tribal

INDIAN CIVIL RIGHTS ACT
Enactment, 29, 128, 330
Exhaustion of tribal remedies, 334
Habeas corpus, 336, 337–338
Implied remedies, 335–337
Internal tribal affairs, 335
Interpretation, 333–334
Non–Indian rights, 338–342
Public Law 280, pp. 237–238, 239–240
Scope, 128, 330–342
Tribal attorneys, 65
Tribal criminal jurisdiction, 161
Tribal sovereign immunity, 91, 335–336

INDIAN CLAIMS COMMISSION
Jurisdiction, 354–355

INDIAN CLAIMS COMMISSION ACT
Enactment, 354
Scope, 354–357